M000170155

HOW TO DO THINGS WITH DEAD PEOPLE

HOW TO DO THINGS WITH DEAD PEOPLE

HISTORY, TECHNOLOGY, AND TEMPORALITY FROM SHAKESPEARE TO WARHOL

ALICE DAILEY

CORNELL UNIVERSITY PRESS

Ithaca and London

Copyright © 2022 by Cornell University

First published 2022 by Cornell University Press
Printed in the United States of America

Librarians: A CIP catalog record for this book is available
from the Library of Congress.

ISBN 978-1-5017-6365-6 (hardcover)
ISBN 978-1-5017-6366-3 (epub)
ISBN 978-1-5017-6367-0 (pdf)

For Adam

Freedom of thought always has to be reinvented.
　　—Michel Serres

Contents

Illustrations

ACKNOWLEDGMENTS

This book has three origins that I want to acknowledge. The first was the Histories Project directed by Michael Boyd at the Royal Shakespeare Company (RSC) in 2007–2008. I had not given Shakespeare's history plays much thought until I saw Boyd's stunning production of *Richard II* in the summer of 2007, an experience that led to my returning to England, in the excellent company of Regina Buccola, to see all eight plays over a four-day weekend in spring 2008. When I began to teach a course on the histories at Villanova, I had the benefit of an enormous cache of production photos from the Boyd cycle that were generously shared with me by John of Gaunt himself, RSC cast member Roger Watkins. My fascination with these plays has been indelibly shaped by those productions, Roger's photos, and the experience of seeing and thinking with Gina.

The book's second origin was a 2010 exhibition at the Guggenheim Museum in New York titled *Haunted: Contemporary Photography/Video/Performance*, which I attended as I was writing my first essay on the histories and preparing to teach them for the first time. In the wake of seeing *Haunted*, I became interested in Andy Warhol's electric chair paintings, and I formed from that exhibit my earliest intuition that the paintings and their subject had something to teach me about the history plays. This intuition led me to an essay in the exhibition catalog by Peggy Phelan, whose work I only passingly knew at the time. Along with *Mourning Sex*, *Unmarked*, and her writing on Andy Warhol, Phelan's essay on *Haunted*, "Haunted Stages: Performance and the Photographic Effect," was my entry point into performance theory and eventually into the scholarship of Phelan's students Rebecca Schneider and Daniel Sack, whose work has been important to my thinking in this book.

The third origin of this project was my timely introduction to the art of David Maisel, whose photograph of an X-ray of a sculpture belonging to the Getty Museum, *History's Shadow* (GM1), is the cover image of this book. I am indebted to a college friend, Alan Rapp at Monacelli Press, for distinguishing the murky contours of my aesthetic curiosity and inviting me to what would become a formative gallery show: Maisel's *History's Shadow* at Yancey Richardson in 2014. Maisel's work—especially *History's Shadow* and *Library of Dust*—has significantly shaped this project, and I am deeply grateful to the artist for the gift that his photographs have been to me. The Maisel photograph on the book's cover generated my early thoughts about much of what came to occupy this book: the temporality of X-rays, the sensation of being observed by inanimate objects, the afterlives and afterdeaths of historical and aesthetic artifacts, the intermediality of those artifacts and their collapse of linear time, the ontological status of the reproduction, and the aesthetic generativity of death. Although I do not address Maisel's photography directly in these pages, I am everywhere indirectly addressing it—using it to think through and toward many of the major claims this book makes. The cover image by Maisel has been my polestar, map, and muse.

I am indebted to a generous, supportive community of scholars, especially in my home city of Philadelphia. Lauren Shohet offered invaluable comments on every chapter of this book, and her own wide-ranging interests have made her an inspiring colleague throughout my career at Villanova. This project was made better by Melissa Sanchez's incisive, thoughtful reading of the full manuscript—reading that was critical to my late-stage thinking and revising. Long after this book is out in the world, I will continue to be enriched by Melissa's magnanimous feedback and her example of scholarly generosity. Joseph Drury, Matt Kozusko, Zachary Lesser, and Kristen Poole have been readers, dear friends, and fonts of moral support through the tricky process of bringing this unusual project into being. I have learned from collaboration and conversation with Rebecca Bushnell and Gina Bloom, whose curiosity about territory new to early modernists has been a precedent for my own. I am grateful for the many colleagues who have listened, read, commiserated, offered insight, and otherwise supported me in this work: Beth Burns, Brooke Conti, Travis Foster, Matthew Harrison, Andrew Hartley, Peter Holland, Wendy Beth Hyman, Shawn Kairschner, Farah Karim, Jeremy Lopez, Genevieve Love, Jim Marino, Paul Menzer, Marissa Nicosia, Chelsea Phillips, Holly Pickett, Richard Preiss, Donovan Sherman, Tiffany Stern, Andrea Stevens, Maggie Vinter, Sarah Werner, and Katherine Schaap Williams. I owe special thanks to Jonathan Walker for leading me back to David Bowie, an old love and one of this project's genii. For mentorship that keeps giving, I thank Linda Bannister, Lowell Gallagher, Holli Levitsky, and James Simpson. And I thank the women scholars before me who have written much of the very best work on Shakespeare's history plays, especially Phyllis Rackin, without whose *Stages of History* my project would not have been possible.

I owe thanks to graduate research assistants who worked on various stages of this project—Brendan Maher, Amanda Piazza, and Casey Smedberg—and to our English subject librarian Sarah Wingo, who helped both them and me. This book would have taken a great deal longer to complete without the many kinds of support provided by my department chairs Heather Hicks and Evan Radcliffe and the time and resources made available by my home institution, Villanova University. I owe particular thanks to the Villanova Publication Subvention Program and College of Arts and Sciences for supporting image reproduction. I am indebted to the Shakespeare Association of America, the Blackfriars Conference of the American Shakespeare Center, the World Shakespeare Congress, and the American Society for Theatre Research for opportunities to try out several of the ideas developed in the book. I thank the artists whose work appears here and the many people who helped me with images and permissions, especially Lisa Ballard at Artists Rights Society and Robbi Siegel at Art Resource. Portions of the first chapter appeared in my earlier article "Little, Little Graves: Shakespeare's Photographs of Richard II," *Shakespeare Quarterly* 69, no. 3 (2018); I thank the journal for permission to republish this material. I am grateful for the dedication and hard work of my wonderful editor at Cornell University Press, Mahinder Kingra; the press readers, who offered invaluable feedback; the production teams at Cornell University Press and Westchester Publishing; my copyeditor, Karen Brogno; and my indexer, Kate Mertes.

For their gifts of friendship pure and true, I am indebted to Carl Bradley, Arianna Brooke, Jean Lutes, Niki Rosas-Baines, Taije Silverman, and especially Sondra Rosenberg.

I lost my mother, Margaret Leary, during the writing of this book. I am grateful every day for the love of literature that she imparted to me and for the family she made during her too-short life; for my father, Steven Leary, who always believes in me; and for Joyce, Kent, Paul, Vangie, Mahlia, and Molly, with whom I am thankful to share all that my mother gave us. To the Daileys— Patrick, Suzi, Jake, and Ryan—the family-by-marriage who have so enriched my life lo these many years: thank you for your love and support.

There are no thanks deep enough for my beloveds, Josh and Adam. To you I belong, and to you I am grateful, at the end of a long day's work, always to return.

HOW TO DO THINGS WITH DEAD PEOPLE

Introduction

The Luminous Spiral and the Cigarette Box, or Technologies of the Afterdeath

This is a strange book. This book is a manifesto on the imperative of thinking strangely.

In this book, I consider Shakespeare's English history plays among reproductive technologies and representational media spanning several centuries, such as selfies, Victorian spiritualist photographs, minimalist sculpture, Andy Warhol's Factory-produced portraits, and capital punishment machines. These artifacts, along with the many others studied here, have in common with Shakespeare's histories a preoccupation with undead afterlives—with how that which appears still or unchanging hosts an other that is dynamic, participatory, and charged with the potential to initiate change. I argue that like the history plays, media such as spiritualist photographs figure a relationship between the living and its dynamically undead other, an other who is often also a self. The representational technologies I explore in this book seek to dramatize, picture, or otherwise render visible this other/self, whose ontological indeterminacy reflects its liminal state between past and present, dead and alive, here and gone. Giorgio Agamben describes this state in his essay on Melville's "Bartleby, the Scrivener": "What shows itself on the threshold between Being and non-Being, between sensible and intelligible, between word and thing, is not the colorless abyss of the Nothing but the luminous spiral of the possible."[1]

How to Do Things with Dead People tarries in the luminous spiral, arguing that Shakespeare constitutes history at the threshold of possibility between dead and alive, object and subject, and that his histories occupy this threshold with a multitude of other reproductive technologies that my study only begins to address. Although some of the technologies that this book sets in conversation with the history plays are conventionally associated with specific mechanical devices, such as the still camera or X-ray machine, I show how such technologies generate and depict phenomena that are not chronologically confined. Shakespeare's histories contain photographic selfies and X-ray images, just as the glitchy machinery of the electric chair mirrors the reproductive operations of the plays' English throne. The throne and the electric chair share conceptual infrastructures that transcend the specific chronologies of technical innovation attending either apparatus. To observe such infrastructures at work and to generate conversation among them, as this book does, is therefore neither a historicist nor a presentist project, because those infrastructures cannot be properly located in either the past or the present. Identifying the common underlying phenomena that such technologies reproduce enables movement beyond distinct histories of literary production or mechanical innovation. Such work opens a transhistorical, intermedial conversation about the generative forms, ontological questions, and representational aesthetics that collect around the undead dead.

The strange thinking I experiment with in this book is compelled by the strangeness of historical materials themselves. Consider, for example, an object from the collection of the National Portrait Gallery in London: a cigarette box of Richard II's relics that was found in the museum's basement in 2010. Discovered in the process of a cataloging project, the box contained fragments of wood thought to be from Richard's coffin, a piece of leather from a pair of gloves, and some fabric, all taken by the Gallery's first director, Sir George Scharf, at the exhumation of Richard's Westminster Abbey tomb in 1871 (Figure 1). Scharf attended multiple royal grave openings during his nearly 40-year career with the Gallery, including those of Henry VII, Edward VI, and James I. What facilitated the identification of Richard's relics was a sketchbook kept by Scharf in which he made detailed drawings of Richard's skull and desiccated brain, drawings dated the day before the cigarette box (Figure 2).[2] The contents of the box were discovered by assistant archivist Krzysztof Adamiec, who remarked in a subsequent interview that "it just looked like a simple, empty box of cigarettes. But when I opened it up there were strips of leather and pieces of wood. It was very exciting for me—it's one of the biggest pleasures of this job to literally feel that you are touching history."[3]

For Adamiec, opening the box to reveal its contents opens a miniature portal into the past, one that generates both tactile and affective contact across centuries and joins the moment of his discovery to prior time. Through its opening, the

FIGURE 1. Cigarette box of Richard II's relics collected by Sir George Scharf, August 31, 1871 (NPG7_3_6_2). © National Portrait Gallery, London.

"simple, empty box" comes to function like a wormhole—a wormhole through which he "literally . . . touch[es] history" in a collapse of space-time. That history is multiple, itself a nexus of wormholes. The box likely dates from the early 1870s, when Scharf visited the tomb of Richard II and collected the objects. Those objects were themselves discovered in the box that is Richard's second resting place, his first having been opened in 1413 when his remains were moved from his original grave at Kings Langley, Hertfordshire, to be reinterred at Westminster Abbey with those of his queen, Anne of Bohemia. (Shakespeare's Henry V refers to this reinterment in his soliloquy the night before the Battle of Agincourt: "I Richard's body have interred new, / And on it have bestowed more contrite tears / Than from it issued forced drops of blood" [*H5* 4.1.277–79]).[4] The cigarette box of Richard's relics marks the juncture between Adamiec's present and the boundless pasts it bears into that present, which include the pasts of Richard's two burials and disinterments, of Scharf's collection, of the cigarette box's storage within another box of Scharf's effects, of the royal hand that once wore the glove, of the glover who sewed it, of the animal from whose hide it was made, of the tobacco and tree and laboring human bodies that generated a box of cigarettes, ad infinitum.[5] To "touch history" is not to make contact with an object fixed in a past time but to index the very unfixedness of time—the inhabitation of the present by an expanse of not only pasts but futures. For as Jacques Derrida's *Archive Fever* would remind us, Scharf's act of relic collection is itself a futureward gesture, one that stages a later encounter with Richard's remains.[6] That future moment of the past's return—a return reprised here and now as you, my reader, encounter the photograph of the cigarette box—is anticipated by the

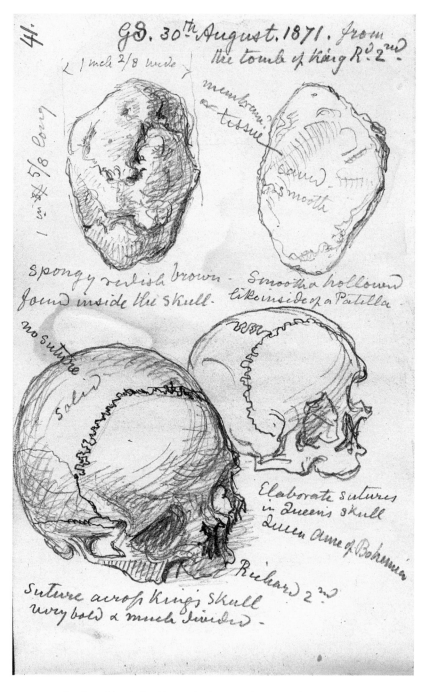

FIGURE 2. Sketches of the skull and brain of Richard II and the skull of Queen Anne of Bohemia by Sir George Scharf, August 30, 1871 (NPG7_3_4_2_97_pg41). © National Portrait Gallery, London.

very acts of collecting, storing, dating, photographing, and cataloging relics from Richard's tomb. Encounters and reencounters with the revenant pasts of the cigarette box are composed by the mechanism of the souvenir itself (*Souvenir*, v., "to remember"). In this sense, the souvenir—a technology through which the past returns to be re-experienced in the present—is not unlike a history play, which scripts the reappearance of pasts in an expanse of potential futures played out through bodies yet unknown.[7] The death that renders historical figures "dust, / And food for—" "For worms," as Hotspur and Hal collaboratively remark near the end of *1 Henry IV*, opens worm holes and wormholes through the corpse of history, making the dead available as participants in live encounters that unfold now and in the time to come (*1H4* 5.4.85).

The context in which the cigarette box was identified—a cataloging project undertaken by the National Portrait Gallery—situates its various artifacts as adjuncts to visual portraiture, especially the portraiture represented by Scharf's drawings. Notably, on the page of Scharf's sketchbook I have chosen for reproduction here, Scharf labeled the larger of the two skulls, in the bottom left foreground, "Richard 2nd" and the smaller "Queen Anne of Bohemia"— rather than "the skull of Richard II" and "the skull of Anne of Bohemia." Scharf produces an unusual kind of royal portrait, one that does not consign the couple to a static past but reproduces them in his present as currently dead, making them available as such for indefinite futures. They are figures whose histories continue to unfold into the present as they are disinterred in 1871 and as Scharf's drawings are digitized and cataloged. Like the cigarette box's staging of future encounters through the mechanisms of preservation and return, Scharf's drawings of Richard's skull and brain host subsequent encounters through images archived for future viewing. In this way, the images function as uncanny visual representations of the brain and soul described by Shakespeare's Richard II at the end of the play that bears his name: "My brain I'll prove the female to my soul, / My soul the father, and these two beget / A generation of still-breeding thoughts" (*R2* 5.5.6–9). Neither the stillness of Scharf's drawings nor the inert state of Richard's brain—a "spongy redish brown" object measuring a mere one and five-eighths by one and two-eighths inches—relegates the brain to the past. Through our rendezvous with it in the archives of the National Portrait Gallery or the pages of this book, Richard's brain is "still breeding": still returning, still reproducing, still generating live encounters.[8] If Scharf had Richard's lines about his brain in mind when he chose it to draw—rather than choosing, say, his femur—we might observe that the brain Richard describes in *Richard II* begot an 1871 portrait of itself.[9]

The itinerary of another dead king made famous by Shakespeare, Richard III, suggests other kinds of return that may yet be in store for Richard II. In view of the afterdeath of Richard III's scoliotic spinal column, which has been fabricated repeatedly to appear in theater and screen productions of Shakespeare's *Richard III* since its exhumation in 2012, it is not difficult to imagine replicas of Richard II's artifacts breeding future generations in the theater.[10] Richard's description of himself in "a little grave, / A little, little grave, an obscure grave," and his reference to "the hollow crown" where "Keeps Death his court" almost beg for stage reproductions of the cigarette box and skull, perhaps to be held and contemplated by the character of Richard himself (*R2* 3.3.52–53, 3.2.156, 158). Given that the Scharf archive dates from the reign of Queen Victoria and that its 2012 discovery occurred during the reign of the wrong Queen Elizabeth, would the appearance of these objects in a staging of *Richard II* constitute anachronism, a preoccupation—an "unpardonable sin," as Margreta de Grazia puts it—for scholars concerned with the historicity of Shakespeare's plays?[11] Since the historical Richard II is always already dead at the beginning of any production of *Richard II*, what, precisely, would be anachronistic about the character of Richard peering into the facsimile of a box that holds his own future/past remains in a play that repeatedly figures him imagining his own future/past remains? Or does the problem of anachronism arise when we look backward from Scharf's futureward-looking archive to re-see Richard's "little grave" as an uncanny anticipation of the cigarette box, itself something of a miniature coffin for Richard? In consigning the remains of Richard to a cigarette box, is Scharf restaging a scene from the play? And if the text of *Richard II* is before me now as I pose these questions, in what sense is reading the play through Scharf's archive "looking backward," as though Shakespeare's play were fixed in some prior time? In sum, what does "anachronism" mean in relation to the textual, dramatic, and material production that occurs and recurs around a literary-historical figure like Richard II?

These questions, which will themselves reappear in different forms across this book, expose the analytic imprecision of the term "anachronism" and its relative uselessness for describing the phenomena that circulate in and around Richard II. Alexander Nagel and Christopher S. Wood usefully propose "'anachronic' . . . as an alternative to 'anachronistic,' a judgmental term that carries with it the historicist assumption that every event and every object has its proper location within objective and linear time."[12] This assumption is confounded by the phenomenal afterdeaths of Richard II. The cigarette box of his relics is a site where not only time frames but multiple media—themselves complexly anachronic—intersect. In its anticipation of the past's return in the present through future reopenings, such as the one activated by the archivist's (or archivists') hands-that-hold and visual-cortex-that-recognizes, the archive composed by Scharf works like a theater, a site where history appears "as the recomposition of remains *in and as the live*," to borrow a formulation from performance theorist Rebecca Schneider.[13] Like a theater, the Scharf archive generates multitemporal effects that transcend the boundaries marked off by the historical periods and academic disciplines that conventionally organize scholarly work. To encounter the archive here, on a page of this book, is to encounter a photograph that is also—at minimum—a text, a theater, a portrait, a corpse, a technology, and a constructed material artifact that is multiply mediated by human bodies, including yours and mine. The result is a history that is not past but still: still becoming.

This is not to say anything especially revelatory about history. We know already that history is manifold and intermedial, that it is under continuous negotiation, and that it is resistant to closure. These are the lessons of post-structuralism and post-colonialism. In the field of early modern literary studies, the principal of this book's several homes, our ideas about history have been informed by diverse models of overlapping temporality, such as the palimpsest posited by Jonathan Gil Harris; David Kastan's shapes of time; the rough, thick embodied time described by Matthew D. Wagner (after Husserl); Gilles Deleuze's pleat or fold; and Michel Serres's crumpled handkerchief.[14] We have at our disposal, then, a rich vocabulary of metaphors for describing what has variously been called polychronicity or multitemporality, and we have absorbed the skepticism imparted by post-structuralism and post-colonialism about generating monolithic notions of reality. And yet early modernism as a field has remained committed, by and large, to the methods of historicism, which idealize the retrieval of a past located in the historical archive, however broadly construed. In its core commitment to recovering the contexts of literary production, historicism insists on the pastness of the past—on its marked difference from the present. Although we acknowledge that history is multifarious and indeterminate, we continue to reproduce a critical methodology that seeks to stabilize the past by constructing authoritative narratives about it, narratives founded on archives that are themselves radically contingent and politically determined. It is a methodology that cuts us off, via the taboo of anachronism, from engaging with the phenomenology of media that we date after the "early modern period," even if those phenomena occur inside early modern texts. It is a methodology that discounts as hermeneutically unstable—if indeed it can see at all—the wormhole effect of the cigarette box, an effect that detonates the very concept of linear temporality from which historicism draws its logics of contextualization. What, for example, can that darling of historicism, the medieval political theology of the king's two bodies, tell us about the temporal effects of the cigarette box or the Richards it restores to us through its opened portal?[15] Alas, not much.

We need not look to such remarkable objects or even to the domain of live theater to be confronted with historicism's insufficiencies. The literary texts studied in this book reveal those insufficiencies at every turn. This revelation is one of the book's aims: to expose the limits of historicism through the very corpus of early modern drama that would seem most to lend itself to historicist methodology: Shakespeare's English chronicle plays. As an ahistoricist study of historical drama, this book jettisons received definitions of literary context that confine our thinking about the histories to the immediate cultural affordances of fifteenth- and sixteenth-century England. Contesting the dominant critical assumption that historical consciousness means chronological specificity, this project rethinks what history is and does by contextualizing the plays within the ongoing human enterprise of representing and relating to the dead. *How to Do Things with Dead People* describes Shakespeare's historical drama as, fundamentally, a reproductive technology by which living replicas of dead historical figures are animated in the present and re-killed. Considering the plays in such terms exposes their affinity with a transhistorical array of technologies for producing, reproducing, and interacting with dead things—technologies like literary doppelgängers, photography, ventriloquist puppetry, X-ray imagery, glitch art, silk-screening, and cloning. By situating the plays in this broader, intermedial context—one that includes current as well as developing technologies, especially technologies of imaging—*How to Do Things with Dead People* deconstructs conventional period boundaries that mark off Shakespeare's reproductive arts as substantively different from our own. This methodological shift enables a wholesale rethinking of what constitutes the context of a work of literature and challenges many basic assumptions about linear temporality that underwrite the theses of historicism and periodization.

Conventional scholarly work on the history plays has been organized by several presuppositions about how time works and what historical drama can and cannot do. Chief among these is the assumption that time is fundamentally linear—an assumption that excludes the dead people of history from participation in the present or future. According to this logic, historical drama can bring likenesses of the dead into an active present, either through text or on stage, but the dead themselves remain dead and irrecoverable. These assumptions underwrite formative scholarship on the plays, such as Phyllis Rackin's important *Stages of History*, which describes Shakespeare's histories as nostalgic for past kings and heroes who are never to be recuperated.[16] For Rackin, historical drama is a site of absence that exposes "the inadequacies of theatrical representation to validate the historical record," a position that Brian Walsh echoes in his subsequent claim for "the poverty of theatrical representation" and the "double absence" of historical figures from either the present time or the stage.[17] Such influential readings of the histories—readings that have gone relatively uncontested—rely on the binaries of now/then, present/absent, and living/dead that artifacts like the cigarette box, as well as the plays themselves, profitably resist. If we take such binaries as given, we miss the density of roles performed by the dead in these plays, who serve as mirrors and doubles, as speakers and audiences. They are actors in embedded mini-theaters, sites for constructing sovereign time, opportunities for temporal experimentation, and generators of futures that are still unfolding.

How to Do Things with Dead People reads the dead as undead sites of ongoing potential, as my echo of J. L. Austin's *How to Do Things with Words* (1962) suggests. Austin defines a "performative utterance" or "speech-act" as language that does not describe the world but, rather, enacts what is declared.[18] Words are generative; they *do* things. Like words, I argue, the dead are enlisted to *do*, serving a generative function for the living by acting as mediums for temporal conjecture, ventriloquism, identity extension, and world-building. The dead are not simply past, nor are they merely sites of mourning or nostalgia. In the technologies I study, still and silent bodies function as figures with ongoing potential—as material for construing what is yet possible and for imagining a future that has not yet arrived.

The conversation that this project introduces through its range of artifacts rejects linear schema that situate the past and the historical dead in a dimension from which we have progressed, either temporally or teleologically. Thus the phrase in my subtitle, "from Shakespeare to Warhol," does not mean to imply a narrative of historical development. Were this book's title not already more than long enough, it would include at least several more to's and fro's, moving in multiple temporal and spatial directions, to suggest the project's investment in dismantling the fiction of linear time and its attendant teleologic. That teleologic—by which we understand ourselves, our culture, and our politics as the fulfillment of an evolutionary process that has advanced us to steadily higher forms of expression—is undone by the history plays' inbuilt theoretical machinery. In their varied and sophisticated engagement with the mechanisms of historical construction, Shakespeare's histories reflect on the very processes by which teleological narratives come into being. The plays dramatize how those narratives, such as the narrative of genealogical succession that posits Henry VI as the natural heir of Henry V and therefore of the English crown, are underwritten by a host of technological mechanisms that fabricate not only history, sovereignty, and power but the more foundational concept of hereditary reproduction. Heredity, I argue, is but one of many ostensibly organic processes that are exposed by Shakespeare's histories as forms of technological artifice. By staging the machinery that generates narratives of paternity, succession, authenticity, and even linear time, the histories denaturalize and demystify the teleologic that would position our own critical, techno-political constructs as inherently more developed than those represented by Shakespeare's plays.

My movement between the book's diverse materials is facilitated by an eclectic body of theoretical resources drawn from a broad range of disciplines. As with the phrase "from Shakespeare to Warhol," the inclusion of twentieth- and twenty-first-century theorists in my study is not meant to suggest a developmental arc that positions contemporary theory as an explanatory apparatus for earlier literature. On the contrary, quite often in this book it is the Shakespearean text that offers the more refined articulation of phenomena that contemporary theorists seek to explain.[19] As I treat them in my study, the history plays talk back to many of the theorists I bring into conversation here, including Roland Barthes, Stanley Cavell, Jacques Derrida, Lee Edelman, Michael Fried, Joseph Roach, and Susan Sontag. Further, I seek to unsettle our canon of acknowledged theorists by expanding what constitutes an admissible theoretical resource. This is most explicit in the book's multiple forms of engagement with the life and art of Andy Warhol, a keen theorist of replica-production, who, like a modern-day Sir George Scharf, perseverated over death and obsessively documented and archived his day-to-day life.[20] Set in conversation with Shakespeare's *Richard III*, Warhol's corpus—his body as well as his body of work—exposes the limits of both conventional engagement with Richard's disability and academic queer theory. Reading Shakespeare, Warhol, and the character of Richard III as kindred dramatist-theorists yields new insight into three figures who have each generated a canon of scholarship unto themselves.

In contrast to literary criticism written during the heyday of theory in the 1980s and 1990s, which either produced or was produced by critics who identified with discrete schools of thought, the work of this book is far more catholic in its approach to theory. By adapting theoretical concepts from discourses like visual studies and art history, performance theory, bioethics, philosophy, queer theory, and crip theory, I seek at once to expand the conceptual frames we use to think about early modern literature and to persuade scholars in these contiguous fields of the vitality of early modern studies. Although labels like "deconstruction" and "queer temporality" might usefully describe some aspects of this project, I decline to summarize its methodology in overdetermined or totalizing terms. Instead, I seek to maximize the potential that a varied conceptual vocabulary offers for both dilating and refining analysis. Some of the materials I bring into conversation with each other here have been partially constelled in other fields that study death, replica-production, performance, and imaging technologies. Yet none of those constellations has included history plays. My argument will be not merely that Shakespeare's histories belong in dialogue with these other phenomena but that the plays theorize, with fascinating depth and diversity, many reproductive technologies that we associate with modernity and postmodernity, such as the photographic technique of double exposure or its biomedical incarnation, the clone. At the heart of the project's insistence on alternative contexts for thinking about Shakespeare's history plays lies a determination to practice, methodologically, what we know about history's resistance to order and closure. When pursued with discipline, such praxis dismantles the boundaries imposed by periodization and disciplinarity, unsettling the very categories of dead and alive.

One of my aims in opening scholarly conversation about Shakespeare to a figure like Andy Warhol is to contest inherited notions of what constitutes viable literary criticism. The hegemony of historicism and cultural materialism, which locate their hermeneutic authority in the historical archive, has not only limited our conception of literary context but enforced narrow definitions of scholarly discipline and critical legitimacy. Moreover, as the profession has begun to observe, the archive-centric decoding instantiated by historicist critical practice can alienate students of literature by making them reliant on a professorial mediator to transmit the valid meanings of a text. By contrast, this project insists on the necessity of methodological experimentation and of expansive, liberatory thinking. In its confrontation with entrenched notions of scholarly rigor and legitimacy, often defined as strictly period-based expertise, *How to Do Things with Dead People* develops a critical praxis rooted in the feminist tradition of dissent to which I am indebted. Against compulsory deference to what Derrida calls "the patriarchive," I offer this book as a celebration of scholarly freedom, of openness to intuition and failure, of inclusive forms of intellectual rigor, and of unabashed critical pleasure.[21] This book solicits us to feel the urgency of strangeness—to feel, as a living necessity, that our understanding can only be enlarged by reaching toward that which at first seems strange. In embracing strange thinking about history, technology, and temporality, this book insists that we must welcome strangeness as fundamental to cultivating a diversity of scholarly perspectives and as vital to the survival of humanist disciplines.

How to Do Things with Dead People focuses on six of Shakespeare's medieval chronicle plays. I purposely take up some of the most celebrated of the histories—*Richard II*, *1 Henry IV*, and *Richard III*—alongside plays that have attracted far less critical and theatrical attention—*2 Henry IV*, *1 Henry VI*, and *3 Henry VI*. My aim in mixing the popular and unpopular is to suggest how a more elastic approach to the question of context can disclose what is worth studying in the less-discussed plays and challenge dominant assumptions about the histories we know well. The arrangement of the chapters is regnal order is both accidental and not. Dramaturgic techniques and preoccupations do link plays within the first and second tetralogies, making organization by tetralogy logical. But the placement of the plays I study here from the first tetralogy (1 and 3 Henry VI and Richard III) after the plays of the second tetralogy (Richard II and 1 and 2 Henry IV) has much more to do with how this project developed than with any argument I am making about their order—either compositional order or regnal order.

Chapter 1, "Little, Little Graves: Shakespeare's Photographs of Richard II," works with performance and photographic theory to examine representations of the king's corpse, grave, and mirror image in Richard II. The chapter opens with Alexander Gardner's famous portrait of Lewis Payne, who was hanged in 1865 in connection with the Lincoln assassination conspiracy. In Camera Lucida, Roland Barthes observes that the photographed Payne is at once dead and not yet dead: "He is dead and he is going to die."[22] The photograph captures a moment when Payne was still living while addressing itself to a viewer who is necessarily looking from a future vantage point after that moment has passed. I observe how the many static, inset images of dead Richard in Shakespeare's play function according to a photographic phenomenology that enshrines Richard as an image for his own morbid, future speculation. As the only character in the play who can frankly contemplate the king's corpse, Richard uses that corpse to both engender and populate the future time after his death.

Chapter 2, "Haunted Histories: Dramatic Double Exposure in Henry IV, Parts One and Two," identifies a pattern of spectral representation in the two plays, tracing their habit of depicting living characters as haunted by their own deaths—deaths that are at once historically past and dramatically imminent. The chapter thinks about these spectral representations as forms of double exposure, a photographic technique that has a long association with beliefs in ghosts and spirits. By superimposing an image of the living and an image of the dead, ghostly double exposures generate a visual field in which figures in different metaphysical states are made to occupy a single space and time. Working from Derrida's concept of "hauntology," the inhabitation of the self by its spectral other, the chapter sets episodes from the Henry IV plays in conversation with several forms of photographic double exposure, including X-rays, Victorian spiritualist photographs, and Duane Michals's photo sequence, The Spirit Leaves the Body (1968). Like images that represent the coincidence of deadness with aliveness, the Henry IV plays produce a temporality that is hauntological and therefore incongruous with conventional models of ontology, linear time, or teleological order.

Chapter 3, "Dummies and Doppelgängers: Performing for the Dead in *1 Henry VI*," studies the dynamics of observation and performativity between living and dead characters in *1 Henry VI*. My discussion is framed by Jeff Wall's *Dead Troops Talk* (1992), a staged, large-scale photo that reimagines a scene from the Soviet-Afghan war in which men blown apart in an ambush reanimate to speak to each other. Because it is a still photo, however, their speech must be supplied by the viewer. Wall's photo and the critical literature around it illustrate how the dead men's still, silent absorption in their liminal state hosts scenes of histrionic ventriloquism for viewers while attributing speech to the dead themselves. I observe this fundamentally theatrical phenomenon in a series of scenes in *1 Henry VI*, a play that repeatedly figures living characters ventriloquizing the dead, who act as silent, sentient onlookers to the performances of the living. Working with performance theory, art criticism, philosophy, and psychoanalysis, the chapter challenges critical truisms about both the history plays and performance phenomena by examining how living characters like Lord Talbot appropriate the dead as dramatic doppelgängers through whom they conjecture hypothetical and future actions.

Chapter 4, "The King Machine: Reproducing Sovereignty in *3 Henry VI*," examines the play's preoccupation with glitches in reproduction, demonstrating how ideas about what is inherited across generations are often explicitly articulated in death scenes and in descriptions of capital punishment.[23] Such moments expose how hereditary succession must be supplemented by technologies of killing and artificial reproduction to construct sovereignty as the mystical juncture between a mortal body natural and an immortal body politic. The chapter uses Derrida's seminars on sovereignty and the death penalty, bioethical discussions of cloning, and Andy Warhol's electric chair paintings as theoretical resources for conceptualizing the intersection of death, time, historical representation, and natural and artificial reproduction. Immortal, divine kingship is constructed in Shakespeare's *3 Henry VI* through the cooperation of naturalized and artificial reproductive technologies that generate sequences of would-be (but not quite) clones: Henry IV, Henry V, Henry VI. The problem of imperfect replication is vividly illustrated in the figure of "crookback" Richard of Gloucester, whose glitched body develops into an important component of the play's meditation on successful reproduction.

Chapter 5, "Fuck Off and Die: The Queercrip Reign of Richard III," rethinks *Richard III* in light of anti-utopian queer theory and its offshoot, crip theory, a radical field of disabilities studies that reclaims the term "cripple" to aggressively confront assumptions that underlie ableist heterosexism. Rather than fetishizing the future signified by the child of heterosexual coupling, Richard empowers himself to murder the line of royal heirs who stand between him and the throne by identifying with his own crip body, embracing ableism's reading of it as a sign of doom or death. The chapter returns to the figure of Warhol—his writings, biographies, Marilyn Monroe portraits, and skull paintings—as a kindred queercrip performer who, like Richard, proliferated his own disfigurement and morbidity through deformed, moribund offspring. Like the queer and disabled artists at the center of current crip theory, who use their bodies performatively to contest ableist heterosexism, Richard and Warhol identify with their social and corporeal otherness to stage fictitious distinctions between normal and defective, straight and queer, alive and dead. The chapter observes how the afterlives of both figures generate forms of postmortem reproduction that insist on a future for the dead, queer, and crip.

The book ends with an autobiographically inflected postscript on David Bowie, who died and was multiply reincarnated during my work on this project. This short meditation alludes to the many possible paths that are suggested but not taken by this book—paths through music, memoir, film, television, dramatic adaptation, and countless other media and art forms that resonate with the history plays' engagement with the dead. Many of the book's observations about representations of the dead in the English chronicle plays could likewise apply, more locally, to other early modern historical drama. While limiting, for sheer manageability, the scope of the book to six of the chronicle plays, I suggest the interpretive possibility that a reconsideration of temporal and contextual models has for other plays in the canon by introducing each chapter with an epigraph from *Macbeth*. Like the book as a whole, these epigraphs are invitations addressed to the future—provocations toward innovative, ongoing, and inclusive scholarly conversation about the place of Shakespearean drama among arts and technologies of the afterdeath.

CHAPTER 1

Little, Little Graves

Shakespeare's Photographs of Richard II

> The dead / Are but as pictures.
>
> —*Macbeth*

In the climactic moments of the deposition scene in act 4 of *Richard II*, when Richard is forced to abdicate his throne to the usurper, Henry Bolingbroke, Northumberland presses Richard to sign articles declaring himself guilty of "grievous crimes . . . against the state" (4.1.213, 215).[1] In response, Richard initiates a pause in the transactional business of the scene to stage an interlude of self-reflection. He declines to turn his tearful eyes on the proffered articles and instead asks to see a looking glass, proposing to "read" his sins in the image of his unkinged face (4.1.267). What he sees in the mirror, however, is neither a document of sin nor the face he expects, one "bankrupt of his majesty" (4.1.257). Rather, Richard discovers the face he had when he was king:

> Was this face the face
> That every day under his household roof
> Did keep ten thousand men? Was this the face
> That like the sun did make beholders wink?
> Was this the face which faced so many follies,
> That was at last outfaced by Bolingbroke? (4.1.271–76)[2]

In the famous speech from Marlowe's *Doctor Faustus* echoed here—in which Faustus admiringly wonders, "Was this the face that launched a thousand ships?"—Faustus's verb tense consigns the face of Helen of Troy to the past, even as he seeks immortality by kissing it.[3] Shakespeare repeats and amplifies this past-tense verb and, through it, conjures for Richard a particular form of immortality. Looking at himself in the mirror, Richard the living character describes the image of a bygone face—a face, marked by the past tense "Was," that registers a temporal discrepancy between the reflected Richard and the reflecting Richard. As a face fixed in a prior time, the image declares its archaic relationship to the speaker's present tense, documenting its own obsolescence. By simultaneously figuring himself as a thing past and as someone presently looking at that past thing—as the imaged face that "Was" and the speaking face that is—Richard multiplies himself to populate different moments in time. He pauses the action of the scene to generate a picture of his past self that encodes a Richard who postdates his own demise.

Shakespeare's mirror scene indexes at least four Richards: the speaking character; the past King Richard he sees in the mirror; the dead, has-been, or ex-king presaged by the image and eventually produced by the assassination of act 5; and the historical, dead Richard II who antecedes the play. These Richards do not legibly correspond to those described by the medieval political theology of the king's two bodies, which has been indelibly linked with *Richard II* since Ernst Kantorowicz's 1957 reading of the play. In Kantorowicz's account, the precept of the king's two bodies explains how the disruptive potential of a king's physical death is offset by reference to the abstract, immortal institution of kingship, which persists intact from one mortal king's reign to the next. Appropriated from theological distinctions between Christ's mortal human body (*proprium et verum corpus*) and the church (*corpus mysticum*), the juridical construct of the king's two bodies establishes a fiction of continuity to negate the material fact of human mortality.[4] Kantorowicz's influential reading of *Richard II* describes the mirror scene as a pivotal moment in the play's representation of this concept, one that dramatizes the catastrophic splitting of Richard's body politic from his body natural. Because Richard lacks a legitimate heir who would inherit the immutable properties of kingship, Richard's royal soul ascends to be enthroned in heaven "Whilst [his] gross flesh sinks downward here to die" (5.5.112).

The historicist project of contextualizing *Richard II* in the political imaginaries of Ricardian and Elizabethan England has been heavily indebted to Kantorowicz, who declares the king's two bodies "not only the symbol but indeed the very substance and essence" of the play.[5] This thesis summarizes how medieval political theology serves in his reading as a historical context, a hermeneutics, a metaphysics, and an aesthetics. "For Kantorowicz," Victoria Kahn observes, "a legal fiction is distinguished from a literary fiction only by its institutional home," a summation that could double as a precept of New Historicism.[6] As this brief look into the mirror moment suggests, however, our historicized understanding of the concept of the king's two bodies cannot accommodate the Richards constructed by his temporally staggered moment of self-reflection. The critical convention of reading *Richard II* as the literary illustration of a historically localized legal-theological concept artificially limits our appreciation of such moments' temporal aesthetics. The teleological relationship between mortality and immortality described by medieval Christian metaphysics is complicated not only by the temporal dislocation Richard observes in moments like the mirror scene but, more broadly, by the genre of historical drama itself, in which the lively, speaking king is always bound to his deadened, inert negative, and vice versa.

I want to propose an alternative conceptual framework for describing the aesthetic and temporal effects of such moments, one suggested not by Ricardian or Elizabethan political theology but by the photographic theory of Roland Barthes. In his influential, enigmatic, and final book, *Camera Lucida* (1980), Barthes traces his response to a childhood photograph of his deceased mother. From this and a series of other old photos, he theorizes the effects of the photographic medium. One image of interest to him is a famous portrait of Lewis Payne, who was hanged in 1865 in connection with the Lincoln assassination conspiracy (Figure 3). The portrait was taken by Alexander Gardner aboard the USS *Saugus* as the condemned man awaited execution. Barthes's fascination with the photo lies in its temporal effects, which he observes to be "vividly legible in historical photographs: there is always a defeat of Time in them: *that* is dead and *that* is going to die." The photo captures a moment when Payne was still living while addressing itself to a viewer who is necessarily looking from a future that succeeds both the photographed moment and the subject's death. In the viewer's consciousness, the photograph pictures multiple temporal dimensions organized around the delimiting horizon of death, figuring "an anterior future of which death is the stake."[7]

In his moment of reflection in the mirror, Richard inhabits all of the subject and object positions mapped by Barthes, including Barthes's own. Richard is at once the photographed Lewis Payne, Payne's photographer, and Payne's viewer: He is the man facing inevitable death, the documentarian whose image technology makes this moment available for an afterlife of future viewing, and the timeless viewer beyond the grave to whom death appears as already completed. Richard is dead and Richard is going to die. In distinction from *Camera Lucida*'s meditation on Payne, however, the immediate viewer for whom Richard is both dead and going to die is not a separate consciousness, such as Barthes or the audience or reader of the play. More locally, that

FIGURE 3.   Lewis Payne, in sweater, seated and manacled. Photo by Alexander Gardener. Washington Navy Yard, D.C., 1865. Library of Congress, Prints and Photographs Division, Civil War Photographs, LC-DIG-cwpb-04208 (digital file from original negative), LC-B8171-7773 (black-and-white film negative).

viewer is Richard himself, a Richard both identical to and temporally discrete from the face reflected in the image. In one sense, then, the mirror moment illustrates the technological feats of historical drama, a form in which a theatrically alive dead king can reflect on a mirror image of his own past face in a moment that both anticipates and recalls the corpse he will be in the play's final scenes. But this moment also accomplishes something particular to

Richard II that photographic theory illuminates: It pauses the play's forward action to generate still pictures of Richard that come into view from a future perspective. This arrested past is defined by an end that has both already and not yet come, an end in which he is "at last outfaced by Bolingbroke" and murdered by the assassin Exton, Richard's own Lewis Payne (4.1.276).

Camera Lucida famously analogizes photography to theater, arguing that both are arts of death—that they are kindred technologies for reproducing and looking at dead things:

> If Photography seems to me closer to the Theater [than to painting], it is by way of a singular intermediary (and perhaps I am the only one who sees it): by way of Death. We know the original relation of the theater and the cult of the Dead: the first actors separated themselves from the community by playing the role of the Dead: to make oneself up was to designate oneself as a body simultaneously living and dead. . . . Now it is the same relation which I find in the Photograph; however "lifelike" we strive to make it . . . , Photography is a kind of primitive theater, the kind of *Tableau Vivant*, a figuration of the motionless and made-up face beneath which we see the dead.[8]

In Barthes's account, early drama theatricalized the past by staging "bod[ies] simultaneously living and dead" in a representational form analogous to the photo of Payne. Barthes's observation has been of significant interest to performance studies for the way it theorizes dramatic stagings of dead figures via living bodies. What neither Barthes nor performance studies takes up—and what this chapter considers at length—are the temporal effects generated by stilled, inert images of the past embedded within dramatic action unfolding in the present, whether on stage or in text. Implied but not explicitly theorized in Barthes's account of both the dramatic and photographic mediums are the present viewers for whom the subject appears alive and dead—the "we" in the final phrase of this passage. Because both photography and drama address themselves to viewers, it is "we [who] see" in the play or photo the superimposition of living and dead. Static images like Richard's mirrored face embed a living audience who occupy a temporal dimension beyond the past represented in the picture.

Although *Richard II*'s many composed or even Mannerist moments have invited comparison to iconography, pageantry, and painted portraiture, these forms of visual representation—while strictly contemporary to the play—operate by a different phenomenology than the one that organizes its static images of Richard.[9] To describe the discrete image aesthetics that organize moments like the mirror scene, this chapter brackets both the body logic of medieval political Christology and the orthodoxies of historicist critical praxis that would confine us to acknowledged contemporaneous visual forms. I argue that the temporal effects produced by the play's still images of Richard are photographic and therefore most clearly elucidated by photographic phenomenology. More precisely than our inherited paradigms for reading *Richard II*, the image theory articulated by photographic theorists such as Barthes and Susan Sontag exposes the play's pictures of a past or dead Richard as sites of aesthetic objectification and scopophilic anticipation. At the same time, however, *Richard II* exploits aspects of photographic temporality that are not fully accommodated by these theorists' accounts of the photographic phenomenon. As I will argue, the temporal effects that Richard produces through pictures like his mirror image at once anticipate *Camera Lucida* and expose what is elided by Barthes's meditation. The chapter ultimately posits *Richard II* as a compelling work of photographic theory in its own right, one in which Richard manipulates the technology of self-imaging to secure his perpetual survival—even in the face of his inevitable death.

In positing photography as a hermeneutic for *Richard II*, I do not seek merely to substitute a postmodern, secular, Barthes-inflected model of historical representation for Kantorowicz's medieval, Christological model of corporeal transcendence. I invoke photography to rethink the very assumptions of linear developmental temporality that inform our notions of secularism and historicism. In other words, I turn here to the secular aesthetic principles articulated by photographic theory to critique the secular model of temporality that presents the king and Christ as its transcendent exceptions. Our readings of the play often foreground *saecula*, defined periods with real or imagined end points: Richard's reign, England's period of divine-right kingship, the Eden before the usurpation, the Middle Ages, the Elizabethan era. The representational aesthetics of *Richard II*, by contrast, demonstrate how the play's embedded images perpetually reproduce multiple, simultaneous temporal dimensions, some with no fixed period. The hermeneutic shift afforded by photography exposes a Ricardian remainder that not only eludes historicized notions of visual art but, more broadly, eludes what Jonathan Gil Harris has critiqued as historicism's "national sovereignty model of temporality."[10] The play's production of images of a dead Richard, especially in its pivotal middle scenes, constitutes time in terms that are not fully compatible with the Christologic of the king's two bodies or the logic of the *saeculum* or period. Like photographs, these pictures do not merely figure the past; they present what Rebecca Schneider has called "the future that subsists" in the image, a future "that necessarily contains" subsequent "moment[s] of looking."[11] Even Richard's tragic death functions as a site for producing his ongoing presence—his open-ended future as a viewer at his own grave.

Contextualizing *Richard II* more broadly than post-Kantorowicz criticism has done productively exposes the play's resonance with transhistorical media by which humans create and look at effigies of a dead past. To think in such terms, I argue, does not necessitate reproducing the logic of periodization by plotting a longer developmental history of camera technology, for example, or suggesting that Shakespeare, not Daguerre, invented the Daguerreotype.[12] Rather, the play constructs static Richard images according to a logic of visually aided retrospection and anticipation that the camera would realize, not invent. If photography and historical drama bind the living to its dead double, so too do these representational forms continually construct the living beholding the dead—Barthes beholding Payne, Richard beholding Richard. Although *Richard II* spectacularly reconsigns the king to his coffin with each iteration, its many static, deathly stills of the king develop across the play into an essential component of Richard's perpetually anticipatory image aesthetics. These still images—the play's little, little graves—host at once the stilled past and a future of beholding still.

I. Becoming a Specter

Before Barthes introduces the photographs of his mother and Lewis Payne in part 2 of *Camera Lucida*, he reflects in part 1 on photographs of himself, lamenting that they capture only his "pose" and not his experience of consciousness. "In the process of 'posing,'" he writes, "I instantaneously make another body for myself, I transform myself in advance into an image."[13] This transformation creates awareness for Barthes of the objectification inherent in the photographer's work, an objectification I will return to repeatedly in this book.[14] The experience of being photographed is one in which he is "neither subject nor object but a subject who feels he is becoming an object: I then experience a micro-version of death (or parenthesis): I am truly becoming a specter."[15] While photography "produce[s] effects that are 'lifelike,'" the image it generates is "another body"—an "effigy" that "embalms" the subject as an object or dead thing.[16] Photographers' efforts to introduce liveliness—"they make me pose in front of my paintbrushes, they take me outdoors (more 'alive' than indoors), put me in front of a staircase because a group of children is playing behind me"—are comically ineffectual, "as if the (terrified) Photographer must exert himself to the utmost to keep the Photograph from becoming Death. But I—already an object, I do not struggle."[17] For Barthes, the photograph's failure to register consciousness effects a translation from subject into object—a death.

A complex, abstract form of this death appears in the Queen's exchange with Bushy (one of Richard's favorites) after Richard has departed for Ireland, a departure that creates an opening for the banished Bolingbroke's fateful return to England. In act 2, scene 2, the Queen develops an extended metaphor of childbirth to express foreboding of Richard's ruin, which she experiences as already completed. The metaphor describes the heir that she would ideally be birthing—the living copy of Richard who would extend the king's patrilineage into the future. But this future is negated as it is engendered, both by the Queen's description of it as "unborn sorrow" and by her reference to "fortune's womb," a birthplace of cycles and vicissitudes rather than straight lines of genealogical or teleological succession (2.2.10). A passage from Samuel Daniel's verse chronicle that is Shakespeare's likely source for the pregnancy metaphor imagines the sorrow-child supplanting the would-be royal heir in the womb. The royal couple are

> bigge with sorrow, and both great with woe
> In labour with what was not to be borne:
> This mightie burthen wherewithall they goe
> Dies undelivered, perishes unborne.[18]

In Daniel's metaphor, sorrow is a royal baby its parents can neither bear nor be delivered of—the tragic fruit of their marriage that precludes its own future by dying in utero. The elaboration of the birthing conceit across Shakespeare's scene similarly enwombs and entombs the future-looking outcome of procreative succession with its own spectral twin, death. The effects are uncanny, resequencing birth and death to proleptically posit Richard's end as the royal couple's child.

Even before the Queen births the "prodigy" of Richard's usurper, the metaphors she exchanges with Bushy objectify her figurative offspring in a way that renders it static, inert, and stillborn (2.2.64). The Queen describes fortune's progeny as at once the feeling of "sorrow" and a material object, a "something" (2.2.16, 26, 12). In an exceptionally intricate reply, Bushy further objectifies her grief by transforming it into an image:

> Each substance of a grief hath twenty shadows,
> Which shows like grief itself, but is not so;
> For sorrow's eyes, glazed with blinding tears,
> Divides one thing entire to many objects—
> Like perspectives, which, rightly gazed upon,
> Show nothing but confusion; eyed awry,
> Distinguish form. So your sweet majesty,
> Looking awry upon your lord's departure,

Find shapes of grief more than himself to wail,
Which, looked on as it is, is naught but shadows
Of what it is not. Then, thrice-gracious Queen,
More than your lord's departure weep not: more is not seen,
Or if it be, 'tis with false sorrow's eye,
Which for things true weeps things imaginary. (2.2.14–27)

Just as the photograph converts Barthes from a conscious subject into an object of the gaze, Bushy's imagery translates the Queen's figurative progeny into an objectified "it" or "thing" by foregrounding the role of the gaze in discerning the "substances" or "forms" of grief from its false, skewed, and over-replicated copies. Bushy attempts to tutor the Queen in distinguishing between the "substance of a grief" and its "twenty shadows," "perspectives," and "shapes" through a conventional Platonic lesson on the difference between the original and its replicas. But his language does not distinguish clearly between the two, emphasizing how grief is apprehended through sight, already an image of itself—a stilled visual object whose original is no less inert than its copies. The Queen's metaphorical progeny is not a conscious being in Bushy's formulation but an object that can be duplicated or viewed from different angles, like the multiplied images produced by a prism (here, a tear) or a distorted anamorphic picture that becomes legible only when viewed askance.

As Scott McMillin has noted, Bushy's lecture on how to see correctly is internally incoherent, suggesting at once that the truth can only be viewed from an oblique angle and that looking at it "awry" creates distortion.[19] As the news of Bolingbroke's rebellion arrives later in the scene, Bushy's "perspectives" metaphor proves itself not only incoherent but largely beside the point: The problem for the Queen is neither the angle from which to view the "something" coming toward her nor the difficulty of discerning false images from real ones. She struggles to name a future that arrives ahead of its time but appears as something already past. The Queen's understanding of the dreaded object's situatedness in time is much closer to the phenomenology of the photographic image than it is to that of anamorphic painting.[20] If she could clearly say what she clearly knows, it would be something like, "Richard is dead and Richard is going to die."

Although Bushy bungles the contemporary representational technology of the perspective picture, his analogy suggests the appropriateness of the image as a figure for describing the Queen's sorrow. In particular, it exposes how images can host two temporal points of view at once, or what Peggy Phelan has referred to as "the double now" that comprises "the photographic effect."[21] His references to images as "shadows" anticipate early theorists of photography who conceptualized the photographic negative as a shadow vestige of what had passed live in front of the camera. In 1835, William Henry Fox described the process through which he created his first photographic negative as "skiagraphy," a term meaning "writing in shadow."[22] In a staged 1857 photograph titled *The First Negative* (Figure 4), Oscar Gustave Rejlander literalized this idea by imagining photography as an "art of fixing shadows," a process that translates the living subject into a static image from which future replicas might be made.[23] Like Bushy's references to shadow, these early attempts to theorize photography represent the image as always already distanced from the original in space and therefore time—a belated shape or negative of that which is definitionally past, even as it reproduces future copies. In Barthes's terms, Bushy constitutes the Queen's shadow progeny as a "this-has-been"; as such, "it is already dead."[24] But the conversation that takes places in this scene also supplements the theoretizing work of Barthes, Fox, and Rejlander by suggesting that the photographic image is not merely a site where objectification happens and temporal registers intersect or overlap. It is a medium for representing those very phenomena, which precede the specific technology of the camera, a device for producing what Jean-Christophe Bailly calls "new and yet long-imagined images."[25] The camera mechanically generates pictorial artifacts imagined in *Richard II*—artifacts that reveal precisely the kind of temporal awareness Bushy and the Queen are attempting to describe.

In its intuition of the death-effects of the photographic image, the Queen's figurative pregnancy—both proleptic and retrospective of Richard's end—disrupts not only the ideal of unbroken linear succession but the underlying fiction of linear time. Her exchange with Bushy offers a compressed meditation on the terms by which both historical drama and photography reproduce the figures of the past—terms that are markedly different from those mapped by the king's two bodies, in which an anthropomorphized divine kingship is regenerated, undisrupted, through the temporal sequence of conception, pregnancy, and delivery of an heir. Kantorowicz describes how "the dying king and the new king became one with regard to the invisible and perpetual Crown which represented the substance of the inheritance. . . . It was an old conceptual property of juristic thought to personify the inheritance; that is, to treat the estate, as it passed from the testator to the heir, as a person."[26] By contrast, the Queen's heir is a nonperson—an image that reverses anthropomorphism by creating "something" or "nothing" and confounding the sequential relationship between progenitor and progeny (2.2.12, 32). She puns on Bushy's "'Tis nothing but conceit" to observe the normal sequence of conception in which the progeny of sorrow would be "still derived / From some forefather

FIGURE 4. Oscar Gustave Rejlander (1813–1875). *The First Negative*, 1857. Photo by Patrice Schmidt. Salted paper print, 22.4×15 cm. Inv.PH02011-13. © RMN-Grand Palais/Art Resource, N.Y.

grief" (2.2.33–35). The sorrow she has conceived has no discernible origin, however; it permutates the temporal sequence of parent and successor:

> For nothing hath begot my something grief,
> Or something hath the nothing that I grieve.
> 'Tis in reversion that I do possess—
> But what it is, that is not yet known what,
> I cannot name; 'tis nameless woe, I wot. (2.2.36–40)

The Queen is not pregnant through a linear procreative process but through a retroactive one—through "reversion," a legal process in which someone already in possession comes into ownership through the prior owner's death. Christopher Pye has observed that "her unborn sorrow is also a returning sorrow"; it is "something that comes toward her from an already established futurity."[27] Instead of descending from a progenitor, the Queen's offspring derives from a postgenitor, a postcreation through death, like a photograph or history play. The representation of the royal couple's future as dead is thus not merely a prophetic anticipation of later events in the play. The exchange between Bushy and the Queen registers the temporal effects of both a photograph of and an Elizabethan play about Richard II, who is dead before the play begins and dead again at its end. In the liveness between these two deaths, Bushy and the Queen figure Richard's future as nonetheless bound to the inert condition of a stillborn image.

Looking at the photo of Payne, Barthes writes, "I read at the same time, *This will be* and *this has been*; I observe with horror an anterior future of which death is the stake. By giving me the absolute past of the pose (aorist), the photograph tells me death in the future. What *pricks* me is the discovery of this equivalence."[28] The exchange between Bushy and the Queen registers precisely this equivalence—this *punctum*, as Barthes calls it: The heir to Richard is its own objectified, unnamed image. For the Queen, this equivalence is experienced as the *punctum*—a piercing recognition, Freud's uncanny, "that class of the terrifying that leads back to something long known to us."[29] She is "heavy-sad" with "heavy nothing"—pregnant with an image, a shadow, a future death (re)generating itself as a picture in her womb (2.2.30, 32).

II. Graved in the Hollow Ground

From this abstract, "nameless" image of Richard's end, the play progressively gives name and distinct shape to representations of his death, many generated by Richard himself. The news that his favorites, captured and executed by Bolingbroke, are "graved in the hollow ground" initiates an extended meditation on death that will ultimately materialize in the play's final spectacle of Richard's coffin (3.2.136). Editors of the play have identified in Richard's morbid resignation a fatalism bordering on causality. Charles R. Forker writes, "Characteristically, Richard anticipates and, in a sense, invites the worst before it actually happens," and Andrew Gurr remarks on Richard's "responsibility for his fall."[30] What critics observe as Richard's death wish or prophesy is the suicidal effect of his self-objectification, especially the figuring of himself as a corpse. He is not only a subject becoming an object, as Barthes puts it, but the documentarian or photographer who "knows . . . very well, and himself fears . . . this death in which his gesture will embalm [him]."[31]

But Richard's self-embalming gesture also creates several temporal effects that compete with his apparent fatalism. Provoked by the news of his decapitated favorites, Richard sinks into despondency:

> Let's talk of graves, of worms and epitaphs,
> Make dust our paper and with rainy eyes
> Write sorrow on the bosom of the earth.
> Let's choose executors and talk of wills—
> And yet not so, for what can we bequeath
> Save our deposed bodies to the ground?
> Our lands, our lives and all are Bolingbroke's;
> And nothing can we call our own but death,
> And that small model of the barren earth
> Which serves as paste and cover for our bones. (3.2.141–50)

Richard seems to identify with the worm-eaten, luridly inert "deposed body" he describes. He imagines himself as skin filled with bones—a corpse pie with a coffin crust. Simultaneously, however, he figures himself and his men in preparation for a future after death. Specifically, he invites them to write documents that will outlast their deaths, such as the epitaph and will. Although engaged in morbid anticipation of the grave, Richard suggests how his voice will linger as text after his body has been buried. Like his meditation on his mirror image, Richard's proposal to "talk of graves, of worms, of epitaphs" multiplies him across several temporal dimensions through a present speaking voice, a future dead body, and a set of artifacts that will extend his voice into a postmortem future.

Richard's monologue develops from this multitemporal preparation for death into a meditative interlude on dead kingship:

> For God's sake let us sit upon the ground
> And tell sad stories of the death of kings—
> How some have been deposed, some slain in war,
> Some haunted by the ghosts they have deposed,
> Some poisoned by their wives, some sleeping killed,
> All murdered. (3.2.151–56)

The past tense of Richard's story of the deposed, murdered king illustrates the passivity that tends to be read as Richard's participation in his own death. He takes his ruin as a foregone conclusion—as something that has already happened in conformity with a genre of tragic king stories into which he inscribes the events of his own life. As in the preceding reference to writing his will and epitaph, however, Richard's invitation to storytelling posits a role for him apart from that of the dead. He is the historiographer whose stories persist beyond the grave—whose point of view, anchored in the future, allows him to reflect back on his own past death. While it narrates him into the grave, Richard's storytelling role again multiplies him—into subject and storyteller, chronicled king and king's chronicler. Further, in his inclusion of kings "haunted by the ghosts they have deposed," Richard suggests a future for himself that does not depend on his surviving the usurpation—a future as a ghost who persists to trouble his usurper. As Maggie Vinter observes, Richard's reference to haunted and haunting kings identifies a potential agency for the deposed king that becomes available to him through death.[32]

As Richard foresees, his death will be the end result of the still-unfolding usurpation, but from the broader perspective of historical drama, it is also merely a function of time. Regretting that Richard returned from Ireland only a day after his army dispersed because they believed their king dead, the Earl of Salisbury describes the source of Richard's ruin as time itself. He laments:

> One day too late, I fear me, noble lord,
> Hath clouded all thy happy days on earth.
> O, call back yesterday, bid time return
> And thou shalt have twelve thousand fighting men.
> Today, today, unhappy day too late,
> Overthrows thy joys, friends, fortune, and thy state. (3.2.63–68)

The forward march of time from yesterday to today creates a "late" day and a "late" Richard whose only hope of avoiding doom is the reversal of time.[33] Death is not simply a function of the plot but of the temporal progression that fixes Richard as a subject (and object) of a completed period and makes him available to the dramatist of history as a character absorbed in postmortem self-reflection. Time itself is Richard's antagonist. "Time hath set a blot upon my pride," he laments (3.2.77). It is futile to try to change the course of events because "Death will have his day"—and, indeed, death already has (3.2.99). As the play advances from scene to scene in the unfolding time of reading or performance, the day of death that has already past grows nearer in the future.

For Barthes, the *punctum* of the historical photograph is time. Time pierces with a death that has been and will be. Like the photograph of Payne, the play represents the figure of Richard in a form that both depends on his being already dead and presents him going-to-be-dead. The play's representation of Richard at once repeats scenes of his aliveness and punctures aliveness with its own temporal progress, restoring Richard to his grave. Richard observes this very *punctum*:

> For within the hollow crown
> That rounds the mortal temples of a king
> Keeps Death his court; and there the antic sits,
> Scoffing his state and grinning at his pomp,
> Allowing him a breath, a little scene,
> To monarchize, be feared and kill with looks,
> Infusing him with self and vain conceit,
> As if this flesh which walls about our life
> Were brass impregnable; and humored thus,
> Comes at the last and with a little pin
> Bores through his castle wall, and farewell, king. (3.2.156–66)

The crown frames a static icon of power that the king imagines to be made "of brass impregnable." The theatrical king enjoying his pompous "little scene" at court entertains a fantasy of changelessness—the scripted performance of the generic role of "a king." This figure is pierced by the "little pin" of Death, the true ruler who renders the "hollow crown" a grave, a verbal and imagistic echo of "graved in the hollow ground" (3.2.136). Encircled in the grave of the crown, the mortal body or "flesh which walls about our life" is a grave within a grave. Just as the *punctum* of time reveals Lewis Payne a "that-has-been," the pin of death discloses the king's mortality, piercing him with what Barthes would call the "lacerating emphasis" of his pastness.[34] Death shares the crown with the king in a configuration in which, Vinter notes, "King Richard and King Death are superimposed upon each other."[35] The living king is doubled by his spectral other—haunted or spooked, as I will describe this phenomenon more fully in chapter 3—by a death that is at once in the future, in the past, and always already in the present.

Even as he observes the effects of time—the death that, like Bolingbroke's usurpation, comes "at last"—Richard is again improvising its subversion. The scene that takes place inside the hollow crown is decidedly theatrical, as though the crown were a miniaturized precursor to *Henry V*'s "wooden O" in which "Are now confined two mighty monarchies," the court of "antic" Death and the lesser court of the king (*H5* Prologue.13, 20).[36] The theatricality of antic Death complements the references to "breath," "scene," and "pomp" in the passage, all of which describe the king's courtliness as a dramatic show of power—a performance of "monarchiz[ing]" that is more spectacle than substance. As in the earlier references to storytelling and epitaphing, Richard's extended metaphor reverberates with an authorial voice, as many critics have observed—the voice of a playwright scripting a drama that unfolds in the circumscribed temporal dimension within the hollow crown.[37] This dramatist's voice, I suggest, represents another form of Richard's postmortem consciousness, one analogous to his function as epitapher and viewer of self-generated images of his death. The king's court is organized by a linear time that terminates in death. By contrast, Richard's authorial metaphor-construction happens in the perpetual present. In positing himself as corpse, chronicler, epitapher, and playwright, Richard both reproduces and subverts the deathly *punctum* of time.

III. There Lies

Richard will remain alive until the final 60 lines of act 5, but the play has already created several graves for him—still images that translate him from conscious subject into unconscious object. Act 3, scene 3, outside Flint Castle, offers several more invitations to imagine Richard already dead. The opening argument between the Earl of Northumberland and the Duke of York—over whether omitting Richard's royal title symbolically decapitates the king—sets particular conditions for the entrance of young Henry Percy a few lines later. When Percy announces that the castle is "royally manned," Bolingbroke corrects him: "Why, it contains no king" (3.3.21, 23). Percy's reply does not entirely resolve the question of whether the castle is royally manned: "Yes, my good lord, / It doth contain a king. King Richard lies / Within the limits of yon lime and stone" (3.3.24–26). Percy models his syntax from Bolingbroke's, making Richard the object rather than the subject of the declaration that Flint "doth contain a king": syntactically, the king is immobilized in the container of the castle. The suspension of the epitaphic "King Richard lies" at the end of the line compounds the opening image of a decapitated king by suggesting that he lies dead. The reference to "the limits of yon lime and stone" amplifies this sense, figuring Richard lying in a stone tomb sprinkled with quicklime, used to prevent the putrefaction of dead bodies.

Richard's subsequent appearance on the battlements at Flint presents quite a different image of him, but it is no less objectifying than these veiled references to the object of his corpse. He is again described as an image: "Mark King Richard how he looks," says Bolingbroke; "See, see" (3.3.61–62). York's response, "Yet looks he like a king," registers the difference between the visible effigy of Ricardian kingship and the political and military power concentrated in Bolingbroke (3.3.68). As he draws the rebels' eyes to Richard's eye, York observes how power is concentrated in the gaze: "Behold, his eye, / As bright as is the eagle's, lightens forth / Controlling majesty" (3.3.67–69). But as in Bushy's metaphors of the perspective picture, Richard has become the thing seen rather than the seer, the beholden rather than the beholder, and it is Bolingbroke and his rebels who "See, see." Richard's gaze is merely a theatrical spectacle—"so fair a show" (3.3.70). Once the organ of Richard's controlling gaze, his eye has instead become the picturesque object of the rebels' beholding.[38]

Faced with the spectacle of the vastly superior army Bolingbroke has amassed to confront him at Flint Castle, Richard breaks into an explicit representation of his imagined burial in the common street, a meditation that extends his visual objectification into a sustained meditation on the dead object of the king. His image of "a little grave, / A little, little grave, an obscure grave" that is "hourly trample[d] on" by his former subjects leads his faithful cousin, Aumerle, to cry and Richard to exclaim:

> Aumerle, thou weep'st, my tender-hearted cousin.
> We'll make foul weather with despised tears.
> Our sighs and they shall lodge the summer corn,
> And make a dearth in this revolting land.
> Or shall we play the wantons with our woes,
> And make some pretty match with shedding tears;
> As thus, to drop them still upon one place
> Till they have fretted us a pair of graves
> Within the earth; and, therein laid? 'There lies
> Two kinsmen digged their graves with weeping eyes.' (3.3.152–53, 156, 159–68)

In Richard's elaborate conceit, he and Aumerle are reproduced several times over: They are a pair of weeping graveside mourners, the dead men laid in the grave, the subjects of a conventional "There lies" epitaph, and their own epitaphers. In Richard's production of his dead image, his eye's camera—a word derived from the Latin word for "chamber"—entombs him in a picture of its own making.[39] His eye thus makes two graves for him: the grave dug by weeping and the grave of his self-objectification as a corpse "within the earth." The image translates Richard from weeping subject into object of the grave and gaze. Crucially, the gaze is Richard's own. While other characters—the Queen, Northumberland, Percy, York—construct indirect, "awry," or figurative images of a dead Richard, he asserts the authority of representing himself as explicitly dead (2.2.21). He anticipates the phenomenon of the selfie, which has been described in media studies as at once a camera, a stage, a text, and a mirror.[40] Richard's selfie is the process and product of optical self-objectification that enshrines him as an image for his own morbid, scopic, future gratification.[41] By inventing and reading his epitaph, Richard captions this dead image, asserting not only pictorial but textual authority to project his perspective beyond the grave.[42]

The epitaphic utterance with which Richard concludes his conceit entails him in a perpetually deictic postmortem gesture toward his own corpse.[43] As Scott Newstok recounts in his study of epitaphs, Queen Elizabeth was reported to have made a similarly epitaphic remark in an early speech to Parliament: "When I have expired my last breath, this may be inscribed on my Tombe: 'Here lies interr'd ELIZABETH / A virgin pure untill her death.'"[44] Elizabeth sets an intention to reign unmarried and dictates her own epitaph to that effect, suggesting what "may be inscribed" on it by others after her death. Newstok rightly observes in such remarks a tension between suicidal self-erasure and what he calls "self-projection."[45] Richard's epitaphic utterance is similarly self-deadening or suicidal, but in its construction of him as both the corpse and the epitaph's later reader, rather than as the living person who dictates her future epitaph, it is even more radically self-projecting. Unlike the future imagined by Elizabeth, in which the interred corpse and epitaph will occupy the same space "here" at her tomb, Richard gestures "there," reading his epitaph from a temporal and spatial distance beyond the corpse. By relegating himself to the grave and then reading his own epitaph over it as a persona distinct from the corpse that lies in it, Richard exercises his exclusive prerogative to imagine the death of the king. When Percy and Bolingbroke flirt with the question of whether "the king lies" in Flint Castle, the doubleness of their language betrays their nascent treason.[46] In openly describing himself in a grave indexed by his own "There lies," Richard constructs a truly exceptional royal exceptionalism—his unique privilege to kill off the king and survive to point at the dead body "there."[47] As the only character in the play who can frankly contemplate the king's corpse, Richard is the only character who can use that corpse generatively to constitute and inhabit the future time after his death. Notwithstanding his usurpation and murder, the future belongs to Richard.

In its expression of both finality and anticipation, Richard's grave image foresees the mechanisms of *Camera Lucida*, whose authorial voice similarly testifies to the futurity implicit in images of the dead. As in Richard's account of his grave, *Camera Lucida* inscribes the consciousness of Barthes as the beholder of the book's photos. The photograph of Barthes's mother that catalyzes his meditation is not even reproduced in the book. It is effaced by the voice of Barthes, a voice captured in perpetual reflection on the superseded image of his mother. The open-ended future of looking represented by Barthes's authorial voice is built into photographs, which are necessarily "addressed [to] a futured viewer," in Rebecca Schneider's words.[48] The image that remains when the photograph is taken inscribes both a past moment and future ones. These "crosse[d] temporal registers" of the already and the not-yet, Schneider argues, are embedded in the word "remains," which denotes both what has been left behind and what "remain[s] before . . . as both *ahead of* and prior to."[49] Richard's meditation on his tear-fretted grave multiplies this already-multiple sense of "remains," creating an image of mortal remains that he remains to behold as well as a textual remainder that he remains to read. These remains, in turn, are produced within the inexhaustibly re-readable, re-performable medium of historical drama, which represents "an encounter," Schneider writes, between the past and "the *still*, or *ongoing*, or *live* mode of return."[50]

In anticipating his death, inscription, reading, and performance, Richard generates what performance theorist Daniel Sack, after Giorgio Agamben, calls "potentiality," or "a present moment's outlook toward the future."[51] Whereas "stillness and silence often read as negation," Sack writes, Richard demonstrates the productivity of his own dead body, or what Sack calls the "live potentiality the still-posed image casts into the future."[52] This form of potential underwrites the generativity of both *Camera Lucida* and *Richard II*. While Barthes fears that being photographed translates him from subject to object, his act of authorial reflection instantiates him in the continuous act of beholding, an act anticipated by the photographic image itself. Unlike Richard, however, Barthes registers no awareness of how his perpetually viewing consciousness supplants the photographic subject, particularly his mother. By contrast, Richard's simultaneous production of a still image and its viewer explicitly discloses the dead image's potential to constitute a future. In strategically deploying the position of viewer that he generates through stilled images of a dead self, Richard recognizes and exploits a feature of the photographic phenomenon unremarked by Barthes, positing himself as at once the photographic-epitaphic subject, object, creator, mediator, and viewer. Although it represents him dead, Richard's self-authored grave scene inscribes him as its authoritative beholder in a scripted, anticipatory, perpetually potential gesture. Richard's image engraves his future.

IV. Was This the Face?

The range of effects created by Richard's anticipatory self-objectification are fully realized in the mirror scene at the end of his deposing in act 4, scene 1. As the opening of this chapter suggests, the mirror image functions in the play as one of Richard's graves, temporally demarcating the living speaker from his dead effigy. Although portrait painting would seem to offer the most historically specific analogue for this framed, truncated, static-image-within-the-play, the mirror moment produces several effects that are unlike those of painting. As Susan Sontag points out, painting makes no claim to having captured a real moment in time, let alone to being created through a process that transfers light from one object onto another, as photography does. She writes, "A photograph is not only an image (as a painting is an image), an interpretation of the real; it is also a trace, something directly stenciled off the real, like a footprint or a death mask. . . . A photograph is never less than the registering of an emanation (light waves reflected by objects)—a material vestige of its subject in a way that no painting can be."[53] Barthes makes a similar point, though in slightly different terms: "Painting can feign reality without having seen it. . . . Contrary to these imitations, in Photography I can never deny that *the thing has been there*"; "In Photography, the presence of the thing (at a certain past moment) is never metaphoric."[54] Barthes and Sontag articulate what Rejlander pictured in *The First Negative*, where the photograph is imagined to derive from the shadow cast by a material object. What Sontag, Barthes, and Rejlander observe about the photograph and its real physical referent is equally true of the mirror image: it certifies through the effects of light the presence of what is imaged.

Because it represents something that was present but is already past, Richard's mirror image works more like a photograph than either a conventional mirror image or a painting.[55] As in a photographic portrait, the mirror image of the erstwhile King Richard testifies that he was the nonmetaphorical king—a lord who kept "ten thousand men," not "a mockery king of snow" (4.1.250). Given its belatedness, however, the figure he sees in the mirror is a death mask of his kingship—an image of what was there that is "stenciled off the real," like the shadowy outline depicted in Rejlander's *The First Negative*. Richard observes in his image what Barthes observes in photography: What is pictured "has been absolutely, irrefutably present, and yet [it is] already deferred"; "There is a superimposition here: of reality and of the past."[56] Richard's call for the mirror and his reading of its flattened, static image as an effigy of his belated kingship thus functions as another expression of his royal rights, including his exceptional authority—dramatized across the scene—to declare his kingship a thing of the past. Like the epitaph of the previous scene, this still, replica-Richard is inherently a deadened object but one that points reflexively to where kingship was: in the man who (still) holds the looking-glass.[57]

Thinking about the mirror image as a kind of proto-photo brings into view Richard's creation of nostalgic longing through his gestures toward an objectified, bygone king. The mirror vision of his spent kingship does not make an explicit political argument for divine right. Rather, it simply figures him as a king who once was, thereby presenting what Sontag calls "an invitation to sentimentality" and "an object of tender regard."[58] In her analysis of the role photographs play in spurring or dulling political action, Sontag argues that "while [photography] can goad conscience, it can finally, never, be ethical or political knowledge. The knowledge gained through still photographs will always be some kind of sentimentalism."[59] In Richard's case, however, sentimentalism functions *as* political knowledge by certifying his bygone kingship and therefore the crime of his deposing. Describing his mirror image as contemporary with his current face would not achieve the same effects: The sentimental, romantic, and political truth claims of the moment depend on the image as a representation of pastness. Although the reflected face is produced simultaneously with Richard's description of it, his temporal staggering of the two faces anticipates what Sontag describes as the photographic "enterprise of antiquing reality" by which Richard "offers instant romanticism about the present" and renders himself an "instant antique."[60] Through Richard's eyes—as through the photographer's—"the now becomes the past."[61] Richard generates nostalgia for himself not simply to lament his loss but to create an unkillable self who survives that loss—a postmortem Richard capable of nostalgia.[62]

The impermanence of Richard's image is built into the mirror, a symbol of transience.[63] Appropriating the destructive forces of time that make images "brittle," Richard proceeds to shatter the glass, drawing an analogy between the transience of his kingship and the transience of its two-dimensional effigy: "A brittle glory shineth in this face—/ As brittle as the glory is the face! / For there it is, cracked in an hundred shivers" (4.1.277–79). Like the earlier epitaphic moment, Richard's act is at once destructive and reproductive, proliferating the still image of a past Richard into a hundred photographic copies. In his dismissive response to Richard's action, "The shadow of your sorrow hath destroyed / The shadow of your face," Bolingbroke highlights the image's status as copy, pointing out the gesture's histrionic and artificial qualities (4.1.282–83). He identifies both the face and the conceit of its brittleness—integral to Richard's project of objectifying and sentimentalizing a lost past—as synthetically generated replicas.

Bolingbroke's depreciation of Richard's gesture recalls Bushy's earlier distinction between "each substance of a grief" and its "twenty shadows" (2.2.14). Richard quickly adapts the moment to this Platonic model, generating a new conceit that relocates loss from the visible image of the mirror to an invisible, internal object:

> 'Tis very true, my grief lies all within;
> And these external manners of laments
> Are merely shadows to the unseen grief
> That swells with silence in the tortured soul.
> There lies the substance. (4.1.285–89)

Moving beyond his initial suggestion of the mirror's doubled faces, one revealing the past and another the present, Richard appropriates the language of substance and shadow into an alternative yet related model of the doubled self: the expressive, visible body and the mute, invisible soul. By claiming "There lies the substance" in a gesture toward the "unseen" soul, Richard creates another epitaph that points to his interior self as a grave. If Bolingbroke has declared Richard's visual representation of ruined kingship inauthentic—too figurative to denote a real death—Richard responds by epitaphing his own soul, excavating inward to the "substance" and finding it, too, lying dead. He shares the Queen's funereally pregnant condition, bearing within a teeming death—a "grief / That swells with silence," or what he will call in the final soliloquy before his murder, "A generation of still-breeding thoughts" (4.1.287–88, 5.5.8). Through this rhetorical gesture toward an entombed interior self, Richard invents a new memorial to objectify the nostalgic pathos of his lost kingship.[64] In the process, he again asserts himself as its only reader, creating through this—his most morbid self-representation—a future beyond his grave.

Given Richard's skillful production of future selves, even at the height of morbid self-objectification, is it any wonder that the play must finally produce him in his coffin, as gratuitous as this spectacle may seem after his lurid, onstage murder?[65] Might we not otherwise expect him to upstage the final scene with an epitaph over his own corpse? (Cue David Tennant—in Figure 5.)

The image aesthetics of *Richard II* create a perpetual perspective for the king, one that becomes legible when we expand the play's conceptual range

FIGURE 5. David Tennant as Richard II, dir. Gregory Doran, RSC at the Barbican, 2016. Ref: 182188. Photo by Keith Pattison. © Royal Shakespeare Company.

to include the phenomenology of the photograph. These image aesthetics are particular to the character of Richard; in Shakespeare's body of work, their closest analogue may be the little container of the sonnet, in which the subject is fixed for perpetual viewing by a speakerly voice that strategically anticipates the eye of the reader. In sonnet 55, for example, the speaker describes the addressee persisting beyond both the natural span of life and the time-bound edifices of the grave and monument. But the nameless young man has, in fact, been lost to history, while the speaker of the poem is suspended in the perpetual present, inscribing his own postmortem survival by generating both a textual afterlife and an audience of "eyes" trained on his lines till doomsday.[66]

By capturing himself in poses of morbid fixity, Richard similarly recalls his own future stillness and enacts his aesthetic afterlife, an afterlife ensured by his perspective on his grave just as by every sonnet's, play's, or photograph's implicit beholder. Reading the play's inset, still images of Richard as gravesites where the future is constituted through the past highlights the images' resonance with other phenomenal afterdeaths of Richard II, such as those that unfold around the cigarette box with which this book began.[67] Such reading also reframes the notion of a double or multiple king that has become so integral to our reading of the play to reflect, with greater precision, the play's local, embedded representational technologies. Viewed in these terms, the corporeal-temporal paradox of "The king is dead; long live the king" neatly articulates the mutually constitutive mechanisms of finality and futurity in Shakespeare's photographs of Richard II.

CHAPTER 2

Haunted Histories

Dramatic Double Exposure in *Henry IV,* *Parts One* and *Two*

> Enter the Ghost of Banquo, and sits in Macbeth's place.
> . . .
> The time has been
> That when the brains were out, the man would die,
> And there an end. But now they rise again.
>
> —*Macbeth*

Having usurped the throne of Richard II and obliquely conceded to his predecessor's murder, Henry IV begins his reign—dramatized in Shakespeare's two *Henry IV* plays—facing both an insurrection in the north and a faction of discontented peers, noblemen who feel slighted by Henry after having helped him to his crown. Their rebellion in *1 Henry IV*, led by young Harry Percy ("Hotspur"), culminates in the king's victory at the Battle of Shrewsbury in the final act of the play. There, Hotspur is killed by Henry's feckless son, Prince Harry (aka Hal), who redeems his prior waywardness by valiantly fighting in his father's cause.

In the lead-up to battle, Sir John Falstaff, Prince Harry's ne'er-do-well companion from the London taverns, receives a commission from the king and an order to muster troops in the king's cause. Having taken bribes to exempt suitable candidates from military service, Falstaff makes his first military appearance in *1 Henry IV* describing the ragtag squadron of decrepit undesirables he has conscripted in their place:

> Slaves as ragged as Lazarus in the painted cloth, where the glutton's dogs licked his sores—and such as indeed were never soldiers, but discarded unjust servingmen, younger sons to younger brothers, revolted tapsters, and ostlers trade-fallen, the cankers of a calm world and a long peace, ten times more dishonourable-ragged than an old feazed ensign; and

such have I to fill up the rooms of them as have bought out their services, that you would think that I had a hundred and fifty tattered prodigals lately come from swine-keeping, from eating draff and husks. A mad fellow met me on the way and told me I had unloaded all the gibbets and pressed the dead bodies. No eye hath seen such scarecrows. (*1H4* 4.2.25–38)[1]

Falstaff's reference to a painted likeness of Lazarus marks the play's second allusion to the biblical parable of a sore-covered beggar who dies while vainly awaiting scraps from the table of a rich glutton (Luke 16:19–31). Earlier, in his final tavern scene before departing for the war, Falstaff likens the inflamed face of his syphilitic companion, Bardolph, to the purple robe worn by the parable's rich man, who spends an eternity in hell because he let the beggar Lazarus starve to death instead of sharing food with his fellow man. In its visual resemblance to the "burning, burning" rich man, Bardolph's face presents Falstaff with "a death's head, or a *memento mori*" (*1H4* 3.3.32, 29–30). As Falstaff's description of his soldiers unfolds in this later moment, Lazarus the beggar also comes to stand in as a figure of death, one of the "dead bodies" Falstaff has "unloaded [from] all the gibbets and pressed" into service to be killed in war. During the ensuing Battle of Shrewsbury, Falstaff remarks that "there's not three of my hundred and fifty left alive, and they are for the town's end, to beg during life" (*1H4* 5.3.36–38). The few of his corpse-soldiers who survive will begin the cycle of begging and dying again by turning back into Lazarus.

The aim of the parable of Lazarus the beggar is to illustrate the virtue of charity through reference to the eternal punishment awaiting those who ignore fellow creatures in need. But like Falstaff's account of his troops, who are at once alive and dead, men and spectral "scarecrows," the parable complicates the categories of dead and living by extending the two characters' actions beyond the span of their time on earth. Lazarus is "carried by the Angels into Abraham's bosom" after his death, and when the rich man dies, he is able to see Lazarus from his place of torture (Luke 16:22).[2] Observing Lazarus's comfort, the rich man calls out for Abraham to send Lazarus to relieve his thirst with a drop of water, a request Abraham denies. Resigned to his torment, the rich man then asks instead if Abraham might send Lazarus to the man's five living brothers to warn them of the torment awaiting them if they fail to change their ways. Abraham's refusal leads the rich man to plead, "But if one came unto them from the dead, they will amend their lives." Abraham responds, "If they hear not Moses and the prophets, neither will they be persuaded, though one rise from the dead again" (Luke 16:30–31).

This reference to rising from the dead echoes the story of the other New Testament Lazarus, the brother of Mary and Martha who is brought back from death after lying in his tomb for four days (John 11:1–44). The state in which this Lazarus returns is not made explicit in John's narrative. Visiting the tomb where Lazarus lies, Jesus commands that the dead man emerge. "Then he that was dead, came forth, bound hand and foot with bands, and his face was bound with a napkin. Jesus said unto them, Loose him, and let him go" (John 11: 44). The narrative does not state that Lazarus is alive; rather, the man who "was dead" emerges from the tomb looking distinctly corpselike, still wrapped in his funeral shroud and apparently unable to unwrap himself. The doubleness or ambiguity of Lazarus's risen state echoes Jesus's earlier, ambiguously double announcement of Lazarus's death. Jesus tells his disciples, "Our friend Lazarus sleepeth, but I go to wake him," by which they understand him to mean that Lazarus is slumbering. He must clarify that he uses the term metaphorically—that in saying that Lazarus is asleep, he means that "Lazarus is dead" (John 11:11, 14).

In the context of a soliloquy that describes living men as corpses, Falstaff's reference to Lazarus invokes two biblical figures who present a variety of post-mortem states that collapse life and death. Luke's Lazarus, the beggar, enjoys an eternity in Abraham's bosom in a conventional Christian afterlife that posits the time on earth and the time beyond as connected to each other through a state of continuous sentience. The rich man's wish first to be comforted by Lazarus and then for Lazarus to visit his brothers suggests that the dead persist in a lively state, either by interacting with beings who occupy the afterlife or by returning to the land of the living to interact, as haunting revenants, with those who have not yet died. The Johannine Lazarus—Mary and Martha's brother—is another kind of revenant. His life ends and restarts, though it is difficult to define what he is when he emerges from his tomb. A zombie? A miracle? A sleepwalker? A ghost? Will he die again? Is his death in the future, the past, or both?

These questions likewise haunt Falstaff's conscripts. They are corpselike, looking as though they have already died once, and yet by Falstaff's account they are also "food for powder, food for powder. They'll fill a pit as well as better. . . . Mortal men, mortal men" (1H4 4.2.66–67). As men who are at once already dead and destined to die again, Falstaff's troops summarize the existential state of characters in history plays, themselves revenants of the historical dead. Thomas Nashe's famous description of seeing Lord Talbot onstage, presumably in an early performance of Shakespeare's 1 Henry VI, articulates the double status of historical-dramatic figures as already dead and to-be dead:

How would it have joyed brave Talbot, the terror of the French, to think
that after he had lain two hundred years in his tomb, he should triumph
again on the stage, and have his bones new embalmed with the tears of
ten thousand spectators at least (at several times) who in the tragedian
that represents his person imagine they behold him fresh bleeding.[3]

Historical drama resurrects the dead in order to restage their deaths through
the living body of an actor—in order to dispatch the dead again and again in
an ever-renewable cycle of dramatic resurrection and rekilling. As a spectator, Nashe attests that Talbot's past and future morbidity are both present to
the audience of such plays who, when they weep for Talbot, weep for a Talbot who is always already "bones"—who has been dead long enough to have
decomposed into a skeleton—and yet is "new embalmed" as though recently
killed again, even as he bleeds afresh. Especially moribund in appearance,
Falstaff's conscripts similarly dramatize the fundamental state of all theatrical characters resurrected from the distant past, who occupy a double status
as alive and dead. Coupled with the allusion to Lazarus, itself a double reference indexing multiple forms of revenance, Falstaff's description of his
troops as already-dead men is more than a hyperbolic representation of their
decrepitude or a proleptic anticipation of their impending doom. It is a summary of how historical drama operates as a mechanism of double exposure—as a spectral technology that superimposes dead and alive through the
reproductive work of live theater. What Marvin Carlson has described as the
haunted nature of all theater—"its ghostliness, its sense of return, the uncanny but inescapable impression imposed upon its spectators that 'we are
seeing what we saw before'"—is amplified in history plays, which resurrect figures from the past.[4] Not only is historical drama therefore spectral, but "spec-
trality is itself theatrical," as Rebecca Schneider argues "—a *coup de théâtre*" in
which the actor's body "*enable[s] the specter to reappear across the surface of live
encounter.*"[5]

Within the spectral double-exposure technology of historical drama, moments like Falstaff's account of his conscripts produce further, embedded double exposures. The double exposure created by Falstaff is both related to and
distinct from the production of dead doubles that I trace in chapter 1. Richard II
produces photographic images of himself that enable him to occupy the
place of a viewer who looks down on—and therefore back at—his dead self
from a future vantage point beyond the grave. Through these morbid selfies—
images of the dead king that only he has the prerogative to generate—Richard
inscribes a perspective for himself that survives his own death. By figuring

Richard in such moments as both the speaking viewer and the dead person generated through his self-embalming imagery, *Richard II* creates double exposures embedded within the double-exposure medium of historical drama—moments in which a dead and living Richard are figured simultaneously. This representational technique is expanded beyond the selfie in the *Henry IV* plays, which depict a host of characters as revenants—as men who have returned from the dead to die again. The two parts of *Henry IV* repeatedly figure the living as dead and the dead as living not only in the description of Falstaff's Lazaran conscripts but in an extensive series of episodes that include Falstaff's fake death at the end of *1 Henry IV*, the false account at the opening of *2 Henry IV* that Hotspur survived the Battle of Shrewsbury, and Prince Harry's mistaken impression late in *2 Henry IV* that his sleeping father is dead. Coupled with what I will describe as the two plays' suggestively spectral relationship to one another, such incidents constitute what I argue is an extended pattern of double exposure in *Henry IV*—a pattern that thematizes the figure of the revenant.

As in chapter 1's discussion of photographic phenomena in *Richard II*, this chapter invokes imaging technologies at once to elucidate features of Shakespearean dramaturgy and to situate that dramaturgy among representational mechanisms that I argue are not period- or media-specific. The forms of photographic double exposure that I explore here—spiritualist photography, X-rays, and a narrative photo sequence—all have close associations with theatrical performance, which is to say that these imaging technologies are themselves intermedial. Their production and consumption rely on theatrical forms of presentation—of exposure—that predate the camera or radiograph by centuries. As chapter 1's engagement with the photographic theory of Roland Barthes argued at length, portrait photography is itself a spectrographic, theatrical technology that entails posing as oneself to produce a lifelike image or effigy. It is "a micro-version of death" that renders the sitter as a photographic "specter."[6] The technique of double exposure amplifies the spectral effects of drama and photography, particularly when used to stage relationships between different states of being such as dead and alive, fleshly and ghostly. As a theatrical genre peopled by revenants from the chronological past, historical drama necessarily participates in a nexus of representational forms that include double-exposed photographs—forms that are preoccupied with boundaries between the living and dead: with haunting, with specters, with revenants.

The revenant, or "that which comes back," is a fundamentally deconstructive figure, one at the heart of Jacques Derrida's notion of "hauntology."[7] In *Specters of Marx*, Derrida posits the revenant or specter as the figure of past and future death that haunts any notion of the present, living self. He writes:

This Ego, this *living individual* would itself be inhabited and invaded by its *own specter*. It would be constituted by specters of which it becomes the host and which it assembles in the haunted community of a single body. Ego = ghost. Therefore "I am" would mean "I am haunted": I am haunted by myself who am (haunted by myself who am haunted by myself who am . . . and so forth).[8]

Derrida coins the term "hauntology"—a portmanteau of "haunting" and "ontology"—to articulate the implications of this spectral inhabitation of the self. All ontology is hauntology, he argues, exploiting the punning collapse of difference hosted by the two words themselves, which are aurally identical in their French pronunciation. Any concept of being must account for the inhabitation of the living by its own specter, that which "is neither living nor dead, present nor absent."[9] Derrida takes as his exemplar for the concept of hauntology the ghost of Hamlet's father, and he returns repeatedly to Hamlet's declaration that "the time is out of joint" to articulate hauntology's temporal implications—to illustrate how the dead king-as-revenant represents an untimeliness that "strikes a blow at the teleological order of history."[10]

Through consideration of the *Henry IV* plays, this chapter argues that Shakespeare's representation of history is fundamentally hauntological and that our study of the histories must therefore attend to the specter in ways that historicist criticism has not, in spite of its "desire," as Stephen Greenblatt famously framed it, "to speak with the dead."[11] By Derrida's terms, Greenblatt missed the mark; five years after Greenblatt's *Shakespearean Negotiations*, Derrida asserted in *Specters of Marx* that "there has never been a scholar who really, and as scholar, deals with ghosts."[12] In their critique of the New Historicist model of history, Peter Buse and Andrew Scott observe that

Greenblatt's desire . . . may on first sight seem to share a Derridean openness to the iterative traces of history, but his subsequent examination of historical cause and effect shows this imagined conversation to be little more than a phonocentric fantasy, "the dead" simply acting as shorthand for the current mortal state of the previously living people to whom he would like to talk. The "desire to speak with the dead" does not therefore represent a negotiation or reading of the spectral traces that constitute historicity, but rather a wish to dissolve those traces into a proleptic ontology.[13]

In contrast to New Historicism's preoccupation with the past as past and therefore as markedly distinct from the present and future, this chapter develops its understanding of history from Shakespeare's dramatized hauntology—

from "the spectral traces that constitute historicity" in the *Henry IV* plays and from the way those traces return to unsettle chronology, telos, and historical fixity.[14] Against Derrida's exaltation of *Hamlet* as the hauntological text *par excellence*, I suggest that Shakespeare theorizes the figure of the revenant and its implications for historicity earlier and with greater complexity in the *Henry IV* plays. Not only do *1* and *2 Henry IV* stage an extended series of revenant moments; they also posit the revenant in a complex variety of guises, none of which are literal ghosts. These range from Falstaff's zombie soldiers to surrogates who die in the king's place to a new king who establishes his rule by reference to his own dead double. By situating *Henry IV*'s production of revenants among other visual and theatrical technologies for rendering spectral selves, I argue that the plays construct historical consciousness in terms that cannot be accommodated by historicist criticism.

I. I Have Seen My Death

Double exposure is a photographic technique that has a long association with beliefs in ghosts and spirits. Some of its earliest practitioners were spiritualist photographers like William H. Mumler, who described the camera as a mediating instrument through which the spirits of the dead made their presence visible to the living.[15] Popular in the United States and Europe from about 1870 to 1930, spiritualist photography constituted a central form of proof for proponents of spiritualism, an area of occult belief that asserted that the dead are not sequestered from the living but continue to relate to us in what Crista Cloutier describes as "a dynamic interaction between the living and the dead."[16] Most spiritualist photographs were produced by double exposure, a process whereby one photographic negative is exposed twice so that events captured at two different times occupy the same visual field and therefore appear to have occurred simultaneously.[17]

Mumler's famous portrait of Mary Todd Lincoln with the ghost of her deceased husband is typical of early photographic encounters between the dead and the living (Figure 6). Clients for Mumler's portraits came to his studio, often for multiple sittings, in the hopes that the spirit of a deceased loved one would appear in one of the resulting photographic prints. Successful spiritualist portraits depict what the rich man in Luke's Lazarus-the-beggar parable desires for his surviving brothers: communication from someone dead. For spiritualists, an image like the Lincoln portrait authenticated a vision of the physical and spirit worlds as colocated with each other, producing what Molly McGarry calls a "nineteenth-century *memento mori*."[18] The sitter and the

Figure 6. *Mary Todd Lincoln with the "Spirit" of Her Husband*, c. 1872. Photo by William H. Mumler. From the Lincoln Financial Foundation Collection.

deceased occupy the shared space and time captured by the photograph in an image that argues that the dead remain with us. The dead participate in the pictured moment. They conform to the conventions of formal portrait sitting as though fully aware of the photographic occasion while also revealing their metaphysical otherness through a ghostly or semitransparent appearance.[19]

Controversies surrounding spiritualist photographs frequently turned on the identity of the ghost. When subjected to legal investigations for fraud, photographic ghosts were often identified as either living people who had associations with the photographer or as rephotographed photographs.[20] In the case of one group of portraits taken by British photographer Frederick Hudson in 1872, the sitter and spirit appear to be the same person, a man named Frank Herne who claimed to be a spirit medium (Figure 7). For ardent spiritualists invested in the authenticity of such photographs, phenomena like the duplicate Herne or other incontrovertible evidence of double exposure did not discount spiritualist belief. Rather, the appearance of doubles—either double sitters like Herne or the outlines of physical objects in the room, which could appear doubled if the camera had been moved slightly between the first and second exposures—merely suggested that spirits used photographic double exposure to produce evidence of their existence.[21] In the case of Hudson's pictures of Herne, defenders argued that the spirit who looked like Herne "was Herne's double, the image of his astral body. Some also thought it to be the spirit brother of Herne's own spirit, answerable to the name of Willie."[22] These explanations assume that at the time the photograph was taken, the living Herne also already existed in his postmortem form. In an illustration of Derridean hauntology, spiritualists argue that Herne's living body coexists—temporally and spatially—with its own undead form, the spirit or ghost, which is both Herne's past and future self. That form is and is not Herne: It is his spirit but also his spirit's twin—himself but also different, also "Willie." Double-exposure technology renders these two coexisting entities visible as two distinct figures.

The coexistence and correspondence between sitter and ghost visible in the Herne photo is implicit in spirit portraits like that of the Lincolns, even though they figure two different people. In such portraits, the ghost figure is a synthetic production of double exposure generated in response to the primary subject's desire to see her- or himself accompanied by the dead—a desire that generates the photo through patronage of Mumler's studio. Although the ghostly image of Mr. Lincoln might easily be identified as a rephotographed photograph, such details did not trouble resolute spiritualists, who reasoned that spirits—whose forms may be radically different from those they took in life—sometimes find it necessary to imitate photographs in order to appear recognizable to the living.[23] The ghost is an accessory to Mrs. Lincoln's act of photographic self-reflection,

10

Herne + Double.

Figure 7. *The Medium Florence Cook and Frank Herne*, 1872. Photo by Frederick Hudson (British, died 1889). From Album of Spirit Photographs. Albumen silver prints from glass negatives, 25.9 × 19.1 cm. The Metropolitan Museum of Art, New York. Image source: Art Resource, N.Y. © The Metropolitan Museum of Art.

an accessory that must conform to her idea of the past in order to authenticate the persistence of her husband in a future beyond the grave. The photographed spirit appears different from a living person in its semitransparency at the same time that it intentionally replicates the living sitter's remembered image of the dead. In its self-justifying logic, the ghost's imperative familiarity reinforces the spectral inhabitation of the living with the dead. The ghost of Lincoln who appears in the photo is at once Mrs. Lincoln's other and her self—her memory returned to her as the image of another.

Spiritualism—and related areas of Victorian occult belief in energies and fluids, animism and effluvium—found an unlikely ally in the discovery of the X-ray in 1895. German physicist Wilhelm Conrad Röntgen discovered the X-ray while conducting experiments with Crookes tubes, which are glass vacuum tubes charged with electricity.[24] He noticed that when he covered a tube with cardboard, a fluorescent screen in the room lit up. This suggested that certain light rays, which he initially termed "X-rays," were able to penetrate the cardboard to illuminate surfaces several feet away. He then began to experiment with different objects to ascertain what the rays could penetrate. This eventually led him to ask his wife, Anna Bertha Röntgen, to place her hand between the Crookes tube and a photographic plate. The result was the first radiograph or X-ray image, a photo of the bones of Anna's hand (Figure 8). Because the rays penetrate skin and muscle but not bone or metal, the photo shows the skeletal structure of the hand "surrounded by a ghostlike aura of flesh," as Corey Keller puts it.[25] On seeing the image, Anna is reported to have declared, "I have seen my own death!"

The X-ray's capacity to reveal what could not be seen by the naked eye bolstered beliefs in phenomena like spirits, vital forces and fluids, auras, and psychic energies, which occultists believed could be revealed by particular people, conditions, and technologies. Allen W. Grove writes, "X-rays' ghostly pictures immediately captured the imagination of a people who for sixty years had associated photography with ghosts, and the . . . belief that the photographic plate could detect ghostly rays invisible to the human eye appeared prophetic in light of Röntgen's discovery."[26] Anna's remark points to an additional connection between X-ray images and spiritualist photography, one suggestive of the imagistic superimposition of the dead and living through double exposure. Although she is looking at a past image of herself, what she describes is her future self—herself dead and decayed into a skeleton. She interprets her skeleton as a *memento mori*. For Anna, the X-ray document of her body's past moment—a moment under radiation—uncannily represents its postmortem skeletal form. Read this way, as artifacts in the *memento mori* tradition, X-rays represent a bygone corporeal moment as an image of decay that is yet to come; they expose the future through an image of the past. The X-ray of Anna's hand might

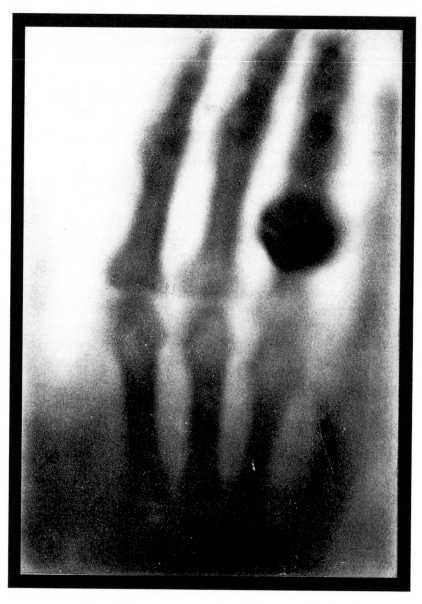

FIGURE 8. The first X-ray image, 1895. The hand of Anna Bertha Röntgen née Ludwig. Photo by Wilhelm Conrad Röntgen. World History Archive/Alamy Stock Photo.

thus usefully be thought of as a spatially tighter, even more localized super-imposition of the past and future body—the living and dead body—than the superimposition represented by Frank Herne's double-exposed portrait. The image of Anna's flesh in a past moment directly overlaps with her future skeletal condition, suggesting, like Herne's portrait, that the living self and its specter co-occur—that they occupy the same space and time, a time that cannot be neatly delineated as past, present, or future.

When viewed in Anna's terms—as a *memento mori*—the X-ray becomes a spectral technology, a mechanism that exposes the spectral other inhabiting the living self. Connecting his concept of hauntology to Freud's uncanny, Derrida describes this spectral other as "a stranger who is already found within (*das Heimliche-Unheimliche*), more intimate with one than one is oneself."[27] Similarly, Nicolas Abraham calls the spectral self a *"familiar stranger"* and a *"bizarre foreign body"* within, a description that is particularly apt for the skeletal figure rendered by X-rays—a figure at once humanoid and alien in appearance.[28] "Wherever there is Ego," Derrida writes, "*es spukt*, 'it spooks,'" meaning that it spooks itself—"'it returns,' 'it ghosts,' 'it specters.'"[29] In a series of declarations that could well describe the X-ray, Derrida writes that "there is some phantom there, it has the feel of the living dead"; the specter "condenses itself within the very inside of life, within the most living life"; "life does not go without death, and that death is not beyond, outside of life, unless one inscribes the beyond in the inside, in the essence of the living."[30] The notion of return that inheres in the figure of the specter or revenant is central here, as in Derrida's other iterations of hauntology. In looking at the X-ray image of her hand, Anna Röntgen views an image of her past hand—an image of herself from the past—returning as an image of her future. Overshadowed by the visible skeleton, the flesh she inhabits as she is photographed is rendered back to her as ghostly. In multiple ways, the X-ray returns her to herself as both a dislocated and colocated ghost—as what Derrida calls "the ghost of the other, and its own ghost as ghost of the other."[31]

The temporal implications of hauntology, illustrated by X-ray images, are explored deliberately by contemporary photographers who use double exposure to represent the various states of being that preoccupied earlier spiritualist photography. In particular, photographer Duane Michals uses double exposure to represent movement between living and dead states through photographic sequences that superimpose bodies, objects, and environments.[32] One of his best-known sequences, *The Spirit Leaves the Body* (1968), begins with a photograph of a nude man lying in a room (Figure 9). The double of the recumbent body sits up, stands, and walks toward the camera until it dissolves. The ghostly spirit produced by Michals's double exposure "leaves the body," as the title of

FIGURE 9. *The Spirit Leaves the Body*, 1968. Photo by Duane Michals. Seven gelatin silver prints with hand-applied text, 3.375 × 5 inches (each image); 5 × 7 inches (each paper). Courtesy of DC Moore Gallery, New York. © Duane Michals.

the work declares. The sequence ends by returning to its beginning—the original image of a nude man lying in a room.

The simplicity of the explanation offered by the title belies the several means by which the sequence undermines the distinctions between dead body and animate spirit that it purports to depict. Rather than representing a straightforwardly linear series of events, Michals's sequence of doubles opens up many of the same questions prompted by Falstaff's troops, by the Lazarus figures, by Victorian spiritualist photography, and by X-rays. When, exactly, does the subject's death occur? Does it not occur in Michals's sequence until the double appears in the second frame? Is that the moment when the recumbent body can be understood as a corpse? If so, what is figured in the first frame? And what is this body's state at the end of the sequence? How is that state different from its state at the beginning? Is there any way in which it can be said to be different, given that the final photograph is a copy of the first? Could this sequence be repeated ceaselessly, its end always a beginning-again? If it could, then what is death? Can we tell the difference between a just-dead body and a living one by looking at it? How is such a distinction complicated by the fact that the body—as well as its transparent double—is that of an actor who is playing both dead and alive, both corpse and spirit? If the spirit dissolves into the position occupied by the viewer, does the viewer reside among the living or the dead?[33]

Like the photographic technologies that produce the portrait of Herne and the Röntgen X-ray, Michals's double-exposure technique renders the ego spooked, haunted by a figure that is at once self and other—what Derrida calls "this non-object, this non-present present, this being-there of an absent or departed one . . . an unnameable or almost unnameable thing: something, between something and someone."[34] By ending in a duplicate of the beginning,

Michals's sequence illustrates the temporal consequences of this hauntology. As a figure of ceaseless return, the specter is destined to come and to come back, such that its "origin and its repetition are coterminous with one another."[35] The specter is not produced by death but inhabits life, which means that it has no identifiable origin or terminus and that life cannot be isolated from death—that life is spectral, haunted. *Es spukt.* The very categories of alive and dead are confounded by the specter. The Michals sequence illustrates this with particular clarity through the absorption of the ghostly double into the viewer. This dissolve at once renders the viewer spectral—the ghost becomes ours, becomes us—and annihilates the boundary between life and death—between past, present, and future, situating us in the realm of the undead and returning the ghost to us again and again as revenant. If we are spooked or haunted by our own spectral selves, who testify that we are always already inhabited by an untimely ghost, then the present is itself untimely, haunted by the past and future. Linear temporality is an unsustainable fiction whose fundamentally teleological claims are dismantled by hauntology. As Buse and Scott summarize, "haunting, by its very structure, implies a deformation of linear temporality."[36] This deformation is central to the photographic practice of Michals, who, without any apparent familiarity with the concept of hauntology, states that an aim of his work is to "play with" and "destroy" linear time.[37] He explores what Derrida calls the *"noncontemporaneity with itself of the living present."*[38]

The theatrical elements of Michals's photography—its use of actors who represent the dead as living and the living as dead, its scripting of sequential actions, its mechanisms for reset and redo—resonate not only with the dramaturgy of history plays but with the theatrical history of double-exposure technologies.[39] Like Michals's sequences, which the artist consistently describes in theatrical terms, spiritualist and X-ray photographs were marked by theatrical modes of production and presentation. Clément Chéroux observes that as a mode of phantasmagoria (the use of optical illusion to produce ghosts or specters), spirit photography doubled as both a form of proof and a form of entertainment.[40] Spirits who appeared in photographs were commonly referred to as "extras," a theatrical and, later, filmic term for supernumerary characters.[41] The photographer was a crucial performer in the production of these images. Cloutier recounts how "in dealing with [his sitters], Mumler's manner was often theatrical."[42] The theatricality of the portrait sitting is mirrored in the central ritual of Victorian spiritualism, the séance, a spectacle in which spirits were brought to show themselves to an audience, usually through the body of a medium.[43] Early in their history, X-rays were linked in the public imaginary with both theatrical spectacles and motion pictures in what Tom Gunning describes as "a widespread culture of display and demonstration."

He writes, "Some impresarios thought X-rays showed even greater entertainment potential than 'animated pictures'; in the 1890s show business trade journals carried advertisements placed by traveling exhibitors who wanted to exchange their motion picture projectors for X-ray equipment."[44] Through their marvelous spectacles of transparency, X-ray exhibitions dramatized the fleshly body as the body double of a skeleton.

The body double produced by Michals epitomizes how these various dramatic-imagistic technologies represent that which appears to be one as multiple, a feature of the revenant articulated by Derrida. The revenant is "more than one: the *more than one/no more one* [*le* plus d'un]"; "*there is more than one of them, there must be more than one of them*."[45] The fleshly form has another form inside of it, before and after it. The living body contains its own deathly future shape, which returns from the past. The portrait sitter is not alone; there is someone else in the room—someone who is at once a revenant from before and an image of the sitter's present wish and metaphysical future. The visible world hosts an invisible one operating in tandem but discernible only under special conditions, and the revelation of what is normally invisible complicates distinctions between past, present, and future. The self's *more than one*-ness and the temporal implications of its multiplicity are of particular interest to Michals, whose double exposures are described by Max Kozloff as representations of a host and its parasite or an ego and its alter, "the guiding analogy of Michals's work." Through Michals's lens, portraiture is revealed to be "a binary form" in which "there will always be a twosome . . . in contrasting states."[46]

This twosome or binary form is multiply conjured by Falstaff's Lazarus allusions in *1 Henry IV*, as are its attendant temporal effects. When Falstaff describes Bardolph's face as a *"memento mori,"* he renders Bardolph as double—as a living image of death (*1H4* 3.3.29–30). Importantly, the phrase locates that death ambiguously in time. Death is an event to come that must be kept in mind during life—hence the phrase's utility as a spur toward moral reform. But it is a future event to be recalled from memory—to be *re*-constituted—in confirmation of Derrida's paradoxical observation that "the future is [the specter's] provenance."[47] Bardolph's face is haunted by revenant-Bardolph; Bardolph's present face is spooked by a future death that must be recollected to return as that which is called back. This temporality of the specter is embedded in the Geneva Bible's translation of the Lazarus parable. In response to the rich man's request that Abraham enlist Lazarus's ghost to warn his brothers of their impending doom, Abraham declares, "If they hear not Moses and the prophets, neither will they be persuaded, though one rise from the dead *again*" (Luke 16:30–31, emphasis mine). This "again" functions like a logical syntactic component of the phrase "rise from the dead," as though to rise from the dead were definitionally to rise from the dead again. "Repetition *and* first time," as Derrida puts it. There is no original resurrection; the revenant *"begins by coming back."*[48] When Falstaff alludes for the second time in the play to Lazarus the beggar, he does so in a description of his conscripts as already-dead men headed off to their future death—as "scarecrows" or specters. His description of his troops articulates, in multiple nested iterations, hauntological and therefore temporal mechanisms shared by X-rays and spirit photographs—mechanisms that unsettle chronological time. As the remainder of this chapter will argue, these mechanisms are a main preoccupation of the end of *1 Henry IV* and of the play's sequel, and like photographic technologies of double exposure, they produce a vision of time utterly incongruous with the notions of historical recovery, conventional ontology, or teleological order that have dominated early modern studies for the past several decades. In Shakespeare's history, it's specters all the way down.

II. To Die Is to Be a Counterfeit

The royal army's signal strategy at the Battle of Shrewsbury that concludes *1 Henry IV* is to protect the king by dressing several people "in his coats" so that the rebels cannot tell which is the real monarch (*1H4* 5.3.25). This tactic dramatizes the attenuation of monarchy initiated by Henry IV's act of usurpation and stages the ontological instability of "real kingship."[49] Having broken the line of genetic succession to claim his title through rebellion, Henry reveals how the king's subject can become the king, thereby evacuating monarchy—especially his own—of its exceptional status. But this device also stages Henry's death repeatedly, even as the deaths of his surrogates facilitate his survival. Combined with the final scenes' extended interest in the production of "counterfeits," the killing off of Henry's substitutes forms one of several theatrical technologies of double exposure generated by the end of the play—technologies that superimpose the living and the dead to stage the temporal multiplicity of the revenant.

When the rebel Earl of Douglas encounters Sir Walter Blunt, one of the king's loyal impersonators, on the battlefield at the opening of act 5, scene 3, he boasts that he has already killed a replica of the king. Addressing Blunt as if he were Henry, Douglas warns, "The Lord of Stafford dear today hath bought / Thy likeness, for instead of thee, King Harry, / This sword hath ended him" (*1H4* 5.3.7–9).[50] Douglas's remarks posit simultaneously dead and living Henrys, the living one he addresses and the "likeness" he has killed. He asserts that Stafford paid for his act of impersonation with his life, but the specific syntax of Douglas's claim—that Stafford "bought / [Henry's] likeness" through death—also suggests that in dying, Stafford obtained the status of

Henry's double and that death rendered Stafford a simulacrum of the king. Implying that a dead person is like Henry IV, and Henry IV therefore like a dead person, this statement is layered with irony. Not only is Blunt another soon-to-be-dead double of Henry, but the Henry who appears onstage in the play is a mere likeness of the dead, historical Henry IV. Douglas's remark that death is at once the price of similitude and the means by which simulacra are generated summarizes the status of characters in historical drama. Such characters are destined, by virtue of their very pastness, to die; to impersonate a dead historical figure is to be scripted into that figure's foregone end. Moreover, because Elizabethan statutes forbade the representation of living persons onstage, the very deadness of historical figures is what makes them available for dramatization. In other words, death is the mechanism by which they become potential dramatic characters—characters who are at once bound to future death and available for continuous dramatic reproduction as animate likenesses who come back. In describing his experience of killing—and thereby producing—a dead double of Henry, Douglas voices the link between impersonation and death foundational to historical drama.

When he kills Blunt in their ensuing combat, proclaiming "here breathless lies the King," Douglas again articulates the logic of the history play, in which costumed likenesses of the king—men "marching in his coats" and "Sembably furnished like the King himself"—are endlessly reanimated and rekilled (1H4 5.3.16, 25, 21). These revenant kings confound linear models of temporal progress. Even as Douglas glories over the misidentified man he has slain, King Henry is both elsewhere dead and still alive—proliferating "like Hydra's heads," as Douglas remarks when he encounters Henry himself in the next scene (1H4 5.4.24).[51] *There is more than one of them, there must be more than one of them.* Through a theatrical mechanism that anticipates both spectral photography and deconstruction's hauntology, moments like the confrontation between Douglas and Blunt enlist a dramatic technology of double exposure—impersonation—to represent the figure of Henry IV as multiple—as dead and alive, past and present. In doing so, such moments reveal historical drama itself to be a spectral technology or double-exposure machine.

The play's interest in the hauntological nature of dramatized history is staged most explicitly when Falstaff subsequently fakes his death to escape being killed by Douglas. Although the stage directions for this moment indicate clearly that Falstaff is pretending death—he "falls down as if he were dead"— an audience seeing the play for the first time would not know that Falstaff has not actually been slain (1H4 5.4.75 s.d.). As Barbara Hodgdon observes, only Falstaff's subsequent speech "codes the moment as something other than a curtain call where, eventually, the two other bodies onstage . . . would also rise to acknowledge spectators' applause."[52] Further, there is no discernible difference between an actor pretending to be a dead character and an actor pretending to be a character pretending to be dead. In drama, as in the Michals sequence, a dead body is not clearly distinguishable from its impersonation by a living actor. As Susan Zimmerman has observed, a corpse cannot be played onstage by anything other than that which it is not.[53] The theatrical liveness of historical figures as well as the deadness of the bodies that represent them onstage are both simulations. By impersonating his own corpse and then resurrecting from "death," Falstaff dramatizes the spectral and simulacral nature of dramatized history. The character is himself a simulated resurrection of a dead historical person who, in this scene, simulates his re-death and then re-simulates his resurrection as a twice-returned revenant—as that which has risen from the dead *again*. The Falstaff who "riseth up" after feigning death is multiply ghosted—to borrow Marvin Carlson's suggestive term—by his multiple specters, past and future (1H4 5.4 .s.d.).[54] He is a walking *memento mori*.

If Falstaff's fake death thematizes the spectro-simulacral nature of dramatized historical figures, his reflections on his corpse-act in the soliloquy that follows radically destabilize the notion of an original from which such simulacra are reproduced. "'Sblood, 'twas time to counterfeit," he declares, "or that hot termagant Scot had paid me, scot and lot too. Counterfeit? I lie, I am no counterfeit. To die is to be a counterfeit, for he is but the counterfeit of a man who hath not the life of a man" (1H4 5.4.112–116). His use of the word "counterfeit" echoes Douglas's remarks earlier in the scene when he encounters what he takes to be another Henry lookalike:

> DOUGLAS: What art thou
>   That counterfeit'st the person of a king?
> KING HENRY: The King himself, who, Douglas, grieves at heart
>   So many of his shadows thou hast met
>   And not the very King. . . .
> DOUGLAS: I fear thou art another counterfeit;
>   And yet, in faith, thou bear'st thee like a king. (1H4 5.4.26–35)

By misidentifying Henry as one of Henry's surrogates, Douglas reveals that there is no immediately visible difference between a real and a counterfeit king. Yet he also seeks to affirm the category of "the very King" by stabilizing the criterion by which such a person might be identified: his bearing. Even as he articulates this criterion, however, he discloses its potential unreliability through the simile "like a king," revealing that a kingly bearing is a kingly likeness. As in the prior scene when Douglas addresses Blunt as Henry IV, his reference to bearing oneself like a king is dense with metatheatrical irony, for the character claiming to be "the very King" is, of course, an actor playing a part—a man dressing, talking, and bearing himself "like a king." As David Scott Kastan observes, the scene discloses how "kingship itself is always and only a counterfeit, a role, an action that a man might play."[55]

On one level, Falstaff's subsequent assertion that the dead are counterfeit constitutes a similarly metatheatrical commentary on his own fraudulent corpse-act. On another, however, it makes a far more profound ontological claim that unsettles the authenticity not merely of kingship but of the play's historical subjects. If it is the case that "To die is to be a counterfeit, for he is but the counterfeit of a man who hath not the life of a man," then the historical Henry IV is not the original from which the play's proliferating copies are made. Rather, as a dead person, Henry IV is himself counterfeit. In this radical declaration, Falstaff declines to fetishize the dead and the past as sites of historical authenticity. But he also resists locating authenticity in the living, as his next sentence suggests: "To counterfeit dying when a man thereby liveth is to be no counterfeit, but the true and perfect image of life indeed" (1H4 5.4.116–18). He asserts that the living are not "counterfeit" per se, but he does not exactly claim them as authentic. On the contrary, he describes the living person as the "perfect image of life"—a likeness of aliveness.

Beyond merely rejecting a chivalric code that valorizes heroic death, as readings of this speech often observe, Falstaff's meditation on counterfeiting ultimately undermines binary distinctions between the living and the dead by rendering both simulacral. In the context of a series of metadramatic episodes, his suggestion that the living and dead are both likenesses creates an analogy between historical and dramatic figures, evacuating both history and drama of the potential to host originality or authenticity. Falstaff articulates Jean Baudrillard's concept of the hyperreal, "the generation by models of a real without origin or reality," or the *precession of simulacra*."[56] Baudrillard associates the hyperreal with "a decisive turning point" that distinguishes postmodern culture—a "transition from signs that dissimulate something to signs that dissimulate that there is nothing."[57] *1 Henry IV* makes the same distinction between representation and simulation in its contrast between Douglas, who believes there must be an original Henry IV on which the king's counterfeits are based, and Falstaff, whose disquisition on counterfeiting ultimately evacuates authenticity altogether. This is not to say that the play is postmodern, however. By exploding the teleologic of an original and its counterfeit, Falstaff compromises the temporal order of before and after that underlies not only concepts of periodization and historical development but also linear temporality itself, without which there can be no pre- or post-*anything*.

Before the final encounter between Prince Harry and Falstaff at the end of *1 Henry IV*, Falstaff acknowledges that Hotspur, too, may be strategically impersonating his own corpse:

> Zounds, I am afraid of this gunpowder Percy, though he be dead. How if he should counterfeit too, and rise? By my faith, I am afraid he would prove the better counterfeit. Therefore I'll make him sure; yea, and I'll swear I killed him. Why may not he rise as well as I? Nothing confutes me but eyes, and nobody sees me. Therefore, sirrah, [*stabbing Hotspur*] with a new wound in your thigh, come you along with me. (*1H4* 5.4.120–27)

Falstaff's reference to Hotspur rising from his moribund recumbency creates a double exposure and another metatheatrical moment, as Kastan notes: "Falstaff's anxious expression voices the reality of the actor playing (counterfeiting) Hotspur, who will, when the scene is over, *rise*."[58] Falstaff's repetition of "counterfeit" in his next statement, "I am afraid he would prove the better counterfeit," registers a fear not that Hotspur plays dead better than he did but that Hotspur would best him if he were to resurrect from not being dead. Like his statement earlier in this speech that a living person is "the perfect image of life," this reference to a potentially resurrected Hotspur as "counterfeit" at once articulates the simulacral nature of historical drama and further collapses differences between dead people, whom he declares counterfeit, and living or undead people, who are lifelike images. His confidence in visual witnessing to certify distinctions—"Nothing confutes me but eyes"—has already been undermined by Falstaff's own fake death, a death that fooled the eyes of Prince Harry himself, who "saw him dead" although he was still alive (*1H4* 5.4.131).

Princes Harry and John enter at the end of act 5, scene 4 to find Falstaff carrying Hotspur's body away. The tableau of Falstaff with a body on his back repeats, from one of Shakespeare's earlier history plays, a moment that is itself a repetition. In an episode of *2 Henry VI* that likewise occurs fewer than 80 lines from the end of the play, Lord Clifford takes up the body of his dead father, the Duke of Somerset, who has been killed in the Battle of St. Albans. Hoisting his father's corpse onto his back, Clifford remarks:

> Come, thou new ruin of old Clifford's house,
> As did Aeneas old Anchises bear,
> So bear I thee upon my manly shoulders,
> But then Aeneas bare a living load
> Nothing so heavy as these woes of mine. (*2H6* 5.3.61–65)

In repeating the action recounted in *The Aeneid* of a son bearing his father away from a scene of war, Clifford substitutes his dead father for the living Anchises.[59] Somerset becomes a dead double for Anchises and Anchises a living double for Somerset in another Shakespearean moment that exploits the ambiguity of an inert body. Falstaff reproduces this tableau at the end of *1 Henry IV*, carrying away the uncertainly dead Hotspur and "hijacking . . . an emblem of father/son affinity, derived from Aeneas' carrying Anchises out of Troy," as John Kerrigan observes.[60] Falstaff repeats the prior episodes with Somerset and Anchises while reactivating the spectral dynamics articulated by Clifford, in which the body on his back doubles as at once living and dead.

For the startled princes who come upon this tableau, Falstaff is also a living dead man. Having delivered an epitaph over Falstaff's presumed corpse earlier in the scene, Harry registers confusion about the status of the figure he and his brother encounter: "Art thou alive? / Or is it fantasy that plays upon our eyesight? / I prithee speak; we will not trust our eyes / Without our ears. Thou art not what thou seem'st" (*1H4* 5.4.132–35). What is it that Falstaff seems? Does he seem to be the ghost of Falstaff carrying a dead body? The ghost of Falstaff carrying its own dead body? The ghost of Falstaff carrying Anchises's ghost? The ghost of Aeneas carrying the ghost of Hotspur? Falstaff's cryptic reply, "No, that's certain: I am not a double man," multiplies rather than resolves this enigma. What, precisely, is "certain" here, in a tableau replicated from *The Aeneid* and *2 Henry VI* in which a character from England's historical past—a character observed to be dead earlier in the scene—carries on his back a (presumably though not definitely) dead character who is also resurrected from England's historical past?[61] Editors gloss the phrase "double man" as having a double meaning: Falstaff's reply establishes that he is not a ghost or "double" and that he is one man—not a two-man man, not both himself and dead Hotspur.[62] In answering Harry's cryptic query with "I am not a double man," however, Falstaff compounds—while seeming to foreclose—the forms of spectral doubleness that the Falstaff/Hotspur (as-Clifford/Somerset-as-Aeneas/Anchises) moment presents. He speaks as one who has come back from the dead again (again)—as a revenant twinned with a revenant. Falstaff is a ghostly double of both himself and Aeneas, the figure on his back a ghostly double of both Hotspur and Anchises.[63] Falstaff is not a "double man" any more than the man he carries. Both are more than one and more than two. Aeneas spooks Falstaff; Hotspur spooks Falstaff; Hotspur spooks Hotspur; Falstaff spooks Falstaff (spooks Falstaff spooks Falstaff, ad infinitum).

Derrida declares, *"There is more than one of them."*

Falstaff answers, *"There are more than two of them."*

III. Hotspur, Coldspur

In suggesting that Hotspur might reanimate from death to rejoin the battle, Falstaff imagines something like a character in a zombie apocalypse—an undead killer haunted by his prior corpse. Such figures are a central interest of *2 Henry IV*, whose compounding specters undermine critical truisms about metaphysical difference, stable originals, historical specificity, and linear temporality.[64] The Induction and first scene of *2 Henry IV* resurrect revenant-Hotspur repeatedly, generating several double exposures of him—moments in which he is represented as both dead and alive, both hot and cold. The allegorical figure of Rumour relates the outcome of the Battle of Shrewsbury that concluded *1 Henry IV*, where Henry's army "Hath beaten down young Hotspur and his troops, / Quenching the flame of bold rebellion / Even with the rebels' blood" (*2H4* 0.25–27). The story Rumour has fomented, however, reports the opposite—that "Harry Monmouth fell / Under the wrath of noble Hotspur's sword" and Henry "Stooped his anointed head as low as death" (*2H4* 0.29–30, 32). Through its multiplication of pasts, Rumour does more than disclose the unreliability of historical narratives or "threaten the ontological stability of bodies and institutions," as critics have argued.[65] Rumour is but one hauntological mechanism among a litany of such mechanisms in the *Henry IV* plays that render being fundamentally spooked and thereby resistant to the presumption that there ever is or was an ontological stability to threaten. Warwick's later complaint that "Rumour doth double" the number of rebel troops resonates with the Induction's narrative duplication of Hotspur, Prince Harry, and King Henry by reversing Hotspur's battle death, killing off Harry, and spawning yet another dead Henry (*2H4* 3.1.92). The play thus opens by spectralizing three key figures, calling Hotspur back from death and visiting upon Harry and Henry deaths that have both already and not yet occurred. Like the other double-exposure technologies this chapter explores, Rumour produces events that resist temporal fixity, opening a play that is preoccupied by signs and news of death in a present time that is spooked by deaths that are at once in the past and in the future.

The question of what happened to Hotspur at the Battle of Shrewsbury is the principal subject of the first scene. Lord Bardolph (a different character from Falstaff's Bardolph) delivers to the Earl of Northumberland, Hotspur's father, "certain news from Shrewsbury" that is the exact inverse of what occurred, reporting the false account of events generated by Rumour (*2H4* 1.1.12).[66] In his response to Northumberland's question, "Saw you the field?" Lord Bardolph explains that he gathered this news and its certainty from a man who had come from the battle (*2H4* 1.1.24). Northumberland's servant Travers then arrives with the opposite news, which he has also gathered from someone along the road—a man who "told [him] that rebellion had ill luck, / And that young Harry Percy's spur was cold" (2H4 1.1.41–42). Like Rumour's double representation of Hotspur, these first two news sources posit a double portrait of him, the dead and the living. Northumberland's response, that this news makes "Of Hotspur, 'Coldspur,'" articulates the apparent binary of hot and cold—metaphors for life and death—while also testifying to the hauntological nature of being—to these states' interdefinition and mutual spooking of one another. Cold is hot's ghost, as the third newsman, Morton, reminds Northumberland after he has arrived and unraveled the full story of the battle. Northumberland, he recalls, knew in advance of mounting a rebellion that his son's "flesh was capable / Of wounds and scars" (2H4 1.1.171–72). To be alive is to be mortal—to occupy a form haunted by eventual death, a hot form spooked by cold.

Northumberland is concerned throughout this scene with visual evidence. Having received conflicting reports of Hotspur's fate from Lord Bardolph and Travers, neither of whom was an eyewitness to the battle, he looks to Morton for more certain certainty. Rumour has ably undermined the reliability of oral accounts, leaving Northumberland to search for other proof in the countenance of Morton: "Yea, this man's brow, like to a title leaf, / Foretells the nature of a tragic volume" (2H4 1.1.60–61). Through the metaphor of a book, Northumberland turns Morton's news into an ostensibly more stable form of information than hearsay and makes himself a firsthand reader of its title page. He then describes Morton's face itself as a kind of ocular proof—a medium through which he views his dead son:

> How doth my son and brother?
> Thou tremblest, and the whiteness in thy cheek
> Is apter than thy tongue to tell thy errand.
> Even such a man, so faint, so spiritless,
> So dull, so dead in look, so woebegone,
> Drew Priam's curtain in the dead of night
> And would have told him half his Troy was burnt;
> But Priam found the fire ere he his tongue,
> And I my Percy's death ere thou report'st it. (2H4 1.1.68–75)

Morton's face, "dead in look," hosts the specter of dead Hotspur. For Northumberland, the appearance of that specter—visible in Morton's trembling, faintness, dispiritedness, dullness, and whiteness—provides evidence of his son's death that secondhand narratives cannot.[67] Himself rendered ghostly by Northumberland's description, Morton functions like a spirit medium through whom Northumberland sees his son's ghost. Looking into the eyes of the man standing before him, Northumberland sees his son's dreaded death as a past event, one that has already happened: "He that but fears the thing he would not know / Hath by instinct knowledge from others' eyes / That what he feared is chanced" (2H4 1.1.85–87).

The narrative Morton goes on to unfold is thus supplementary to the visual evidence of Hotspur's death that Morton's ghostly appearance has already provided. But in telling the story of the Battle of Shrewsbury, Morton further multiplies the specters of Hotspur, reproducing a hauntological history. He recounts:

> But these mine eyes saw him in bloody state,
> Rend'ring faint quittance, wearied and out-breathed,
> To Harry Monmouth, whose swift wrath beat down
> The never-daunted Percy to the earth,
> From whence with life he never more sprung up. (2H4 1.1.107–111)

Although Morton's account asserts that Hotspur did not survive his encounter with the Prince, it leaves open the potential that he may "spr[i]ng up" as some kind of revenant, a possibility entertained by Falstaff in the concluding scenes of 1 Henry IV and articulated moments later in Morton's series of retellings. In addition to remarking how Douglas "had three times slain th'appearance of the King," which attests that seeing someone die does not prove their finality, Morton describes Hotspur and his army as zombies who were dead before they were defeated:

> My lord, your son had only but the corpse,
> But shadows and the shows of men, to fight;
> For that same word "rebellion" did divide
> The action of their bodies from their souls,
> And they did fight with queasiness, constrained,
> As men drink potions, that their weapons only
> Seemed on our side; but, for their spirits and souls,
> This word "rebellion," it had froze them up
> As fish are in a pond. (2H4 1.1.191–99)

In this account, Morton generates double exposures of Hotspur and his men, exposures whose temporal effects resonate with the X-ray and Michals's *The Spirit Leaves the Body*. The men's future defeat and death are projected backward in time, turning their battle bodies into "corpses." Suspended at the end of the verse line, the phrase "your son had only but the corpse" renders Hotspur, in particular, pre-dead. In Morton's image, the past selves of Hotspur and his army are ghosted by their future doom, just as the image of Anna Röntgen's hand discloses her future skeletal form, making flesh spectral. It is unclear from Morton's narrative, however, when this future arrives in the past, because it appears as an effect that precedes the battle. It is "rebellion" (*re + bellāre*, or "to rise up and fight again") that transforms living men into the corpses they have not yet become.[68] By Morton's logic, Hotspur's rebel army enters the battle having already died; his men arrive as revenants, killed by the word "rebellion," which "did divide / The action of their bodies from their souls." They commence the battle as frozen fish—as cold-blooded zombie-things already exhibiting the effects of rigor mortis. In the division of their souls from their bodies, Hotspur's rebels resemble the man in Michals's sequence, whose deathly separation of body from soul cannot be pinpointed in time. It is not an event that happens once in a straightforwardly linear sequence but one that has already happened and happens again.

Morton's news itself constitutes a series of repetitions in which Hotspur is reanimated and re-deadened: the specter of dead Hotspur appears in Morton's face; then Morton recounts how Prince Harry killed Hotspur, but the syntax of his narration leaves open the potential of a zombie return; then Morton tells of a zombie rebel army, led by the corpse of Hotspur, who are killed (again) by Harry and the king's army. Morton's news does not identify a time when Hotspur was last seen alive. Even in the period before the rebel army assembled, when Northumberland "cast th'event of war . . . / And summed the account of chance," it was his "presurmise," as Morton recalls, "That in the dole of blows [his] son might drop" (*2H4* 1.1165–68). Planning for the war involved the anticipation of Hotspur's death. Hotspur was never not spooked by his spectral self. By staging him as a historically dead dramatic character and narratively rehearsing his fate, *2 Henry IV* returns Hotspur as ghost Hotspur, zombie Hotspur, corpse Hotspur, Coldspur Hotspur. He returns as revenant— as Hotspecter. He represents the interhaunting of the past, present, and future—the way in which the death of Hotspur returns as future and past, disturbing linear temporality by haunting the past Battle of Shrewsbury and the present encounter between Morton and Northumberland.

Derrida's term "hauntology" and the notion of "interhaunting" I am deriving from it foreground the specter of death that haunts the living, and this chapter likewise emphasizes how the double exposure technologies of the *Henry IV* plays generate theatrical moments in which living characters are spooked by their own ghosts. However, the conclusion of Morton's digest of news, as well as the very phenomenon of historical drama, highlights the *inter*-aspect of interhaunting: The dead are not left in the past but are endlessly repurposed by the living. The living host the dead, but the dead also host the living, as chapter 3 will illustrate at length. This mutual inhabitation of the dead and living is summarized in Morton's account of how events are beginning to shift in the rebels' favor as their rebellion is translated into a holy cause by the Archbishop of York:

> But now the Bishop
> Turns insurrection to religion.
> Supposed sincere and holy in his thoughts,
> He's followed both with body and with mind,
> And doth enlarge his rising with the blood
> Of fair King Richard, scraped from Pomfret stones;
> Derives from heaven his quarrel and his cause. (*2H4* 1.1.199–205)

Morton describes a reversal of the division between body and soul that marked the rebel army at Shrewsbury—a reunification of the corporeal and transcendental. What catalyzes this reunification is another revenant event: the recovery of Richard II's dried blood from the floor on which it was spilled when he was killed at Pomfret Castle. The resurrection or "rising" of the rebellion from its moribund showing at Shrewsbury is triggered by the revenant of the murdered king, who is repurposed by the Archbishop of York to redirect the course of England's future. The revenant rebel army are parasitically "enlarge[d]"—expanded, replenished, filled up by the desiccated remainder of the dead. Revenant resurrects revenant.

IV. And Is Old Double Dead?

In ruminating over the undead figure of Hotspur, the opening of *Henry IV, Part Two* reverberates with the temporal, metaphysical, and ontological questions raised in the last two acts of *Part One*. These questions not only suffuse *Part Two* with a mood of melancholic doom but surface in critical conversations about the relationship between the two *Henry IV* plays. Not coincidentally, critics have frequently posited a ghostly or parasitic relationship between the two plays. Editor James C. Bulman observes that the dramaturgy of the sequel "has led generations of critics to dismiss *Part Two* as a pale imitation of a glittering original, 'a diminished shadow of its predecessor.'"[69] In this formulation, *2 Henry IV* is a ghost of the first play—"a ramshackle rag-bag of a piece," as Richard David put it, such that when the play turns up, it serves namely to remind us that we are not seeing the prior, real thing.[70] While critiquing such judgments of *2 Henry IV* and asserting that the play, "more than any other of Shakespeare's chronicle plays, broadens one's sense of what history can be," Bulman nonetheless describes it as "essentially parasitic," reinscribing the notion of a preceding original—of a host with a hanger-on.[71] Harry Berger Jr. argues the opposite, suggesting that *2 Henry IV* is the haunted, not the haunter. Across the *Henriad*, he remarks, "earlier textual moments persist like ghosts that haunt and complicate later moments."[72]

Bulman's compelling theory of how the sequel came to be written resolves this apparent debate by suggesting how the plays mutually haunt and inhabit one another. Against arguments that Shakespeare either originally conceived of *Henry IV* as a two-part play or that he conceived the material in *Part Two* only after *Part One* was a theatrical success, Bulman suggests that Shakespeare overwrote *Part One* and used the leftover material for *Part Two* once it became evident that a sequel would draw an audience.[73] He notes, for example, how the repetition of scenes across the plays creates a sense of deflation that is generated by the return of the first play through the second. For example, in the tavern scene at the end of *Part Two*, act 2, scene 4, when Harry and Poins reveal themselves after observing Falstaff in disguise, "their exchange bids an audience recall the comic vitality of their earlier scene [in *Part One*] and, in so doing, recognize the diminished pleasure, and even pointlessness, of goading Falstaff in this play."[74] For Bulman, the tavern scene in *Part One* is suffused with "comic vitality," while the parallel scene in *Part Two* is "diminished" by comparison. While this formulation maps easily onto a reading of *Part Two* as the spectral shadow of *Part One*, it also depends on the return of *Part One* in the midst of *Part Two*—on the revenance of *Part One*, on its presence as an absent presence, on its pastness as not past. *Part One* thus haunts *Part Two* as undead—as specter. Conversely, the future dramatized in *Part Two* also haunts the past dramatized in *Part One*. Prince Harry's ultimate rejection of Falstaff at the end of *Part Two* is promised at multiple junctures in *Part One*, such as in Harry's soliloquized declaration at the close of his first scene with Falstaff that he will "throw off" his "loose behaviour," along with the comrades who encourage it, and in his expressed intention to "Banish plump Jack" when he is king (1H4 1.2.205, 2.5.485). Both the future events' inhabitation of the past and the past's return in the future illustrate hauntology's deconstruction of linear temporality. Beyond merely "broaden[ing] one's sense of what history can be," as Bulman remarks about *Part Two*'s foregrounding of material that does not appear in the chronicle sources, the *Henry IV* plays' mutual haunting of one another resists sequential models of time that underlie conventional conceptions of history.

Like undead Hotspur, Falstaff becomes a focal point in *Part Two* for representing the hauntological nature of being, drama, history, and time. The death that Falstaff audaciously reenacts, fakes, and narrowly avoids at the end of *Part One* haunts him throughout *Part Two*. His first line in the play, "Sirrah, you giant, what says the doctor to my water?" opens his *Part Two* storyline with an X-ray moment (*2H4* 1.2.1). Concerned with how his past behavior is affecting his present health, Falstaff enlists the diagnostic technology of early urinalysis for a glimpse at the invisible body within and for clues to its future trajectory. He seeks what Derrida calls the "ungraspable visibility of the invisible, or an invisibility of a visible X."[75] In the scene that subsequently unfolds between Falstaff and the Lord Chief Justice, who visits him to warn him that he has not forgotten the robbery at Gads Hill dramatized in *Part One*—that the past is not altogether past—Falstaff repeatedly shifts his illness to other characters, only acknowledging his gout in soliloquy (*2H4* 1.2.245–50). He greets the Lord Chief Justice with "I heard say your lordship was sick," and when this tactic does not divert his foe from the purpose, Falstaff turns to rumors of the king's illness: "I hear his majesty is returned with some discomfort from Wales. . . . And I hear, moreover his highness is fallen into this same whoreson apoplexy" (*2H4* 1.2.896–97, 105–10). The Lord Chief Justice meets these deflections by returning repeatedly to Falstaff's physical state: "I think you are fallen into the disease," he replies, suggesting that Falstaff has the sickness he attaches to the king (*2H4* 1.2.120). "You are as a candle," he observes, "the better part burnt out" (*2H4* 1.2.157–58). These reminders to Falstaff about his illness and advanced age provoke Falstaff's outrageous expression of denial: "You that are old consider not the capacities of us that are young. . . . And we that are in the vanguard of our youth, I must confess, are wags too" (*2H4* 1.2.174–78). This ludicrous declaration attempts to recapture the comic audacity of Falstaff's lies in *Part One*, but it falls flat in the face of what Nicholas Grene rightly describes as the Lord Chief Justice's "pitiless enumeration of [Falstaff's] physical symptoms of ageing":

> Do you set down your name in the scroll of youth, that are written down old with all the characters of age? Have you not a moist eye, a dry hand, a yellow cheek, a white beard, a decreasing leg, an increasing belly? Is not your voice broken, your wind short, your chin double, your wit single, and every part about you blasted with antiquity? And will you yet call yourself young? Fie, fie, fie, Sir John! (*2H4* 1.2.179–86)[76]

The previously unarticulated manifestations of illness that sent the aging Falstaff seeking medical diagnosis are here blazoned across his body, figuring the Falstaff who appears before us as decrepit, diseased, and of declining wit. The Lord Chief Justice's description of Falstaff's decay is spectrographic: it generates, through imagery, a living body marked by signs of death.

Falstaff's first scene in the play thus presents him as a spectralized figure—"the type of Old Mortality," as Giorgio Melchiori describes him, or, in the Prince's terms, a man for whom "the grave doth gape / . . . thrice wider than for other men" (*2H4* 5.5.53–54).[77] The Falstaff who concluded *Part One* with a preview of his own corpse returns in *Part Two*, spooked by not only the catalog of past excesses to which his body gives witness but the future death that shadows him. Doll Tearsheet explicitly raises the specter of Falstaff's death in their final scene together before he departs to encounter the rebels. "When wilt thou leave fighting o'days, and foining o'nights," she asks, "and begin to patch up thine old body for heaven?" "Peace, good Doll," he replies, "do not speak like a death's-head, do not bid me remember mine end" (*2H4* 2.4.236–37). His reference to the "death's head" echoes his remark in *Part One* about Bardolph's face as a *memento mori*. As in the other *memento mori* moment, death appears to Falstaff as an event to be "remember[ed]" or recalled as though past. Coupled with the Lord Chief Justice's morbid blazon, Doll's reference to Falstaff's "old body" suggests that he does not need the face of another to show him an image of his end. He need only look in the mirror; the death's head is his own.

Unlike *Part Two*'s Falstaff, who has been described as a character "with a haunted horror of mortality" who is "darkly afraid of death," the aging Gloucestershire justices whom Falstaff visits toward the middle of the play, Silence and Shadow, discuss mortality matter-of-factly alongside market news and other casual conversation, cataloging those of their generation who have already met their end:

> SHALLOW: And to see how many of my old acquaintance are dead.
> SILENCE: We shall all follow, cousin.
> SHALLOW: Certain, 'tis certain; very sure, very sure. Death, as the Psalm-
>   ist saith, is certain to all; all shall die. How a good yoke of bullocks at
>   Stamford fair?
> SILENCE: By my troth, I was not there.
> SHALLOW: Death is certain. Is old Double of your town living yet?
> SILENCE: Dead, sir.
> SHALLOW: Jesu, Jesu, dead! A drew a good bow; and dead! A shot a fine
>   shoot. John o'Gaunt loved him well, and betted much money on his
>   head. Dead! (*2H4* 3.2.32–44)[78]

While remarking how all lives are haunted by the specter of deaths that "shall follow" in the future, Shallow simultaneously constructs specters of the past through the nostalgic reminiscence over his and his peers' prior selves. In recalling how "old Double" "drew a good bow" and "shot a fine shoot" back when he was not yet either old or dead, Shallow renders Double doubly spectral: Both the young and the old Double are past, and yet both return in a conversation characterized by "uncanniness," as Kerrigan notes—a conversation that "brings a buried man back to life." In this way, the question posed by Shallow about whether old Double is dead "articulates a central trope" of the play, Kerrigan observes.[79] Additionally, the conversation takes place between two characters whose names, Silence and Shallow (a portmanteau of "shall follow"?), carry associations with the grave. Like Double, Shallow himself appears in their discussion as multiply spectral. His remark, "I was once of Clement's Inn, where I think they will talk of mad Shallow yet," opens a series of nostalgic recollections about his wild youth, which he imagines persisting in the stories still circulating at Clement's Inn. Present Shallow is doubled by the ghost of his youth, who returns as revenant in the narrative history he imagines, in which his past is continuously reproduced in Clement's present. Shallow is multiplied further by the specter of the future death that "shall follow,"—a specter Falstaff attaches, at the end of the scene, not just to the current, aging Shallow but to his youthful self. Falstaff recalls,

> I do remember him at Clement's Inn, like a man made after supper of a cheeseparing. When a was naked, he was for all the world like a forked radish, with a head fantastically carved upon it with a knife. A was so forlorn that his dimensions, to any thick sight, were invisible. A was the very genius of famine. . . . You might have trussed him and all his apparel into an eel-skin. (2H4 3.2.303–16)

Young Shallow—like "this same starved justice," old Shallow—was a figure of famine—an invisible, dimensionless ghost. Young Shallow was already his old double: dead. As Jonathan Crewe puts it, "the stark-naked Shallow is seen from the start as a remainder—a cheese-paring—rather than a bodily totality."[80] Like zombie Hotspur, young Shallow was ghosted by his future corpse. The "chimes of midnight" that he and Falstaff heard in their riotous nights were as much a death knell as the soundtrack of their youth (2H4 3.2.211).

The scene's double exposures of Shallow represent him haunted by his own spectral selves, revenants who arrive from the past and future to inhabit the present, rendering the present spooked by other times. Just as the moments depicted by the Herne portrait or Röntgen X-ray superimpose bygone, current, and future bodies, so does Shakespeare's rendering of Shallow. Observing the scene's central placement in the play (at act 3, scene 2), Naomi Conn Liebler argues that this placement points to its importance to the play's representation of "an irrecoverable past," a claim that reflects much critical convention around

Shakespeare's histories.[81] While agreeing that this scene does important work—namely, by expanding the play's spectrography beyond its central characters—I argue that it collapses linear time models that would meaningfully distinguish the present from what we conventionally think of as the past or future. In Derrida's terms, the scene "dislocates the linear order of presents" and thereby also dislocates the past and future.[82] This deconstruction of linear order problematizes scholarly truisms about the history plays, such as Phyllis Rackin's assertion that the plays seek "to recuperate a lost, heroic past" but end up "calling attention to the ineluctable absence of that past"; or Graham Holderness's claim that that the history plays "revive the past as vanished, replayable fact, presented to a world in which the pastness of the past is clearly visible."[83] In Falstaff's description of Shallow's body, past, present, and future appear simultaneously. Further, Falstaff suggests that the younger Shallow does not constitute a prior origin or "fact" from which the older Shallow has declined because that Shallow is himself doubly spectral—an image of his future corpse and the fictitious invention of an old man's wish. For Falstaff, that past was never strictly a present. Its events were themselves spectrodramas that collapsed dead and alive, real and counterfeit, time then, now, and to come.

When Shallow calls Falstaff's potential conscripts onto the stage, a scene that is already haunted with "ghosts of futures past" (to borrow a phrase from Molly McGarry) becomes even more crowded.[84] Bulman notes that the conscription episode bears the marks of having been written for *Henry IV, Part One*, in which it would have made more sense, geographically, for Falstaff to muster troops in Gloucestershire on his way to fight the Battle of Shrewsbury. The scene itself, then, represents the potential disarrangement of linear temporality, insofar as the summary Falstaff gives of mustering Lazaran soldiers in *Part One* was likely written after the fully dramatized scene of an identical event that appears in *Part Two*. Both iterations have the quality of a revenant, returning as "repetition *and* first time"—as that which "*begins by coming back.*"[85] In the dramatized iteration in *Part Two*, Falstaff's corpselike conscripts, "unloaded [from] all the gibbets and pressed" into service to be "food for powder" at Shrewsbury, return as reincarnations from the earlier play (*1H4* 4.2.37, 65). Their status as resurrected dead men is emphasized by three of their names, "Mouldy," "Feeble," and "Shadow," though even the more promisingly named "Bullcalf" complains that he is "a diseased man" (*2H4* 3.2.176).[86] Falstaff's play on Shadow's name as he instructs Shallow to "prick him, for we have a number of shadows fill up the muster book," gestures to the practice of "dead pay" by which unscrupulous officers registered dead or nonexistent persons among the names of conscripted soldiers in order to fraudulently collect their pay (*2H4* 3.2.132–33).[87] Like the scene itself, which includes one of the play's several "ghost characters," or characters who appear in the stage directions but have no lines or apparent function, Falstaff's army will be populated by corpses, shadows, and specters.[88] He assembles a revenant of Hotspur's zombie squadron in a scene that is itself a déja vu of Falstaff's Lazarus soliloquy in *Part One*.[89]

Of Falstaff's conscripts, only Feeble declares his willingness to serve and die in the king's cause, a remarkable utterance in a play occupied with hypocrisy, double-crossing, self-dealing, and cowardice. "A man can die but once," Feeble reasons—ironically, alas, given his theatrical context. "We owe God a death. I'll ne'er bear a base mind. An't be my destiny, so an't be not, so. No man's too good to serve's prince. And let it go which way it will, he that dies this year is quit for the next" (2H4 3.2.232–36). Feeble's aphorism, "We owe God a death"—itself a repetition of Prince Harry's claim in *Part One* that Falstaff "owest God a death"—posits human life as borrowed time pitched between two deaths, a prior death and one that must come to pass (1H4 5.1.126). Feeble refers to the debt created by Jesus's sacrifice, in which Jesus died in place of human sinners so that humans might be redeemed from eternal damnation.[90] Jesus died as Feeble's substitute—as his double—in a transaction that leaves Feeble bound both to a death in the past and to the future death that will cancel it out. In other words, Jesus's past death produces the specter of Feeble's future death, leaving Feeble's present spooked. Like Falstaff, Shallow, his moribund fellow conscripts, and all humans redeemed by the Crucifixion, Feeble lives under sentence of death, his life a *memento mori*. As a character in a dramatic scene, however, Feeble is not "quit for the next" year if he pays his debt and dies in battle. He can rise again to be killed again day after day, year after year, century in and century out.

V. Harry Harry

The illness, age, and morbidity that characterize figures like Falstaff and his conscripts are proliferated across the realm in *Part Two*, infecting "the body of [the] kingdom," where "rank diseases grow," and compromising the king himself, who is "much ill" (2H4 3.1.37–38, 111). In dramatizing events around the end of Henry's life, the play both reprises a number of *Henry IV*'s earlier double-exposure techniques and introduces new ones. Like the Michals sequence and the spectacle of corpse impersonation at the end of *Part One*, Prince Harry's scene at his father's deathbed in *Part Two* stages the ambiguous status of the inert, nonresponsive body. Returning once again to court as a truant, Harry finds his father apparently asleep with the crown on the pillow next to him. When a feather near his father's face "stirs not," Harry interprets the sleeping body as dead, though he continues to describe it as asleep: "This sleep is sound indeed. This is a sleep / That from this golden ring01 hath divorced / So many English kings" (2H4 4.3.166–68). Harry's use of sleep as a metaphor for death, even after he is convinced that it is not a sleeping body he is seeing, registers how a living body hosts the image of a dead one—how the state of sleep mimics the state of death, presenting a preview of the sleeper's corpse.[91] The doubleness of the nonresponsive body as alive and dead is heightened in Shakespeare's treatment of his source material for this scene. In Holinshed's account of the episode, Harry is not alone with his father. The others in the room reach a shared agreement that the king is dead and place a linen cloth over his face.[92] Eschewing the cloth, Shakespeare's dramatization lingers in the equivocal appearance of the inert, unshrouded body and the epistemological uncertainty it generates. As in the Michals sequence, where the body whose spirit will leave is identical to that whose spirit is leaving and that whose spirit has left, this moment in the play collapses rather than instantiates differences between living and dead. By disclosing Prince Harry's assessment as mistaken, the scene undermines the epistemological certainty on which claims of difference depend.

Shakespeare's choice to stage the king alone with his son focalizes the conflict between the two characters, making their subsequent reconciliation central to Prince Harry's arc toward majesty. But it also creates the conditions for a psychological interpretation of the corpse young Harry sees in his sleeping father's form.[93] Discovering the missing crown, King Henry rails, "Is he so hasty that he doth suppose / My sleep my death?" suggesting that his son's eagerness to be king drives his faulty supposition (2H4 4.3.190–91). When Harry reenters the scene to find his father awake and therefore alive, he marvels, "I never thought to hear you speak again" (2H4 4.3.220). Henry's response, "Thy wish was father, Harry, to that thought," posits his supposed corpse as his son's issue. In seeing his father as dead, Harry has projected onto his father's body an image of his own desire. The corpse he generates, like the ghost produced by a spirit photograph's double exposure, is a specter of himself—of himself as king, a kingly self who can only come into being through his father's death. In order to think himself Henry V—the clone of Henry IV, as I will formulate it in chapter 4—he must father an image of his dead father that is at once the image of a dead other and the image of a dead self. As Henry puts it in his lengthy chastisement, Harry must "Give that which gave [him] life unto the worms" through a parricidal wish that kills off his own point of inception (2H4 4.3.245).[94] In seeing his father as dead, Harry constructs an image of his future that is spooked by the demise of his own provenance.

To say that the figure of Prince Harry is spooked by the death of his progenitor is not to say, however, that Harry is personally troubled by imaging either himself or his father dead. Like Richard II, he intuits the usefulness of constructing images of his dead self, particularly as he dramatizes the "turn[ing] away of his former self" to "flow henceforth in formal majesty" (*2H4* 5.5.58, 5.2.132). In his final exchange with his father, he creates dead selves to authenticate his worthiness as Henry's son and heir:

> God witness with me, when I here came in
> And found no course of breath within your majesty,
> How cold it struck my heart. If I do feign,
> O let me in my present wildness die. (*2H4* 4.3.278–81)

In describing himself as struck to the heart with cold, Harry presents himself as having been killed by the realization of his father's death. This rhetorically constituted dead self is multiplied in the conditional statement that follows it, in which Harry proposes to die again if he speaks falsehood. Describing himself as "dead almost" from "thinking [Henry] dead," he then goes on to construct a fictitious account of the scene we have just witnessed of him and his sleeping father, offering a specious direct quotation of what he said to the crown when taking it from Henry's side (*2H4* 4.3.284–85). He quotes a self who did not speak his quoted words, ventriloquizing a simulated revenant self from the past. Harry's multiply self-deadening responses to his father's bitter upbraiding preview the dexterity with which he will exploitatively dramatize his cohabitation with his own specter in the final scenes of *Part Two*. Further, he reconstructs, in the present, a past self who is distinct from himself, generating a fictitious revenant Harry. Through his revision of earlier events in the very same scene, Harry not only illustrates the fruits of Falstaff's tutelage in the art of expedient lying but also participates in the subversion of distinctions between historical event, eyewitness account, popular rumor, official record, dramatic representation, and spectral double that have been a central interest of the *Henry IV* plays since Falstaff's fake death at the end of *Part One*.[95] The past is rendered as a counterfeit told to a counterfeit by a counterfeit—a lie whispered to a revenant by a ghost.

When Harry appears for the first time after Henry IV has died, he presents himself as a double for his dead father, accentuating the spectral aspects of his succession. In response to the peers' uneasiness with the new king, whose disposition toward them has not yet been established, Henry V assures them, "This is the English not the Turkish court; Not Amurath an Amurath succeeds, / But Harry Harry" (*2H4* 5.2.47–49). The phrase "Harry Harry" articulates the logics of succession, simultaneity, and indistinction, positing him as he who comes after, is concurrent with, and is the same as his dead father. "Be assured," he promises,

> I'll be your father and your brother too.
> Let me but bear your love, I'll bear your cares.
> Yet weep that Harry's dead, and so will I;
> But Harry lives that shall convert those tears
> By number into hours of happiness. (*2H4* 5.2.56–61)

"Harry" names both he who lives and he who is dead; ensuring continuity from one generation to the next entails the son's occupying the role of self, brother, and father—of living and dead, of self and other self. This formulation is markedly different from the doubled monarch described in the doctrine of the king's two bodies, in which the king is comprised of the mortal body natural and the immortal body politic. As Meredith Evans usefully points out in her reading of rumor and law in *2 Henry IV*, Ernst Kantorowicz's influential study describes the two-bodied king or *corporation sole*—the mystical juncture of "immortal species and mortal individuation"—as a "spectre."[96] Although historicist critical habit might tempt us to map this specter onto Harry's utterance, Harry does not make a claim particular to kingship.[97] Rather, in positing a dead and a living Harry, he names his hauntology, not his royal exceptionalism. He identifies the spectral past and future Harrys colocated in his present self. "Harry Harry" is at once an expansion of self that absorbs the dead father in / as himself and a super-compressed paraphrase of Derrida: "This *living individual* would itself be inhabited and invaded by *its own specter*. It would be constituted by specters of which it becomes the host and which it assembles in the haunted community of a single body."[98] In short, Harry Harry.

The discussion that ensues about the rightness of the Lord Chief Justice's past discipline of young Harry compounds the doubled, spectral figure of Harry Harry. In defending his treatment of the disobedient Prince Harry, the Lord Chief Justice describes himself as a former surrogate for King Henry IV, a deputy carrying out the king's law: "I then did use the person of your father. / The image of his power lay then in me" (*2H4* 5.2.72–73). He invites the new king to imagine a duplicate of this event occurring during his reign to come, suggesting that Harry "Be now the father, and propose a son"—a son who behaves in the future as Harry did in his past (*2H4* 5.2.91). The specter of the dead Henry IV appears in the Lord Chief Justice's thought experiment through his invitation to the new king to imagine himself as the father who has died. The Lord Chief Justice proposes a future inhabited by the past—a revenance of the earlier event through the person of the new king, who is to weigh the merits of his servant's judgment by reinhabiting the figure of the dead king and projecting that figure into a hypothetical future. In his response, the new king takes this thought experiment a step further by respeaking the words he imagines his father to have spoken in the past, telling the Lord Chief Justice:

> I do wish your honours may increase
> Till you do live to see a son of mine
> Offend you and obey you as I did.
> So shall I live to speak my father's words:
> "Happy am I that have a man so bold
> That dares do justice on my proper son,
> And not less happy having such a son
> That would deliver up his greatness so
> Into the hands of justice." (2H4 5.2.103–11)

Through a form of ventriloquism that is a central subject of chapter 3, Harry dramatizes an event in his reign that is at once a repetition of the past and a hypothetical future. His dead father's revenant words, through their echoing return across time, collapse not only past into present into future but history into speculation. The new king expresses his authority by giving voice to the spectral self/other—the Harry Harry—who speaks through him now and in the theoretical time to come. He appropriates the ghost-voice of his dead father both to characterize himself in the past as "a son / That would deliver up his greatness so / Into the hands of justice" and to characterize the gesture he is about to perform in reinstating the Lord Chief Justice, whom he will name his counselor or symbolic "father" (2H4 5.2.117). In the same way that the rebel army is "enlarge[d]" through the appropriation of Richard II's dried blood, the new King Henry parasitically annexes his dead father, announcing the character of his kingship through the theatrical gesture of speaking as his father's ghost (2H4 1.1.203–4).[99]

Harry's ventriloquistic dramatization of an episode from his father's reign is embedded in this scene's broader presentation of his new persona—a persona he forms not only by identifying with his dead father but by identifying his dead father as his dead self:

> Princes all, believe me, I beseech you,
> My father has gone wild into his grave,
> For in his tomb lie all my affections;
> And with his spirits sadly I survive
> To mock the expectation of the world. (2H4 5.2.121–25)

Projecting his former wildness onto his father's corpse, Harry buries his old self in his father's coffin. What transcends the grave in Harry's formulation is his father's spirit, which survives in him. By again appropriating his dead father, he thus generates two spectralized Harrys: the Harry in the coffin, at once his father's corpse and the corpse of his own dead "affections," and the Harry who wears the crown, the father's spirit embodied in the reformed son whose prior self is dead.

Henries are proliferating (again), double exposure upon double exposure. Although the newly crowned Henry V warns Falstaff in his final dismissal of the fat knight, "the grave doth gape / For thee thrice wider than for other men," it is Harry who is the figure of increase here, propagating spectral selves who spook the coffin and the crown alike (*2H4* 5.5.53–54).[100] In translating Falstaff into a dreamlike figment of his imagination—"I have long dreamt of such a kind of man"—Harry makes Falstaff into another one of his shadows, another phantasmatic self through whom he performs the hauntological assemblage of Harry Harry (*2H4* 5.5.49). In the same way he ventriloquizes his father's voice to articulate the terms of his reign, he empties out and appropriates Falstaff through a theatrical gesture of double exposure in which Falstaff becomes the ghost of his "former self," at once Harry and Harry's other (*2H4* 5.5.58). The royal plural through which he performs the play's concluding banishment is thus both the agent and the effect of cannibalizing Falstaff. "Be it your charge, my lord," he orders the Lord Chief Justice in his final lines in the play, "To see performed the tenor of our word" (*2H4* 5.5.70–71).

Taking a cue from Falstaff's own corpse-act, Harry exploits the spectral, the ghostly, the spooked aspects of his identity. He opens the reign of Henry V declaring, "*There are more than three of them, more than four of them. There are at least V of them.*"

CHAPTER 3

Dummies and Doppelgängers
Performing for the Dead in *1 Henry VI*

Nothing is but what is not.

. . .

There are two lodged together.

—*Macbeth*

1 Henry VI begins with the funeral of a dead king
and the question of why he died, a question that goes unanswered by Henry
V's casketed corpse. The play's opening series of formal elegiac remarks, delivered by the Dukes of Bedford and Gloucester, are quickly disrupted by the
Duke of Exeter, who announces Henry V's lifeless state with a candor that
jars against the high mythologizing of his peers.[1] "Henry is dead," Exeter
declares, "and never shall revive: / Upon a wooden coffin we attend" (1.1.18–
19).[2] His remarks index the inert object of Henry's corpse within the inert
object of the coffin. Neither the material remains of Henry V nor the box that
holds them offers answers to Exeter's subsequent questions about whether the
king's death was caused by "the planets of mishap" or "the subtle-witted
French" (1.1.23, 25). Dead men tell no tales.

But that does not mean they aren't listening. After his blunt declaration that
"Henry is dead," Bedford directly addresses the late king:

Henry the Fifth, thy ghost I invocate:
Prosper this realm, keep it from civil broils;
Combat with adverse planets in the heavens.
A far more glorious star thy soul will make
Than Julius Caesar or bright. (1.1.52–56)

Bedford imagines Henry V as present in some conscious, perceptive state between current corpse and future astral body. This representation of Henry as sensible of their proceedings is repeated after a messenger delivers news of the English losses in France. Both Bedford and Gloucester respond to the news with a warning about disclosing it within Henry's hearing:

> BEDFORD: What say's thou, man, before dead Henry's corpse?
>   Speak softly, or the loss of those great towns
>   Will make him burst his lead and rise from death.
> GLOUCESTER: Is Paris lost? Is Rouen yielded up?
>   If Henry were recalled to life again,
>   These news would cause him once more yield the ghost. (1.1.62–67)

In Bedford's construction of a future tense for Henry, Henry is not at all what we would call "dead." On the contrary, this exchange represents "death [as] a fictitious event," to borrow a formulation from Bert O. States. In their conversation around the coffin, "Death comes to have the status of a fiction," as States puts it; death is "something that may well be true but isn't real, something toward which we can willingly suspend our belief, if not our disbelief."[3] Bedford and Gloucester treat Henry as a sentient presence—a conscious being potentially capable of corporeal resurrection. Gloucester's hypothetical scene reanimates Henry and then hastens him back into his coffin, imagining a series of events in the subjunctive mood in which the king would come back to life only to be instantly rekilled by what he hears. Both men devise a response for Henry that he does not have, verbally fashioning alternative Henrys who react to the news as they script and pose him. They calibrate the messenger's speech around a Henry who is necessarily an avatar for their own reactions to the news from France.

Criticism on the history plays takes as axiomatic that this opening funeral scene expresses nostalgia for the reign and person of Henry V, whose untimely death only two years after he was named heir apparent to France left his nine-month-old son King Henry VI of England.[4] In her influential study of the histories, *Stages of History*, Phyllis Rackin names Henry V the "lost center" of not only *1 Henry VI* but all eight of Shakespeare's English chronicle plays. He is "the desired object of theatrical recuperation [and] nostalgic yearning," she writes—an "ineluctable absence."[5] Contemporaneously with Rackin's 1990 book, the discipline of performance studies developed a parallel discourse about absence and loss, one that describes performance, like history, as always receding into the past. For theorists like Peggy Phelan and Herbert Blau, who helped shape the field, performance is defined first and foremost by its disappearance—by its constitutive ephemerality.[6] In his influential 1996 book *Cities of the Dead*, Joseph Roach summarizes historical and performative loss in the term "surrogation," by which he means the imperfect performative process through which we attempt to replace, substitute for, or re-create the dead in what he calls a "doomed search for originals." For Roach, this search "is the most important of the many meanings that users intend when they say the word *performance*."[7] Roach situates the historical past and performative present along a linear temporal continuum in which "the purity of origins," as he puts it, is subject to further "erasure" with every subsequent iteration: "Performance, in other words, stands in for an elusive entity that it is not but that it must vainly aspire both to embody and to replace."[8] Performance theory's theses about erasure, loss, and failed performative replacement have, in turn, influenced subsequent work on the histories, producing claims of compounding loss—historical and theatrical—such as in Brian Walsh's conclusion that Shakespeare's history plays represent a "double absence."[9]

If we were to read this moment in *1 Henry VI* as an illustration of "double absence" or "surrogation," we might argue that Bedford and Gloucester are performing as stand-ins for Henry in a nostalgic gesture that can only affirm Henry's irrevocable absence from both England and the stage. But something else is also happening here. Henry is functioning as a surrogate for *them*. Silent in his dark chamber, Henry becomes available to his survivors as a kind of dummy or puppet—a proxy through whom they conjecture possible consequences of the news from France. The scene thus prompts a revision of Roach's notion of surrogation. Although in historical drama living performers do surrogate or stand in for the dead, the dead are also enlisted as performative avatars for the living. Surrogation, then, is not merely a process of linear degradation through which originals are replaced by imperfect substitutes. It is a bidirectional process through which the dead likewise substitute for those who survive.[10] Because they are mute and motionless, the dead can be translated into sites of potential. Stilled and speechless bodies like Henry's are latent with an ongoing theatrical dynamism that exposes the inadequacy of critical assumptions about the pastness of the dead.

In chapter 2, I observed a related form of surrogation at the end of *2 Henry IV*, when the newly kinged Henry V appropriates, first, his dead father and then the spectralized Falstaff to dramatize aspects of himself. As in Richard II's construction of his dead image, Henry V's annexation of the dead and silenced at once multiplies him and exposes his inhabitation by moribund counterparts. Bedford and Gloucester perform a similar form of appropriation in their use of the casketed Henry V to respond to the messenger's news. Just as Henry V ventriloquizes his dead father, so, in turn, do his survivors instrumentalize the dead Henry V. What is different about the Bedford and Gloucester moment is the temporal origin of the dead man's response. At the end of *2 Henry IV*, Henry V ventriloquizes words from the past, albeit invented ones, that he attributes to his deceased father so that his past father is quoted by the present son. Bedford and Gloucester, by contrast, devise responses for the dead Henry V that he is imagined to generate in the present, while dead. In their admonishments to the messenger, they treat Henry as a participant in the scene, and they conduct themselves— they act—with attention to his presence. They appropriate him as an extension of their concern about the news but also, more precisely, as an audience to their conversation. The dead Henry V becomes enlisted in a specifically theatrical dynamic in which his observation affects the performances of the living.

My suggestion that the dead Henry V functions as both a ventriloquist's dummy and an audience highlights the intermedial nature of what is staged in this moment. Bedford and Gloucester use the mediums of their living bodies—specifically, their bodies' capacity to generate speech—to create the impression that movement originates somewhere else: in the passive corpse of Henry V, which is translated into a medium for their reaction to the messenger. Through this displacement of their action onto inanimate matter, Bedford and Gloucester demonstrate how a static object can function as a theatrical participant, one that is not only made to act in the scene but that generates reciprocal actions—such as "speak[ing] softly"—from others (1.1.63). While we might be tempted to dismiss this necrodramatic phenomenon as a symptom of premodern superstition about the sentience of the dead, it is a phenomenon, I argue, that transcends the chronological periods that the play represents. What is more, this phenomenon is not limited to historically remote figures whom we can dismiss, from our imagined superior vantage point, as naive. Rather, the necrodrama—or, more broadly, the object drama—staged in this scene is reproduced in contemporary criticism and art, including art that does not explicitly figure the human and therefore does not as naturally lend itself to the kind of anthropomorphizing that takes place with Henry's corpse. The transhistoricity of the theatrical dynamic staged at Henry's funeral illustrates how humans appropriate dead people and insensate objects in the timeless endeavor to represent ourselves to ourselves.

I. A Dialogue of the Dead

Consider, for example, Jeff Wall's 1992 photograph titled *Dead Troops Talk (A Vision After an Ambush of a Red Army Patrol near Moqor, Afghanistan, Winter 1986)*. Like much of Wall's best-known works, *Dead Troops Talk* (Figure 10) is a large-scale transparency exhibited in a lightbox. Given its format, the monumentally sized photo marks a juncture between theatrical, photographic, and filmic

FIGURE 10.   *Dead Troops Talk (A Vision after an Ambush of a Red Army Patrol near Moqor, Afghanistan, Winter 1986)*, 1992, by Jeff Wall. Transparency in lightbox, 229.0 × 417.0 cm. Courtesy of the artist.

media.[11] Although the image mimics documentary war photography, it is entirely a fiction—a digitally composed tableau that was meticulously staged, section by section, in Wall's studio using performers, costumes, set dressers, and special-effects makeup. The image figures a fantastical afterlife in which men who have been blown apart in battle carry on what Wall has described as a "dialogue of the dead."[12]

Susan Sontag has written of this image, "The figures in Wall's visionary photo-work are 'realistic' but, of course, the image is not. Dead soldiers don't talk. Here they do."[13] And yet, as anyone looking at the photo can see and hear, they don't. Despite its affinity with glowing, celluloid war movies and its kinship with dramatic staging, Wall's image is conspicuously still and silent. As a photograph, it cannot represent dialogue, a durational form of communication. When people talk, sounds follow one another in a linear temporal sequence, as do the facial contortions required to produce them. Without the addition of banderoles or speech bubbles filled with text, a single still photo can only arrest the body in an attitude of speech; it cannot represent speech's duration. Wall's title, *Dead Troops Talk*, thus names a durational form—speech—that does not match the static form of the single-frame image. In cooperation with the permanent present tense of the photo's title, the men's static gestures suggest the capacity for speech without ever realizing it.

The figures in the photo neither progress beyond the moment captured by the camera nor turn outward in acknowledgment of us. If they seem to carry on conversation, it is survivors like Sontag who talk for them, filling their imagined speech bubbles with invented words, as the conclusion of her meditation on the photo illustrates. Sontag all but ventriloquizes their voices:

> These dead are supremely uninterested in the living: in those who took their lives; in witnesses—and in us. Why should they seek our gaze? What would they have to say to us? "We"—this "we" is everyone who has never experienced anything like what they went through—don't understand. We don't get it. We truly can't imagine what it was like. We can't imagine how dreadful, how terrifying war is; and how normal it becomes. Can't understand, can't imagine. That's what every soldier, and every journalist and aid worker and independent observer who has put in time under fire, and had the luck to elude the death that struck down others nearby, stubbornly feels. And they are right.[14]

In Sontag's reading of the photo as an antiwar image, the troops' talk is not arrested by the still picture but made available through that picture as an ongoing speech act. The soldiers' deflection of our gaze becomes a refusal—a feeling critique addressed to us, about us. This address is fully commutable into language. By not looking at us, they tell us what we look like to them. They tell us that we "can't understand, can't imagine." Wall's silent figures become an audience observing us, upon whom we can perpetually project words about ourselves.

Together, Wall's elaborately produced photograph of "talking" corpses and Sontag's script of their hypothetical speech illustrate how the historical dead become sites of ongoing performance that complicate strict linear time. *Dead Troops Talk* imbues killed bodies with the capacity of continuing observation and durational communication, creating a temporal sphere in which they are at once dead and not dead. This sphere not only includes but depends on audiences like Sontag, whose theatrical ventriloquism of the dead collapses distinctions between them and herself, between dead object and speaking subject, turning the soldiers into doubles for their audience—into media through whom we generate surrogates of ourselves. Sontag's remarks, composed after the moment "documented" by the photo, suggests how the silent potential of the figures allows them to be continuously scripted into ongoing speech, not only among themselves but with us. They are still but also therefore still talking—about us, to us, and through us.[15]

1 Henry VI stages a number of *Dead Troops Talk* moments, in which dead and deadish men function as doubles for the living—as sites for construing potential words, deeds, and exchanges of attention. Christopher Pye has read Bedford and Gloucester's scripting of Henry's hypothetical resurrection as a "fantasy of the sovereign body's phantasmal return," one that articulates the special properties of the monarch's doubled body. Pye notes that the fantasy "was not limited to fictitious monarchs" but that it also informs stories about the dead Queen Elizabeth.[16] This chapter argues, by contrast, that the ventriloquistic performance in the opening scene of *1 Henry VI* has nothing specific to do with monarchy or with the concept of the king's two bodies, nor is it a phenomenon distinct to either medieval metaphysical belief systems or early modern dramaturgy. Rather, I argue, the enlistment of the dead as variously animated and voiced doubles for the living is a central feature both of the play's dramatization of historical temporality and of human representations of the self. Further, the temporality disclosed by these performative exchanges is not neatly linear, as critical assertions of surrogation and nostalgia suggest. It is a temporality that might usefully be called queer—a temporality that exposes what Madhavi Menon calls "the vexed relation between sameness and difference" by undermining distinctions between self and other; dead and alive; past, present, and future.[17]

This chapter centers on the martial English hero, Lord Talbot, who is consistently represented in *1 Henry VI* through doubling mechanisms that are suggestive of figures like the ventriloquist's dummy and doppelgänger. These mechanisms constitute Talbot simultaneously as a living person, an already-dead person, and "a future dead person," to echo a phrase from Carla Freccero.[18] Working with accounts of how theatrical exchange takes place around still objects of visual art such as Wall's *Dead Troops Talk*, I describe Shakespeare's Talbot as a figure constructed in and through performative correspondence with the dead. I bring attention to the play's sustained interest in how the living self is dramatized by its dead double. In this way, my reading rethinks the concept of theatrical surrogation and challenges the conventional scholarly assumption that the histories stage nostalgic longing for an irrecoverable past—an assumption that is organized not by the play's internal theatrical mechanisms but by the linear temporal format of chronicle history.

II. I Prefer Not To

As the messenger delivers the news from France, Bedford and Gloucester experience the dead Henry V as present in the scene. Crucially, he does not register their presence in return. Like Wall's troops, he is confined to his box and does not acknowledge them; he does not reveal himself to them in an act of mutual recognition. As Stanley Cavell argues in his influential 1969 essay on failed acknowledgment in *King Lear*, silence or reticence in interpersonal relationships—the withholding of self-revelation or mutual recognition—generates the same audience-character dynamics that organize theater. Because characters and audiences occupy two distinct existential spaces, the audience has no means to acknowledge the characters onstage, whereas the characters are only present under the gaze of an audience. Cavell famously asks, "How is acknowledgment expressed; that is, how do we put ourselves in another's presence?" His answer: "By revealing ourselves, by allowing ourselves to be seen. When we do not, when we keep ourselves in the dark, the consequence is that we convert the other into a character and make the world a stage for him."[19] Like the audience at a play, the dead Henry V remains "in the dark," inscrutable within his coffin and beyond the shared space of the living. This creates circumstances in which his survivors not only try out various explanations for his death but perform their ongoing obedience to his kingly presence. In Cavell's terms, Henry's lack of an answering acknowledgment of Bedford's or Gloucester's presence sets the stage for a theatrical relationship in which they perform while he observes.[20]

Cavell's discussion of acknowledgment and theatricality is directly influenced by art critic Michael Fried, whose contentious 1967 essay, "Art and Objecthood," defines the presence implied by minimalist art objects as a form of theatricality. Fried's work suggests how an object like a sculpture—or, in Henry's case, a coffin or corpse—can be present to its beholder in a way that creates a "hold upon us [that] is theatrical."[21] In a formulation that could well describe the opening scene of *1 Henry VI*, Fried writes, "Something is said to have presence when it demands that the beholder take it into account, that he take it seriously—and when the fulfillment of that demand consists simply in being aware of the work and, so to speak, in acting accordingly." This "special complicity that the work extorts from the beholder" is a feature of "literalist objects," as Fried terms the products of minimalism.[22] As in Cavell's discussion of failed acknowledgment, Fried stresses how the nonresponsive, "nonrelational" character of the literalist object distances the beholder, creating "a theatrical effect or quality—a kind of *stage* presence."[23] This presence, or the "theatricality of objecthood," arises from the literalist object's hollowness, its suggestion of an outside and an inside that is "almost blatantly anthropomorphic. It is . . . as though the work in question has an inner, even secret, life."[24] Because of its anthropomorphic features, it has qualities of both object and subject—of inert matter and personlike presence.

In his recent book *After Live: Possibility, Potentiality, and the Future of Performance*, performance scholar Daniel Sack extends the claims of Cavell and Fried toward a fuller theory of how withheld acknowledgment organizes the beholder and the anthropomorphized object into a theatricalized relationship.

One of the central points of reference for his study is Herman Melville's "Bartleby, the Scrivener," in which the increasingly impassive—and, eventually, dead—Bartleby generates progressively hysterical responses from the narrator, the lawyer who inscribes the tabula rasa–like scrivener with his own obsessive constructions.[25] Not unlike Wall's dead troops or the dead Henry V, who *will* do something or *would* do something but does nothing, Bartleby operates as an "open and indeterminate ground" on which the lawyer projects an elaborate series of narratives, motives, and emotions, "playing out his own spectacle of tribulation."[26] Characterized by his opaque statement of negative inclination, "I prefer not to," Bartleby is a figure of potentiality, "a withheld realization, a possession of the capacity to do or develop," "a medium prepared for, but abstaining from, articulation."[27] Following Cavell, Sack argues that Bartleby's resistance to verbal or visual acknowledgment of the lawyer's elaborate overtures creates theatrical conditions in which the lawyer becomes a performer for Bartleby, the darkened audience. He writes,

> Contact with a life suspending its potentiality—a life withholding and displaying its capacity to perform without acting upon such a capacity—can provoke the beholding subject to perform him- or herself, to take the stage while that obdurate other seems to look on. To put it somewhat differently, . . . the potential object becomes an audience facing the beholding subject.[28]

The object and its beholder reverse roles so that the object becomes the beholder of the performance staged for its gaze. In this way, Sack writes, Bartleby "stages a kind of theatrical relationship with his beholder—the lawyer—in a manner analogous to the silent and looming [literal] object's relation" to its audience.[29]

Sack's discussion suggests two ways that Bedford and Gloucester are performing for the dead. As one literal object nested inside another, the corpse and coffin of Henry V function as the "open and indeterminate ground" on which his survivors conjecture a set of hypothetical and future actions for him—actions that project temporally beyond his corporeal death and the present moment of their speaking.[30] In one sense, then, they perform *for* him by substituting their action words for Henry's still silence: Confronted with the hollow, blank box of his coffin—of his corpse—they construct an anthropomorphic interior, a consciousness that acts as a surrogate for their own responses to the messenger. In another sense, Henry's implacable blankness produces the conditions of theater, in which he is positioned as an audience to actions that they perform within his hearing. Both senses of "performing for"—performing in place of and performing in front of—suggest Henry's presence in the scene—through his speaking surrogates and as an audience to their speech. As Sack puts it, "by presenting a posed statement they still acknowledge the beholder as a fellow meaning-maker."[31] Positing Henry as lost beyond dramatic recovery—a conventional claim of literary criticism on the histories—fails to account for how the play includes him in the dramatic present and for how he functions as a site of potentiality, a site for producing action in the subjunctive mood and future tense.[32] Rather than reinforcing the linear temporal scheme that organizes chronicle history, Henry participates in a temporality of the ongoing that is consonant with performance's own terms for staging the past through the medium of the live. "Performance," Peggy Phelan has written, "is the art form which most fully understands the generative possibilities of disappearance."[33] Obscured in his darkened theater and ostensibly gone, Henry, like Wall's dead troops, precipitates performances on his behalf and for his beholding. He functions as "a means without an end," to quote Sack again—a figure who represents "the potential to think forward in time."[34]

III. To Overpeer the City

With these observations in mind, I want to consider a series of episodes toward the end of act 1 and the beginning of act 2 of *1 Henry VI*, which shift from England to the war in France and the English fight to retain territories secured by the victories of Henry V. These episodes take place at Orléans, where the English have mounted a siege. The short scene with the French Master Gunner and his Boy on the walls at Orléans initiates a sequence of beholding moments that delineate what kinds of looking produce the conditions of performance and what kinds do not. The Master Gunner tells the Boy,

> The Prince's spials have informed me
> How the English, in the suburbs close entrenched,
> Wont, through a secret grate of iron bars
> In yonder tower, to overpeer the city,
> And thence discover how with most advantage
> They may vex us with shot or with assault.
> To intercept this inconvenience,
> A piece of ordnance 'gainst it I have placed,
> And even these three days have I watched, if I could see them.
> Now do thou watch, for I can stay no longer.
> If thou spy'st any, run and bring me word,
> And thou shalt find me at the governor's. (1.5.8–19)

The Gunner describes two acts of surveillance, one within the other: the English looking through the iron grate spying on the French and the French, in turn, spying on the English looking through the grate. In both cases, surveillance—looking at another without being exposed to reciprocal view, or "looking without being seen," as Cavell defines spying—positions the lookers at a strategic advantage to those who are beheld.[35] The English "overpeer the city" through the aperture in the grate, in turn forfeiting their audience superiority to the Gunner and Boy who watch them unperceived. The fact that those being watched are unaware of being seen forecloses the problem of performativity. This foreclosure is the very purpose of surveillance: The beheld are not performing for the beholder.

In the next scene at Orléans, the English general Lord Talbot, who has just been ransomed from the French, tells the Earl of Salisbury his story of being captured and humiliated before French onlookers:

> With scoffs and scorns and contumelious taunts,
> In open market place produced they me,
> To be a public spectacle to all.
> "Here," said they, "is the terror of the French,
> The scarecrow that affrights our children so."
> Then broke I from the officers that led me
> And with my nails digged stones out of the ground
> To hurl at the beholders of my shame. (1.6.17–24)

As a prisoner of the French, Talbot was made to display his impotence in a visual "spectacle" that activates the root meaning of "behold"—to hold captive—and turns the marketplace of Orléans into a public theater of power. In contrast to the unaware objects of surveillance described by the Gunner, the captive Talbot is painfully conscious of being looked at, and he revolts violently against the impotent role in which this gaze casts him, aggressively performing his defiance. Importantly, through Talbot's present narration of himself on view in the past, the mute Talbot—the shamed Talbot on display—is covered or enclosed by his retrospective, authoritative narration. As Cavell puts it, "the man who has the word 'I' at his disposal has the quickest device for concealing himself."[36] Even as he is relating his shame, Talbot is narratively ensuring his privacy, constructing a speaking double for his silenced, objectified self, a double who mediates and thereby mitigates his exposure.[37]

In response to Talbot's account, Salisbury offers him a voyeuristic spectacle of the French as "revenge" for the abuse he suffered in the marketplace. Salisbury reverses the market-goers' shaming view of Talbot by positioning him to behold the French:

But we will be revenged sufficiently.
Now it is supper time in Orléans.
Here, through this grate, I count each one,
And view the Frenchmen how they fortify.
Let us look in: the sight will much delight thee. (1.6.36–40)

Salisbury's answer to Talbot's tale of being exposed to the derisive French gaze is to open a peephole into the private mealtime of the Orléaners. Like the spying of the Gunner and Boy, this act of looking is markedly different from the theatrical dynamics of beholding that organize the Bedford/Gloucester/Henry V relationship, for example, or Talbot's public shaming. Fried's career-long discussion of beholding in works of visual art, one that borrows significantly from Denis Diderot's art theory, usefully describes this distinction. Across several works—"Art and Objecthood" (1967), *Absorption and Theatricality* (1988), *Courbet's Realism* (1990), *Manet's Modernism* (1996), and *Why Photography Matters as Art as Never Before* (2008)—Fried traces a fundamental antagonism between theatricality and absorption, or antitheatricality.[38] Theatrical works address, hail, or acknowledge the beholder, revealing themselves through a range of techniques to be performances for their audience's gaze. Antitheatrical or absorptive works are the opposite: They are self-contained; they do not turn outward; they do not compose an outside toward which to turn. The viewer of an absorptive painting is an unacknowledged voyeur situated in a separate world from the painted figures, who "appear wholly oblivious to being beheld."[39] For Fried, as for Diderot, consciousness of being beheld produces performance or theatricality, which artists should shun as antithetical to authenticity. Voyeurism and surveillance operate by this same logic: when unconscious of being watched, people cease performing and reveal their authentic, vulnerable selves, which can be captured by the click of a hidden camera or ambushed by an opportunistic army.

Fried describes the state of absorption as the occupation of a world distinct from the viewer's world. In an absorptive work of art, "it is as though the personage [in the painting] and the beholder inhabit different worlds"; "the personage [is] 'removed to another sphere of life.'"[40] Although the figures in such paintings are visible to the viewer, the viewer's world is invisible to those in the painting, who are fully absorbed in their separate sphere. This invisibility is precisely the advantage conferred by surveillance, as the Gunner's reference to "overpeer[ing]" suggests: the English gain advantage by watching the French unseen, in turn providing insight to the Boy who watches them while obscured from view.

These moments of surveillance represent a distinct contrast to the theatrical dynamics that organize the play's opening scene. The French being surveilled are decidedly "removed to another sphere of life," absorbed in their world, blind to the surveillance opportunity afforded by the grate and unconscious of the watchers on the other side of it. But the sphere occupied by a corpse can be a more ambiguous one, as Fried's and Sontag's respective discussions of *Dead Troops Talk* illustrates. In ventriloquizing the words of Wall's soldiers, Sontag assumes that they are not absorbed in a separate world—that they could look out of the image to address the audience if they chose to. In her view, they decline to acknowledge us because they have nothing to say to us, not because they occupy an existentially separate sphere.[41] Reading Sontag reading Wall's photo, Fried insists instead that the image operates according to an absorptive logic, generating "the ontological illusion that the beholder does not exist."[42] Neither critic is specifically focused on the existential status of the dead per se. And yet the disagreement between their two readings of Wall discloses the ambiguity of the dead troops' state—their potential either to be scripted into a sphere shared by the viewer or to be absorbed in an imagined world that they occupy apart from us. The discrepancy between Sontag and Fried discloses how the dead—even the ostensibly reanimated dead—cannot conclusively be read for signs of an absorptive or theatrical state. This ambiguity lends the dead a special flexibility, one explored by *1 Henry VI*. The opening act of the play suggests that there is a wider gulf separating a dining Frenchman from his English spy than there is between a living Englishman and his dead king. Henry's corpse is markedly less "removed" than are the French diners; by Bedford's and Gloucester's accounts, Henry continues to occupy their sphere of life, generating a theatrical relationship that subverts the basic binarism of life and death. Unlike the unknowing objects of surveillance, Henry's court behave as though they are being overheard. Because they perceive Henry to be listening—because they do not believe themselves invisible or inaudible to him—they perform. The two worlds demarcated by the grate at Orléans are more distinct from each other than those of the living and the dead.

IV. I'll Be a Salisbury

The theatricalized relationship between beholder and beheld that is absent from the scenes of surveillance is reasserted in the events that follow, in which the English are punished for what Maurice Hunt has described as their act of "forbidden looking."[43] When the Boy touches off his explosives, he blows off part of Salisbury's face, specifically his eye: "How far'st thou, mirror of all martial men?" Talbot asks, "One of thy eyes and thy cheek's side struck off?" (1.6.52–53). In Talbot's assessment of Salisbury and Sir Thomas Gargrave, who has been killed by the blast, the victims' capacity for visual acknowledgment stands in as a marker of presence—of life. "Yet liv'st thou, Salisbury?" he asks; "Though thy speech doth fail, / One eye thou hast to look to heaven for grace. / The sun with one eye vieweth all the world" (1.6.60–62).[44] For Talbot, it is not language that renders one present but the capacity for perception—here, visual perception, as opposed to Henry V's postmortem auditory sense. As a sentient presence with one eye and no language, Salisbury becomes a literal object that—or perhaps a literal object *who?*—provokes a series of histrionic performances on the part of Talbot. In Hunt's terms, Talbot "supplies the voice for the silent picture of dying Salisbury."[45] Like Bedford and Gloucester elaborating Henry's postmortem responses—or Sontag, who do the dead troops in different voices—Talbot enlists Salisbury as a kind of ventriloquist's dummy, speaking his part and then responding to his own performance of Salisbury:

> He beckons with his hand, and smiles on me,
> As who should say, "When I am dead and gone,
> Remember to avenge me on the French."
> Plantagenet, I will—and like thee, Nero,
> Play on the lute, beholding the towns burn. (1.6.70–74)

In this highly theatrical passage dense with surrogations, Talbot puts words in Salisbury's mouth, making the near-dead man an avatar for his own speech and revenge. He does the voices of both Salisbury and Salisbury's interlocutor or revenger, who will perform on Salisbury's behalf after he's "dead and gone." In the role of Salisbury's revenger, Talbot generates a second dead interlocutor, Nero, whom he at once speaks to and mimics, in particular reproducing Nero's visual advantage as a beholder—an audience—to the destruction of a city. The messenger's news that the French are gathering to attack provokes another groan from Salisbury that Talbot likewise verbalizes as Salisbury's desire for revenge: "Hear, hear, how dying Salisbury doth groan! / It irks his heart he cannot be revenged. / Frenchmen, I'll be a Salisbury to you" (1.6.82–84). Talbot again translates Salisbury's unintelligible sound into language, drawing from his own ventriloquized words a cue to take up the role of revenger—to perform the role of Salisbury. In this way, the revenge Talbot may have desired for himself after his humiliation by the French is projected onto Salisbury. By ventriloquizing Salisbury, Talbot illustrates Cavell's observation that "the theatricalization of others turns them to scapegoats."[46] Although Talbot describes himself as a surrogate for Salisbury's will, the inert, unintelligible Salisbury comes to function in these passages as a surrogate for Talbot's will.

Act 2 begins like act 1, with a "dead march"—either the funeral of Salisbury or a muffled drumbeat to signal the English army's secret attack on Orléans. As in the opening scene of the play, the dead are enlisted by the living as conscious witnesses to the unfolding action. Renewing his assault on the city, Talbot announces,

> And here will Talbot mount, or make his grave.
> Now, Salisbury, for thee, and for the right
> Of English Henry, shall this night appear
> How much in duty I am bound in both. (2.1.34–37)

Either onstage as a corpse for his own funeral procession or elsewhere lying dead, Salisbury has acquired postmortem omniscience that allows him to visually witness Talbot's assault of Orléans. Talbot performs his assault "for" Salisbury and "for" English Henry—as a substitute acting on their behalf and for their visual gratification: for them "shall this night appear."[47] As will increasingly become his habit, Talbot refers to himself in the third person, foregrounding how the duty-bound Talbot is a character or role, here one performed for an audience of Henry and of Salisbury, the "thee" whom he addresses as though present and sentient.

Following Talbot's successful capture of Orléans in act 2, scene 1, Salisbury's dead body is brought onstage in a replay of both Henry's funeral and Talbot's exhibition at the marketplace:

> Bring forth the body of old Salisbury
> And here advance it in the market place,
> The middle centre of this cursed town.
> Now have I paid my vow unto his soul:
> For every drop of blood was drawn from him
> There hath at least five Frenchmen died tonight. (2.2.4–9)

Salisbury's corpse is "advance[d]" in the marketplace as though Salisbury were the agent of conquest who had captured the town. By posing Salisbury as the conqueror, Talbot again displaces any personal desire for revenge onto his theatrical substitute, the passive body through whom he dramatizes his victory. In this piece of histrionic display, Salisbury's body acts as a surrogate for Talbot's own physical conquest of Orléans. The corpse functions not only as an actor and prop in Talbot's dramatization of conquest but as a silent witness to the fulfillment of Talbot's vow. Talbot uses the corpse to reverse his own earlier humiliation in the marketplace by setting up a Talbot stand-in—a double—in conquest over that exact same space.

These dynamics become even more complex in the lines that follow in which Talbot invokes a new, perpetual audience for the events in Orléans:

> And that hereafter ages may behold
> What ruin happened in revenge of him,
> Within their chiefest temple I'll erect
> A tomb, wherein his corpse shall be interred—
> Upon the which, that everyone may read,
> Shall be engraved the sack of Orléans,
> The treacherous manner of his mournful death,
> And what a terror he had been to France. (2.2.10–17)

In his proposal for Salisbury's tomb, Talbot constructs a perpetual audience to "behold" the events at Orléans in "hereafter ages." Specifically, what this audience will behold are the actions of Talbot, who enacted "ruin" on Salisbury's behalf. His use of the passive voice, "ruin happened," effaces him from the action at Orléans while simultaneously making himself—not Salisbury—the spectacle beheld by his imagined future audience. As in earlier scenes when Talbot interprets Salisbury's groans, Talbot overwrites Salisbury's corpse with a story that foregrounds his own role. Principal among the information written for future generations "Shall be engraved the sack of Orléans"—a sack conducted by Talbot and willed through Talbot's ventriloquized performance of Salisbury. The ambiguity of "Upon the which," referring to the tomb, the corpse, or both, suggests how the dead Salisbury functions as an "open and indeterminate ground," to return to Sack's phrase.[48] On that ground, Talbot proposes to inscribe what is necessarily his version of Salisbury's history, one that underscores his own role. His final item for the epitaph, "what a terror he had been to France," ascribes to Salisbury the "terror" that in every other instance in the play is associated with Talbot, including in his account of being humiliated in the marketplace: "'Here,' said they, 'is the terror of the French'" (1.6.20).[49] The epitaph is as much about Talbot as it is about Salisbury, if not more so. The uses to which Talbot puts the dead object of Salisbury reveal the suggestive ambiguity of Talbot's earlier declaration that Salisbury is "mirror to all martial men," which ostensibly means he is a model.[50] Maimed and muted, Salisbury comes to function as a double for the play's most prominent martial man—a mirror-object that reflects an image of Talbot.

While in the earlier, openly ventriloquistic moments after the explosion, Talbot posited himself as a mouthpiece for Salisbury, his plans for Salisbury's epitaph show how the speechless Salisbury functions as a mirror and a surrogate for Talbot, a corporeal and textual medium through which Talbot constructs his own legacy. By constituting a perpetual audience for that legacy, Talbot projects an image of himself, through Salisbury, into the future. In doing so, he negates his own mortality, dramatizing what States calls "the psychology of avoidance," or the collective and individual denial of human death as substantial, real, and personal.[51] He performs an act of figurative cannibalism, appropriating Salisbury to himself and paradoxically generating his own perpetuity through a mourning gesture that, in Jacques Derrida's term, "den[ies] death and the alterity of the dead other."[52] Talbot's appropriation of dead Salisbury enacts what Carla Freccero describes as the core logic of cannibalism, "the desire to make what is other same, to annihilate or assimilate the other by incorporation."[53] Talbot denies his own future death by denying Salisbury's past death and, in doing so, at once effaces and instrumentalizes Salisbury to construct Talbot's own persistence in "hereafter ages."

What I am proposing in this reading is a form of surrogation that is at once similar and opposite to that articulated by Roach. Roach uses the term "surrogation" to describe the imperfect performative process through which we attempt to replace, substitute for, or replicate the dead. We carry on their legacy by taking up their roles in a system of performative substitutions. Talbot responds to the mortally wounded Salisbury by positing himself as a substitute, a "stand-in," in Roach's terms, who performs Salisbury's speech and action. As Talbot's relationship to Salisbury develops across the events at Orléans, however, these dynamics of surrogation are increasingly exposed as bidirectional. Even as Talbot posits himself as a medium for Salisbury's words and will, Salisbury is functioning as a double, an effigy, or a dummy for Talbot's will. Talbot's use of Salisbury suggests how surrogation is not merely a means through which the living posit themselves as doubles for the dead, whose loss can never fully be repaired. The dead likewise function to surrogate the living, providing a medium through which the living at once constitute themselves in the present and project themselves into the future in an exchange of attention articulated by Sack: "I see you and you see me, therefore we both exist as such, have a presence and common presentness."[54] That co-presence— the co-presence of Talbot and Salisbury after Salisbury's mortal wounding and death—confounds clear distinctions between deadness and aliveness.

As Roach notes, the dynamics of surrogation depend on a certain degree of effacement: Salisbury persists only as he is constituted by Talbot. In Roach's terms, the epitaph Talbot proposes for Salisbury represents "the paradox of collective perpetuation: memory is a process that depends crucially on forgetting."[55] But like scholars of the play who argue that Henry V is its lost center whom all the characters seek futilely to recover, Roach's terms would lead us to describe Talbot's epitaphic gesture as "the relentless search for the purity of origins," which he argues "is a voyage not of discovery but of erasure."[56] This kind of reading gives us an incomplete picture of the dynamics that emerge between Talbot and Salisbury—and, earlier in the play, between Bedford, Gloucester, and Henry V. These scenes do not suggest a desire to recover or replace the dead. On the contrary, they dramatize the ongoing utility of the dead for constituting the living, a utility that can only emerge from their dead state—from blankness, from a body that can be posed, from a hollow interior that can be made to generate words, from a tabula rasa waiting to be inscribed and an epitaph waiting to be engraved. As Sack observes, such blank object-persons work as "fellow meaning-maker[s]" in the now and in the time to come. Salisbury becomes for Talbot "a means without an end."[57]

V. Here Is the Talbot

The theatrical dynamics that organize acts of beholding and performance in Talbot's scenes at Orléans are extended in the encounter with the Countess of Auvergne that immediately follows. In the transitional exchange between Talbot and the Countess's messenger, in which the messenger invites Talbot to visit the Countess, Talbot refers to himself not merely in the third person but using the definite article: "Here is the Talbot. Who would speak with him?" (2.2.37). This oddly phrased response suits the messenger's oddly phrased question—"Which of this princely train / Call ye the warlike Talbot, for his acts / So much applauded through the realm of France?"—in which "Talbot" does not name someone who came to France but someone denoted by his "acts" in France (2.2.34–36). "Talbot" is a name that circulates, by reputation, "through the realm" separately from his body. Talbot's reply that he is "the Talbot" not only acknowledges but compounds this representation of himself as multiple and disintegrated, naming Talbot as someone or something apart from the speaking "I."[58]

The messenger's invitation to Talbot describes another scene of beholding:

The virtuous lady, Countess of Auvergne,
With modesty admiring thy renown,
By me entreats, great lord, thou wouldst vouchsafe
To visit her poor castle where she lies,
That she may boast she hath beheld the man
Whose glory fills the world with loud report. (2.2.38–43)

Anticipating the Countess's dismissive reaction to Talbot in the next scene, this invitation again figures Talbot as doubled or divided, a man constituted of a body and of a reputation that floats free from it. The aim of their meeting, the messenger suggests, is for Talbot's body and "renown" to be brought together in one person, the composite "man," for the Countess to "beh[o]ld." Burgundy's response identifies the dynamic between audience and performer implicit in the Countess's request:

> Is it even so? Nay, then I see our wars
> Will turn unto a peaceful comic sport,
> When ladies crave to be encountered with.
> You may not, my lord, despise her gentle suit. (2.2.44–47)

The Countess's desire to behold Talbot as an object of visual gratification translates military conquest into a performance spectacle, a hybrid comedy-sporting event.[59] In his reply to the messenger, "I return great thanks, / And in submission will attend on her," Talbot verbally performs the posture of humility instantiated by the Countess's anticipated gaze (2.2.251–52).

In many ways, the subsequent encounter that unfolds at the Countess's castle repeats Talbot's earlier shaming before the market audience at Orléans. The Countess echoes the French spectators' derisive deixis of Talbot's captive body, "Here . . . is the terror of the French," by similarly remarking on a disjuncture between the two Talbots, the Talbot she has heard about and the Talbot she sees: "Is this the scourge of France? / Is this the Talbot?" (1.6.20; 2.3.14–15). Instead of "some Hercules, / A second Hector" with "grim aspect," "large proportion," and "strong-knit limbs," she finds him "a child, a seely dwarf," a "weak and writhled shrimp" (2.3.18–22). In response, Talbot is unable to affirm himself by himself; He must bring in others who can "certify her Talbot's here" (2.3.31). In Rackin's influential reading of this scene, the Countess's response places myopic, characteristically French emphasis on the physical body of Talbot against the expansive concept of Talbot's glory—the immortal historical record of Talbot.[60] When read in the context of the preceding scenes, however, the confrontation between the Countess and Talbot demonstrates continuity with the play's representation of Talbot as a double. The scenes with Salisbury dramatize how Talbot's identity is constituted as an effect of surrogation. In narrating to Salisbury his humiliation in the marketplace, Talbot becomes the speaking counterpart or verbal double of his silenced, objectified, past self. When Salisbury is mortally wounded in body and voice, Talbot posits himself as Salisbury's double in an act of surrogation that also turns Salisbury into a double or "mirror" for Talbot. In none of these scenes is Talbot represented as a unitary figure: He is consistently constructed as more than one Talbot, a feature summarized by his third-person self-address. The Countess therefore does not misread Talbot. Rather, in duplicating the theatrical circumstances that organize many of the previous scenes, she posits Talbot in a performative role that makes him a double of himself.[61] In other words, the Countess merely re-creates the conditions in which the play repeatedly casts Talbot as a performer who is at once "I" and "him," self and performative other.

Before he can leave to summon the army that will collectively "certify her Talbot's here" and rescue him from the Countess's trap, Talbot is confronted by another iteration of himself in the form of the "picture" the Countess holds captive in her gallery: "Long time thy shadow hath been thrall to me," she tells him, "For in my gallery thy picture hangs; / But now the substance shall endure the like, / And I will chain these legs and arms of thine" (2.3.35–38). Her identification of his picture as "shadow" and his body as "substance" again makes explicit what has been true throughout the play thus far: that to name Talbot is to name Talbot's doppelgänger. The figure of the doppelgänger, which "lend[s] imagery to a universal human problem—that of the relation of the self to the self," usefully elucidates several features of the play's characterization of Talbot.[62] As Otto Rank observes in two important studies of the doppelgänger, *The Double: A Psychoanalytic Study* (1914) and "The Double as Immortal Self" (1941), literary representations of the double often figure it as a shadow or mirror image of a human body. The Countess's identification of Talbot's "picture" as his "shadow" and his "legs and arms" as his "substance" is consistent with this strand of the doppelgänger tradition. Her framing of the ominous relationship between his body and image expresses the doppelgänger's association with death, "a reminder of the individual's mortality, indeed, the announcer of death itself," Rank writes, "an omen of death."[63] Rank cites numerous examples from later Romantic literature in which the "killing" of the protagonist's painted image, mirror reflection, or shadow brings about the death of the protagonist (as in Oscar Wilde's *The Picture of Dorian Gray*). The Countess's possession of Talbot through his image is often read as a form of "image magic," a kind of voodoo or witchery in which antagonizing an image produces harm to the body it represents.[64] This "image magic" is a version of the doppelgänger topos that Rank identifies as a feature of later psychological fiction, especially works by authors like E.T.A. Hoffmann and Fyodor Dostoyevsky.[65]

The confrontation with death initiated by the appearance of one's doppelgänger is not limited to the realm of fiction. It is a persistent theme in accounts of the image, ranging from African tribes' encounters with Western photojournalists to Roland Barthes's *Camera Lucida*. Rank notes, "The horror of having a portrait or photograph made is . . . to be found all over the world"; some aboriginal peoples "actually fear that they will die as a result of having their pictures taken."[66] Although Rank identifies such beliefs with "primitive people," he links these beliefs about the sinister effects of imaging with the treatment of the doppelgänger in Western literature. As chapter 1 observes, Barthes's *Camera Lucida*, perhaps the most influential work on photography in the twentieth century, likewise associates the photographic image with death. In a formulation that recalls Talbot's many doublings of himself, Barthes describes himself posing in front of the camera, a mechanical viewer that provokes his performance of another self: "once I feel myself observed by the lens, everything changes: I constitute myself in the process of 'posing,' I instantaneously make another body for myself, I transform myself into an image."[67] Barthes has to struggle, he remarks, to communicate "what I am, apart from any effigy" in this "advent of myself as other: a cunning dissociation of consciousness from identity."[68] He describes the experience of being photographed as "a micro-version of death"; he is "a subject who feels he is becoming an object." He concludes that in the photograph he has "become Total-Image, which is to say, Death in person."[69]

Emerging from radically divergent cultures and historical moments, these various considerations of the imaged doppelgänger and its relationship to death suggest how the Countess's "image magic" is more than a category of witchcraft that uses a picture as its medium. As the image theory of both Barthes and Rank's "primitive people" attest, the captivity, immobility, or death imposed by the pictorial double is an effect of imaging itself—of freezing a moment in time, posing a body in a permanently fixed gesture, or rendering what is living in static form. The picture of Talbot is thus ominously macabre, not only in the Countess's description of it as a prefiguration of her intent to capture him but in the fixity of its very form—in its translation of living Talbot into a static, passive object. Further, this pictorial doppelgänger of Talbot is yet another in the play's long sequence of dead Talbots. At Henry V's funeral in the opening scene, the court receives news of Talbot's capture in France. The messenger's detail that "A base Walloon, to win the Dauphin's grace, / Thrust Talbot with a spear into the back" logically leads Bedford to ask,

> Is Talbot slain then? I will slay myself,
> For living idly here in pomp and ease
> Whilst such a worthy leader, wanting aid,
> Unto his dastard foemen is betrayed. (1.1.141–44)

The messenger's answer, "Oh no, he lives," brings Talbot back from the dead state in which he was momentarily suspended as Bedford not only assumed Talbot's death but plotted his own (1.1.145). The play's very first mention of Talbot thus presents an image of him dead with a spear in his back. Later in act 1, the disfigured and dying Salisbury offers a "mirror" double of Talbot as Talbot figures himself in Salisbury's maimed image. And although the epitaph Talbot subsequently invents for Salisbury inscribes a perpetual audience to behold his deeds, so too does it identify Talbot with a corpse and tomb. As the concept of the doppelgänger illustrates, the Countess's baleful, deathlike "shadow" of Talbot is a logical successor to these prior doublings in which the living Talbot is bound to his morbid twin in the kind of hauntological assemblage I explored in chapter 2.

In his response to the Countess's threat to take the substance of his body captive like the shadow that hangs in her gallery, Talbot recasts the metaphor of substance and shadow to assert that in holding his body, the Countess has not achieved his substance:

> TALBOT: I laugh to see your ladyship so fond
>   To think that you have aught but Talbot's shadow
>   Whereon to practice your severity.
> COUNTESS: Why? Art not thou the man?
> TALBOT: No, no, I am but shadow of myself.
>   You are deceived; my substance is not here.
>   For what you see is but the smallest part
>   And least proportion of humanity.
>   I tell you, madam, were the whole frame here,
>   It is of such a spacious lofty pitch
>   Your roof were not sufficient to contain't.
> COUNTESS: This is a riddling merchant for the nonce.
>   He will be here, and yet he is not here.
>   How can these contrarieties agree?
> TALBOT: That will I show you presently. (2.3.44–60)

Talbot undercuts the Countess's threat to turn his substance into shadow by claiming that his substance eludes her; she has captured another of his shadows instead.[70] Talbot's recasting of substance and shadow resembles the dualistic metaphysical model that underlies concepts of the soul. The mortal body is transitory and insubstantial—the "least proportion of humanity"— while the soul is the immortal essence of the human being. Through this reconfiguration of substance and shadow, Talbot rejects the Countess's equation between his captive image and his captive person, suggesting that his personhood lies elsewhere, beyond the container of her castle or canvas—beyond even the container of his body.

Talbot's reference to substance and shadow again posits him as doubled, invoking a form of dualism associated with an earlier understanding of the doppelgänger, one that precedes the association of the double with death. Rank writes, "Originally conceived of as a guardian angel, assuring immortal survival to the self, the double eventually appears as precisely the opposite, a reminder of the individual's mortality, indeed, the announcer of death itself."[71] The English soldiers who emerge at the sound of Talbot's horn to rescue him from the Countess's plot not only ensure Talbot's immediate survival but represent the impossibility of subduing him through his physical person. Talbot's troops are produced as the transcendent doppelgänger or "guardian angel" by which he negates the deadly threat posed by the Countess, proving that Talbot exceeds his mortal body. While the doppelgänger represented in Talbot's picture associates the double with death, the inverse meaning of the doppelgänger as the immortal part of the human being is also potently operable in this scene, exposing how the double can likewise be a figure of perpetuity. Rank writes, "Originally, the double was an identical self (shadow, reflection), promising personal survival in the *future*; later, the double retained together with the individual's life his personal *past*; ultimately, he became an opposing self appearing in the form . . . which represents the perishable and mortal part of the personality."[72] All of the histrionic scenes discussed thus far in this chapter—the scene that unfolds in Sontag's ventriloquistic meditation on *Dead Troops Talk*, the scene with dead Henry and his nobles, the scenes with Salisbury at Orléans, and the scene at the Countess's castle—disclose the doppelgänger's double duty as a site where both the dead talk through the living and the living talk through the dead. The figure of the doppelgänger thus complicates critical truisms about the play's nostalgia, such as Michael Hattaway's assertion that "Talbot is a figure for the nostalgia that suffuses the play."[73] Such claims do not sufficiently address *whose* nostalgia is supposed to suffuse the play. As the recurrence of doppelgängers makes clear, the play and its characters resist the binary distinction between aliveness and the deadness that would produce nostalgia from within the text.

Talbot's dramatic resolution to his predicament with the Countess illustrates the degree to which the history play is itself a genre of doppelgänger literature. Talbot certifies that he is more than a mortal body by staging a piece of theater in which he is surrogated by his troops, a host of Talbot doubles who represent his "substance, sinews, arms, and strength" (2.3.63). Although his men are not dead, they function here much like Salisbury in the preceding scenes—as puppets whose actions Talbot scripts and whose bodies he poses and interprets in order to dramatize aspects of himself. Talbot's enlistment of others in a theatrical scene of self-extension works like a miniature history play: Talbot recovers from the Countess's deadening gaze to come alive again through a staged spectacle in which he is represented through a cast of substitutes.[74] While these substitutes "certify" the presence of Talbot—the living, substantial here-ness that he is impotent to certify on his own—they do so through scripted action. They do not function as autonomous, individuated characters in Talbot's mini-drama but, rather, as automaton-Talbots. In their role as both guardian angels and silent, zombie puppets, Talbot's troops illustrate the double meaning of the double—the doppelgänger's flexibility as a figure for both death and immortality. In its many doublings that theatricalize relations between the living and dead, 1 Henry VI, like the history plays more broadly, confounds the distinction between mortality and perpetuity.

VI. Yourself Your Self in Twain Divide

Talbot's doubleness is most explicitly dramatized when his only son, John, joins him to fight the Battle of Bordeaux. From John's arrival at the beginning of act 4, scene 5, until father and son die two scenes later, all appearances by Talbot include John, generating the double-vision effect of "two Talbots" that is amplified by the fact that they speak to one another almost exclusively in boxlike (coffinlike?) couplets (4.7.21).[75] The verbal exchanges between father and son center on the life-and-death implications of their doubleness. Urging his son to flee the battle that will surely end in death, Talbot rearticulates the model of his divided self that was first introduced by the Countess's messenger:

> I did send for thee
> To tutor thee in strategems of war,
> That Talbot's name might be in thee revived
> When sapless age and weak unable limbs
> Should bring thy father to his drooping chair.(4.5.1–5)

In these words to his son, Talbot figures himself as two separable entities: his name and the body he refers to synecdochally as "limbs." While he imagines his body declining toward death, his name or renown will find revivification through his substitute, John, whom Talbot will later call "my other life" (4.7.1). When John rejects this logic, Talbot insists that he is divisible and that his son can carry elements of him beyond his father's death: "Part of thy father may be saved in thee" (4.5.38).

In his resistance to his father's command that he flee the battle to save himself and thereby the Talbot name, John expresses an alternative understanding of their doubleness:

> Is my name Talbot, and am I your son,
> And shall I fly? O, if you love my mother,
> Dishonour not her honourable name
> To make a bastard and a slave of me.
> The world will say he is not Talbot's blood
> That basely fled when noble Talbot stood. (4.5.12–17)

John regards the question of fight or flight as a crucial test of his faithful doubling of his father, arguing that his own name, "Talbot," hinges on his replication of his father's actions. To act differently than his father—to flee when his father stands—is to fail to double his father. John cannot bisect his father into name and body; in his understanding of what it is to be his father's son, the inheritance of the name "Talbot" depends on the actions performed by the Talbot body. By this logic, his body must remain with his father's to the death in order for him to be worthy of the Talbot name. Failure to double his father's actions would not only bar him from his patrimony, John suggests, but it would have implications for the status of his own body, which would degrade from that of a faithful duplicate to the body of "a bastard and a slave" fathered by some other man. Against his father's suggestion that Talbot's name can be decoupled from what his body performs, John concludes, "No more can I be severed from your side / Than can yourself your self in twain divide" (4.5.48–49). In a statement that posits his father as both unitary and doubled, John declares that he is as indivisible from his father as his father is from himself.

The doubling of Talbot through his son is itself doubled or repeated in the next scene. Rescuing John from a skirmish with the French, Talbot remarks, "I gave thee life, and rescued thee from death" (4.6.5). In response, John suggests how the twice-gifted life that he has received from his father duplicates the filial relationship that was itself established as a form of doubling in the prior scene:

> O twice my father, twice I am thy son:
> The life thou gav'st me first was lost and done
> Till with thy warlike sword, despite of fate,
> To my determined time thou gav'st new date. (4.6.6–9)

As Talbot goes on to relate the events of the battle that led to his son's rescue, this second birth of John—this "new date"—reprises the question of John's legitimacy as a Talbot copy. Talbot dwells in particular on his combat with the Bastard of Orléans, in which he shed "some of his bastard blood" in recompense for the Bastard's bloody wounding of John (4.6.20). His accompanying verbal attack on the Bastard makes explicit what is at stake in this physical encounter:

> "Contaminated, base,
> And misbegotten blood I spill of thine,
> Mean and right poor, for that pure blood of mine
> Which thou didst force from Talbot, my brave boy." (4.6.21–24)

The concern John articulates in the previous scene—that he must prove himself Talbot's son lest he be reputed a bastard—is resolved here by the father's explicit defeat of the bastard/Bastard on his behalf.[76] Completing that defeat, Talbot names his son "Talbot" in an authenticating statement of John's successful doubling. Through John's bloodshed and Talbot's retributive wounding of the Bastard, John is "sealed the son of chivalry"—the true double of Talbot, the play's "noble chevalier" (4.6.29, 4.3.14). John's mother, who was in jeopardy of being "dishonour[ed]" if John failed as a Talbot duplicate, has been erased altogether by this martial encounter. The father alone becomes the progenitor of the son in a fantasy of cloning and paternal authentication that I will return to in chapter 4.

Given the dire circumstances that attend John's arrival at Bordeaux, his decision to stay and fight at his father's side guarantees at once his legacy and his death, a paradox that I will argue in chapter 5 is an inescapable feature of the heteronormative politics staged in the plays.[77] In his concern about what will be said about him if he leaves the battle—"The world will say he is not Talbot's blood / That basely fled when noble Talbot stood"—he anticipates a future in which he persists in the historical narrative (4.5.16–17). In order not to be shamed by that narrative as "not Talbot's son," however, young John Talbot must suffer his father's fate (4.6.51). Failure to do so will make him an un-Talbot, unlike his father and, instead, "like . . . to the peasant boys of France" (4.6.48). Actualizing himself as his father's double and the bearer of his "renownèd name" necessarily entails his death, as he goes on to declare: "If son to Talbot, die at Talbot's foot" (4.5.41, 53). As Alexander Leggatt puts it, insofar as his dramatic function goes, "he is born only to die . . . as though John, in finding his father, has found his own doom."[78] John's paradoxical identity, which requires he die in order to live on in fame as Talbot's son, again illustrates how the figure of the doppelgänger collapses death and immortality. Declaring, "live I will not if my father die," John posits his father as the fatal doppelgänger—the picture of Dorian Gray, of Talbot—whose destruction will trigger his own (4.5.51). The fact that events unfold in reverse, with John's death triggering his father's, confounds any tidy delineation of who is the Talbot and who is Talbot's doppelgänger.

This indistinction is amplified by the mourning scene that follows, which opens on Talbot holding his dead son, asking, "Where is my other life? Mine own is gone" (4.7.1). Talbot identifies as the dead man whose life "is gone," locating his own life in the son who is dead. This articulation of the doppelgänger relationship between father and son—itself a form of Derridean hauntology—is theatricalized in a final moment of ventriloquism that echoes Talbot's scenes with Salisbury: "Poor boy, he smiles, methinks, as who should say / 'Had death been French, then death had died today'" (4.7.27–28). Talbot produces another *Dead Troops Talk* moment, theatricalizing his identity as the undead double of his son by translating John's facial expression into language. In the same way that Sontag's ventriloquism of Wall's soldiers extends their temporal reach beyond the stilled moment represented in the photograph so that the dead keep "talking" through the audience who perform for and as them, Talbot's ventriloquism posits John as still speaking. As a verbal medium, Talbot affects the death of death—"death had died today"—that he articulates through John, simultaneously declaring the end of death and dramatizing John's transcendence of death through the father's postmortem utterance. Talbot ends his life staging a scene of double surrogation in which he at once speaks for his dead son and scripts his son's dead body into speaking its father's words. He does what Shakespeare does in this and every scene of the history plays: he uses the living to speak the words of the dead and the dead to speak the words of the living.

Thomas Nashe's much-quoted account of seeing *1 Henry VI* on the stage addresses precisely this second form of surrogation—the form, I have been arguing, that complicates our notions of surrogation as a linear temporal process by which the dead are replaced over time. Nashe describes how in history plays, the subjects of chronicle history "are revived, and they themselves raised from the grave of oblivion, and brought to plead their aged honors in open presence."[79] The dead figure is "brought to plead" through the body and voice of the actor, but in Nashe's formulation, that actor does not appear as such. It is the actor who is erased so that Talbot speaks the plea scripted by the living playwright. Nashe relates his experience of Talbot in terms that resonate with Shakespeare's construction of the character as a specifically performative phenomenon: a living person playing the dead and a dead man speaking through the living. As Talbot himself demonstrates time and again in the theatrical exchanges he stages throughout *1 Henry VI*, "there is no immortality can be given a man on earth like unto plays."[80] This immortality is generated not only by history plays like *1 Henry VI* but by the scenes of theatrical exchange embedded within them.

Appropriately, Talbot's death does not bring an end to the proliferation of Talbot doubles. Sir William Lucy's confrontation with Joan la Pucelle over Talbot's corpse reproduces, through honorific titles, a host of Talbots like those summoned before the Countess of Auvergne.[81] Talbot is "the great Alcides of the field, / Valiant Lord Talbot of Shrewsbury," as well as

> Great Earl of Wexford, Waterford, and Valence,
> Lord Talbot of Goodrich and Urchinfield,
> Lord Strange of Blackmere, Lord Verdun of Alton,
> Lord Cromwell of Wingfield, Lord Furnival of Sheffield,
> The thrice victorious lord of Falconbridge,
> Knight of the noble order of Saint George,
> Worthy Saint Michael and the Golden Fleece,
> Great *Maréhal* to Henry the Sixth
> Of all his wars within the realm of France. (4.7.60–71)

Learning that all of these Talbots are dead, Lucy threatens that no living Talbot is necessary to menace the French. "Were but his picture left amongst you here," he declares, "It would amaze the proudest of you all" (4.7.83–84). Lucy imagines another Talbot portrait, one that would not replicate the stilled, deathly impotence of the Countess's picture but instead figure the persistence of Talbot's power through his image. Even as she goes on to dismiss Talbot's corpse as "stinking and flyblown" and lying inert "here at our feet," Joan, too, reproduces Talbot in her alarmed suggestion that Lucy "is old Talbot's ghost" (4.7.76, 87). She observes, with marked anxiety, that "He speaks with such a proud commanding spirit" (4.7.88).

Lucy speaks like dead Talbot, which is to say that dead Talbot speaks through Lucy. Within the very scene of the two Talbots' deaths, Talbot's dying promise that he and his son "shall scape mortality" is realized through a speaking double—a doppelgänger who is at once a living character and a dead one's ghost (4.7.22). As he takes the Talbots' bodies off to be buried, Lucy warns that "from their ashes shall be reared / A phoenix that shall make all France afeard" (4.7.92–93). In his closing couplet on the fate of the Talbots, Lucy returns us to the opening scene of the play and to the theatrical phenomena that unfold around the casket of Henry V.[82] The future will be performed through the past. The living will find voice through the dead.

CHAPTER 4

The King Machine

Reproducing Sovereignty in *3 Henry VI*

> What, will the line stretch out to th'crack of doom?
>
> —*Macbeth*

Before the Battle of Tewksbury that will seal the Yorkists' claim to the throne at the end of *3 Henry VI*, King Edward threatens the rebellious Earl of Warwick with a gruesome promise of how he will use the Earl's severed head when the Lancastrians are defeated:

This hand, fast wound about thy coal-black hair,
Shall, whiles thy head is warm and new cut off,
Write in the dust this sentence with thy blood:
"Wind-changing Warwick now can change no more." (5.1.54–57)[1]

Edward's lurid image is not a premonition of Warwick's battle death in the following scene, where his corpse will lie cooling in the field for an indefinite length of time. It is a fantasy of capital punishment—of a judicial decapitation precisely coordinated so that Edward can take hold of Warwick's severed head during the short space of time "whiles" it is "warm and new cut off" and the blood has not yet begun to congeal. The image's constellation of capital punishment, blood writing, and the "sentence" seems on its face a straightforward illustration of Michel Foucault's claim that public execution "inscribed in [the victim] and on [the victim]" guilt and state power: "in him, on him, the sentence had to be legible to all."[2] But Edward adds a second sentence beyond the sentence of death. This sentence will be written not in or on Warwick but with Warwick's bleeding head, which Edward proposes to convert into a writing implement for use on a surface apart from the decapitated body. Warwick's head would be made into a rudimentary fountain pen to inscribe a sentence elsewhere. By reading the earth as the resulting document, Edward enlists an organic surface in the artificial technology of human writing. At the same time that he proposes this synthetic function for dirt, he paradoxically suggests—through contact between blood and the dust from which it originated—a destined absorption of Warwick's death into the organic order.

Both Warwick's head and the dust inscribed with his blood function in this passage as what Jacques Derrida calls supplements—specifically, supplements to the production of Edward's kingship. Derrida develops the term *supplément* across his body of work to describe a prosthetic extension "which comes to replace, imitate, relay, and augment the living being."[3] In his seminar *The Beast and the Sovereign*, he argues that sovereignty in particular is not complete or legible in itself and cannot be constituted without supplements. These supplements are invariably technological in that they instrumentalize people and things to produce what cannot be made manifest on its own. Warwick's head and the organic surface on which it writes are both enlisted by Edward as technologies to supplement the regal title to which he lays claim. In Derrida's terms, both head and dust function in Edward's fantasy as "marionettes"—as technological prostheses for expressing Edward's sovereignty. "Any art of the marionette," Derrida writes, "[is] a question of art, of *tekhnē* as art or of *tekhnē* between art and technique, and between life and politics."[4] By enlisting dust as a writing surface, Edward shows how the prosthetic work of the supplement or marionette collapses distinctions between the natural and the technological, the grown and the made.[5] Edward's expression here of regal rights instrumentalizes head and earth, exposing how grown and made are indistinguishable—how "*techne* or art is at the center of what we take to be natural and original," including the origin of dust itself.[6]

Along with head and dust, Edward's proposed capital punishment of Warwick and the temporal constructs fabricated by it work as supplements to his production of Yorkist sovereignty. In his translated seminars on the death penalty, Derrida describes capital punishment as a necessary supplement to theologically based kingship. Through its mimicry of the lethal power of God, sovereignty "defines [itself] by this right and by this power: over the life and death of subjects. This is how the essence of sovereign power, as political but first of all theologico-political power, presents itself, represents itself as the right to decree and to execute a death penalty. Or to pardon arbitrarily, sovereignly."[7] Further, he argues, the right to determine the end of another's life functions not simply to express but to constitute the immortality of sovereignty. The death penalty engineers a concept of infinitude through its spectacle of finitude:

> The finality of this end as damnation or condemnation to death, its paradoxical finality, is to produce the invincible illusion, the phantasm of this end of finitude, thus of the other side of an infinitization. . . . This is one of the places of articulation with religion and with theology, with the theologico-political. For this phantasm of infinitization at the heart of finitude, of an infinitization of survival assured by calculation itself and the cutting decision of the death penalty, this phantasm is one with God. . . . [8]

In Derrida's thinking, the construction of a divinely ordained sovereignty that transcends time depends on the visible production of finite time by means of control over the moment of death. For theologically grounded kingship, the death penalty is the very mechanism—the supplement—through which an effigy or "phantasm" of timeless divinity is constituted. The death penalty "put[s] an end to finitude; it affirms its power over time; it masters the future; it protects against the irruption of the other."[9] That other is death itself, which always threatens to undermine sovereignty's claim to a transcendent body. Death's status as the other or antithesis of kingship is expressed a number of times in *3 Henry VI*, such as in York's statement, "I will be king or die," and in the play's visual juxtaposition of the throne he occupies in the first scene with the molehill on which he is killed three scenes later (1.2.35).[10]

The death penalty's function in creating the immortality or timelessness of sovereignty is articulated in the sentence Edward proposes to write with Warwick's blood: "Wind-changing Warwick now can change no more" (5.1.57). By this moment in the final act of the play, Warwick has been firmly established as England's "king-maker," the "Proud setter-up and puller-down of kings" (3.3.157).[11] Edward's bloody sentence is more than a jab about Warwick's inconstancy—about his switch from Yorkist to Lancastrian. It is also a reference to the turnover of kings that Warwick has effected throughout the play. As "king-maker," Warwick punctures the institution of hereditary monarchy by exposing kingship as, at best, a cooperation of the made and the grown. To declare Warwick henceforth unchangeable is to declare the crown settled on the house of York once and for all.

This *once and for all* is the essence of changelessness that Edward fantasizes. Warwick's decapitation would freeze him in the "now," making now perpetual. If change is a function of time, Warwick's execution would initiate Derrida's "paradoxical finality," an end to time itself and the beginning of a static now without end—a period of "no more" change, an end to endings, a divine perpetuity in which the future will be absolutely identical to the present. Edward's sentence illustrates how "sovereignty projects an image of itself as absolute and univocal by purifying itself of death," to quote Gwynne Fulton's reading of Derrida.[12] In observing how the phantasm of infinitization is constructed through the finality of the death penalty, Derrida's work explains how an execution such as that proposed for Warwick is essential to Edward's claim to theologico-political kingship. The declaration that Warwick will be arrested in time is a means for Edward to constitute the unchanging, timeless, outside-of-time, or transcendent nature of sovereignty. The ax that would take off Warwick's head works as a time machine—not a mechanism for transport backward and forward in time but one that makes time, fabricating a concept of time on which sovereignty depends: time arrested; time cloned; time, like kingship, always and forever identical to now. By imagining Warwick's execution, Edward imagines that he would initiate a fixed, unchanging now, thereby ending endings. In its production of Warwick's decollation, Edward's prosthetic instrument of capital punishment works as both a time machine and a king machine, manufacturing sovereign transcendence. Since sovereignty is essentially a claim about time, the time machine and the king machine are one and the same.

The concept of the machine is central to Derrida's thought. He defines the machine "as a system [*dispositif*] of calculation and repetition. As soon as there is any calculation, calculability, and repetition, there is something of a machine."[13] In *Technologies of Life and Death: From Cloning to Capital Punishment*, philosopher Kelly Oliver summarizes the significance of the machine in Derrida's work: "The machine appears as a metaphor for technology, certainly; but more than this, it appears as a cipher for the undecidability between original and copy, real and artificial, nature and culture, determinism and freedom, grown and made, chance and choice."[14] The observation that capital punishment functions for Edward as a time machine and a king machine is thus also an observation that in *3 Henry VI*, sovereignty is constructed at the juncture of the antinomies articulated by Oliver. Derrida adds that "in the machine there is an excess in relation to the machine itself: at once the effect of a machination and something that eludes machinelike calculation."[15] This "excess in relation to the machine itself" is a kind of built-in, if unpredictable, glitch—a disruption in calculation or productivity that is nonetheless endemic to the machine's nature. If we think about Warwick as the "king-maker," we can see that he is posited at once as a kind of mechanism—an apparatus for producing kings by repeatedly "setting up" and "pulling down"—and a glitch in another, concurrently running machine: the copy machine of hereditary kingship that occludes its artificial operations through reference to organic replication.

The person of Warwick thus illustrates sovereignty's mutual dependence on the grown or sexually reproduced and the made or artificially produced.

As my brief reading of Edward's threat suggests, this chapter is interested in the construction of sovereignty in *3 Henry VI*, a play that Michael Hattaway has rightly described as "a political essay."[16] *3 Henry VI* dramatizes the defeat of the Lancastrian King Henry VI by the rival house of York, concluding its busy, tumultuous action with the Yorkist Edward IV on the throne. The play begins after Henry's loss at the Battle of St. Albans (staged at the end of *2 Henry VI*) and includes a number of key events in Shakespeare's dramatization of the Wars of the Roses: Henry's entailment of the crown away from his own son to a Yorkist heir; the brutal death of Richard, Duke of York, at the hands of Queen Margaret and Lord Clifford; the rise and fall of Warwick, the "kingmaker"; the murders of King Henry and his son; and the emergence of Richard of Gloucester as a savage Yorkist henchman and malcontented aspirant to the throne. Over the course of these events, Shakespeare stages what I argue is a penetrating study of the mechanisms by which kingship, historical narratives, and dynastic claims are generated. The play shows immortal, divine kingship to be constituted through the cooperation of naturalized and artificial reproductive technologies. These include mechanisms like capital punishment that produce the temporal constructs necessary to the institution of sovereignty—constructs that disclose, in David Wills's terms, "the prosthetic status of time."[17] And they include the biological, cultural, and narrative mechanisms for producing the royal genealogies and future lines of succession that enable kingship to fabricate itself as timeless and undying from one generation to the next.

Scholarly interest in the history plays' constructions of sovereignty has tended to focus on *Henry V*, whose Chorus directly invites the audience of the play to participate in the collective, imaginative work of king-making. While *3 Henry VI* is not as aesthetically satisfying as *Henry V*, this chapter argues that the play represents a sustained, acutely intellectual engagement with questions about how kingship is made. Further, in its perseveration over events dramatized earlier in Shakespeare's English chronicle plays, especially *Richard II*, the play explores the interconnectedness of king-making and history-making. Like its considerations of sovereignty, the play's meditation on historical construction highlights how the past is constituted through a union of found and manufactured material, often eliding distinctions between the two. By exposing the components of the king machine at work, the play denaturalizes and demystifies not only the institution of sovereignty but the temporal, historiographic, and teleological artifices on which that institution depends.

This chapter explores king-making as a form of replica-production that can at once elucidate and be elucidated by current and emerging copy-making technologies. In addition to engaging with the late seminars of Derrida, I set the play in dialogue with contemporary theorists of serial reproduction, especially Andy Warhol and philosopher Kelly Oliver, both of whom explore homologies between execution machinery and cloning. As in the first three chapters of the book, my aim here is to bring Shakespeare's chronicle plays into a transhistorical conversation about aesthetic productions of life, death, and time and to challenge some of the assumptions about history and temporality that inform our critical praxis. This conversation—which maps the conceptual infrastructures shared by the throne and the electric chair, by history plays and Warholian silk screens—dismantles teleological narratives that would posit the play's early modern reproductive technologies as the rudimentary ancestors of modern machines. The uncanny resonance between *3 Henry VI*'s sovereignty machines and our own culture's mechanisms for contriving and naturalizing the marionettes of political power presents a radical—if not devastating—challenge to liberal humanist teleology, a challenge that must inform both our accounts of the past and our accounts of ourselves.

I. Like a Bolt of Lightning

My reading of *3 Henry VI* emerges, foremost, from Warhol's iconic series of electric chair paintings, which I treat here as theoretical resources for thinking about how time, death, historical representation, and natural and artificial reproduction intersect. As in the book's other chapters, however, my reading of Shakespeare through Warhol ultimately develops into a reciprocal reading of Warhol informed by the theorizing resources that emerge from the early modern dramatic text. Like Shakespeare, Warhol used chronicles—in his case, the newspaper—as source material for exploring both the mechanisms by which power is reproduced and the workings of representational media itself. Warhol began painting electric chairs in 1963 as part of a series that eventually came to be known as *Death and Disaster*, which included images of suicides, car crashes, and other miscellaneous fatalities. The original for the paintings was a media image of the electric chair ("Old Sparky") at Sing Sing Penitentiary in Ossining, New York. Dated January 1953, the photo was circulated in advance of the impending executions of Julius and Ethel Rosenberg, who would be electrocuted for treason at Sing Sing in June of that year.[18] Through the technology of silk-screening, Warhol and his assistants copied the photograph onto canvases that had been painted with a ground of one or more colors. Some of the paintings reproduce the wide shot that shows the chair in the broader context of the Sing Sing death chamber, which features a "SILENCE" sign near the top right that lights up when an execution is in progress (Figure 11). Others are cropped more tightly, showing only the chair itself and the floor pad beneath it (Figure 12). In some versions, like *Orange Disaster #5* (Figure 13), the image is replicated in a grid pattern across the canvas, forming what art critic Heiner Bastian describes as Warhol's "black dramaturgies."[19]

The electric chair was introduced in 1888 to automate the process of execution—to remove human agency from the work of putting someone to death by introducing a mechanism that would carry out the state's killing duties. With the electric chair, the role of the executioner—once a human being who could err through inefficiency, cruelty, or incompetence—became abstracted into a machine and mystified into an electrical force that distanced individual agents of the state from the body of the victim. Like the guillotine introduced in France in the late eighteenth century, the electric chair was hailed as an advance in penal technology that would enhance the dignity of executions for both state and victim, guaranteeing that all victims would receive an identical death and putting an end to the barbarous cruelty that characterized

FIGURE 11. *Little Electric Chair* (1964), by Andy Warhol. Image and Artwork © 2021 The Andy Warhol Foundation for the Visual Arts, Inc./Licensed by ARS.

FIGURE 12.   *Big Electric Chair* (1967–1968), by Andy Warhol. Image and Artwork © 2021 The Andy Warhol Foundation for the Visual Arts, Inc./Licensed by ARS.

earlier execution methods. One of the attractions of both the guillotine and the electric chair was the mechanisms' imagined capacity to reduce death to a single instant. If the guillotine's blade ended a life—as its inventor claimed—"like a bolt of lightning," the electric chair delivered the bolt of lightning itself.[20] The ideal of instantaneity was central to both devices' claim to kill humanely and therefore justly and legally. Torture is characterized by a combination of suffering and time—of pain plus duration.[21] Freedom from suffering—an aim of French penal reformers and a guarantee of the Eighth Amendment of the US Constitution—meant freedom from forms of execution that killed over hours or even minutes. The reduction of the killing process to a single instant would eliminate the "cruel and unusual" experience of dying in or over time.

As a technological supplement to state power, the electric chair performs multiple kinds of artificial production and reproduction. It is a time machine that was believed to capture an instant of death—a fraction of time or a moment of non-time—through its technical apparatus, though because "there is no degree zero instant," as Wills observes, it is more accurate to say that the chair fabricated the instant as a unit of time rather than capturing it.[22] Importantly, the chair's temporal mechanisms also include a set of claims about the past and the future. Like the decapitation death that Edward proposes for War-

FIGURE 13.   *Orange Disaster #5* (1963), by Andy Warhol. Image and Artwork © 2021 The Andy Warhol Foundation for the Visual Arts, Inc./Licensed by ARS.

wick, the electric chair certifies a particular version of the past while fixing its victims in a perpetual state of legal unforgivenness.[23] As an apparatus designed for reset and reuse, the electric chair is also a predictive appliance whose very appearance foretells a future in which living bodies will be mechanically processed into corpses—a future of repetition, of the same.[24] Through replication of a programmed set of automated operations, it works as a copy machine that repeats death over and over at the flip of a switch. The chair's death-delivery system functions, more broadly, as a sovereignty machine, a supplement or prosthesis that generates state power by producing a spectacle of lawful killing authority that disciplines the victim's illicit acts. Left unpunished, those acts represent a threat to the state's sovereign, exceptional right to kill with impunity. Punished justly, instantly, painlessly, and ritualistically, those crimes are subdued by a transcendent power—at once natural and technological—that is channeled by electrical wires through the chair-apparatus of the state. The local viewers of the execution, who watch the victim's death in "SILENCE" through the execution chamber's curtain-flanked window like a hushed audience before a proscenium stage, function as proxies for the broader public on whose behalf the state performs its right to kill.[25]

By the period in which Warhol began painting the electric chair, the appliance's notorious glitches had come to compromise its several productive and reproductive claims. The original meaning of "glitch," a term astronaut John Glenn defined in 1962 as "a spike or change in voltage in an electrical circuit which takes place when the circuit suddenly has a new load put on it," is an uncannily apt descriptor for the electric chair's myriad malfunctions.[26] The belief that the chair delivered instantaneous death without suffering was contested by the observation of eyewitnesses, who testified otherwise.[27] Executed immediately following the removal of her husband's corpse from the Sing Sing chair, for example, Ethel Rosenberg required two additional shocks after the normal course of three shocks left her heart still beating. Witnesses to her execution reported that her head was smoking by the time the ordeal concluded.[28] By elongating the death process, such malfunctions reveal both the grisly material reality of death by electrocution and the chair's inability to produce the looked-for "instant" of death. Rather than mechanically duplicating death in a way that would abstract state violence into a current of electricity, the chair came to be marked by its own unsavory counter-history of notoriously unruly effects on uncooperative bodies: It set heads on fire, tortured but failed to kill, and glitched in myriad horrific ways that left victims burned, smoking, or bleeding profusely. Further, a number of its victims were later proved to have been executed wrongfully. Such cases subvert the claims of both past crime and future justice by introducing not only histories of judicial miscarriage but the potential for subsequent wrongful electrocutions. Combined with evidence of victims' horrific suffering in the chair, the specter of wrongful execution—of state murder rather than state justice—compromises the very production of sovereignty concentrated in its prosthetic machinery of death.

These glitches in the system—in the execution system and in the sponsoring system of law—are a focus of Warhol's electric chair paintings, and they expose the interdependence of naturalized and artificial forces in the production of state power, its images, and its narratives. By silk-screening a photograph onto painted canvases, Warhol introduces another set of reproductive operations and glitches in addition to those represented by the execution apparatus. More than any other visual art form, the technology of photography made possible the replication of an image the eye perceived in the physical world—replication that testified to the truth of the past and made possible the persistence of that stilled, original moment for future viewers.[29] Although a photo is technically made through the exposure, over time, of film to light, photography is popularly conceived as capturing a single instant in time, not as representing a duration of time.[30] The kinship between penal and photographic technology's mechanical production of an "instant" is expressed in the colloquial term that came to be used, after the emergence of photography, for the official who lowered the wooden bevel down over the neck of a guillotine victim. This person was referred to as "the photographer," the blade of the guillotine imagined as a camera shutter that closes on a single instant of time.[31]

As in the electric chair's production of time, death, and sovereign transcendence, glitches arise at all stages of the photographic process, compromising photography's claims to faithful historical representation and temporal instantaneousness. Warhol highlights the deficiency and manipulability of the photographic document in his paintings of the electric chair. He adjusts its context through cropping, exposes gaps in the original by highlighting the graininess of the image, accentuates human mediation in the technological artifact by silk-screening over paint, and underscores the fiction of exact repeatability by covering canvases in cloned images that are never precisely the same.[32] Peggy Phelan has written that "Warhol was interested in the invariable errors and mistakes that made the pursuit of the same an always-failed enterprise" and that he "preferred transmutations to transmissions."[33] Transmutation is multiplied by the electric chair's overlapping representation of two imperfect reproductive technologies: the chair itself and the photographic process through which images of the interior of Sing Sing's death chamber are made available to the broader public. By highlighting the potential for error and intervening explicitly in the transmission process, Warhol's electric chair exposes glitches in our technologies for producing either reliable accounts of the past or stable prototypes for the future.

Warhol's grainy replication of the electric chair photograph shows the state's image of timeless power to be contingent on the workings of flawed copy machines—both the chair itself and the photographic technology that disseminates its image of deadly power. As a homologous work of reproduction—a reproduction about reproduction—Shakespeare's 3 Henry VI likewise discloses

how immortal, divine kingship is constructed according to a glitchy cooperation of naturalized and artificial replicative technologies. As Edward's threat-
ing of Warwick shows, the institution of divine kingship—which survives the
death of any individual king, according to medieval political theory—relies on
the finality of the death penalty to constitute its claim to immortality or un-
changeability. For such transcendent power to outlast the life span of a king,
however, the king's body must be serially copied through hereditary reproduction (Henry IV, Henry V, Henry VI). Like the business of cloning corpses
or cloning photographs, the business of cloning kings is an imperfect one in
which aberrations of all kinds can disrupt the claim of naturally immortal
kingship. These aberrations, a main preoccupation of 3 Henry VI, reveal killing and artificial reproduction to be technological supplements to hereditary succession, supplements that fabricate the exceptional ontological claims
of sovereignty by which a mortal body natural is coupled to an immortal
body politic.

As in Warhol's paintings, history itself emerges in the play as a product of
the cooperation between the found and the manufactured, the natural and the
artificial, the grown and the made. In addition to the other kinds of supplement-
assisted production at work in Edward's image of the decapitated Warwick,
the passage exposes history as a technological artifact that, in turn, fabricates
past and future time. In particular, the image suggests how Warwick's execution would have immediate, automatic, retroactive effects that would be declared and read through the record Edward proposes to inscribe with his blood.
Warwick's changeability (not Edward's) led to his decapitation, the hypothetical blood-writing insinuates, and Warwick's decapitation would arrest him in
a perpetually irredeemable, unforgiven, and unchangeable state that permanently fixes him as a traitor. The blood sentence elides the imprudent changeability of Edward, which incited Warwick's revolt—changeability that the
audience of the play observes firsthand. Insofar as the sentence serves as a history of Warwick, it is exposed by the play itself as a partial and slanted one,
just as Warhol's glitchy production of the electric chair image problematizes
the chair's historical claims. In conjunction with the play's extended attention
to historical revisionism, this moment of historiographic construction that attempts to fix Warwick's legacy reveals the technological nature of history-
making. There is no history without reproductive technology, be it oral, written,
pictorial, or dramatic. The play presents history as a supplement to kingship,
one that is fundamentally technological and therefore glitchy in its production of the past. Like dust, decapitated heads, and sovereign timelessness, history itself is revealed as another marionette, a puppet of what Derrida calls
the "prosthstate."[34]

II. The Chair of State, Where Now He Sits

Beginning and ending in a litany of deaths recounted around the "chair of state," Shakespeare's play, like Warhol's series on the electric chair, is preoccupied with transmutation—with errors inherent in the reproduction of state power and the stories told and performed about it. The terms established by Warhol's paintings highlight several features of *3 Henry VI*. First, although hereditary monarchy draws its power from a cooperation of transcendent and natural processes—of divine anointing and hereditary succession—the play discloses how the institution relies on human agents and technological supplements to manufacture the appearance of the natural and divine. Like Warhol's electric chair, the play posits a mystified image of enthroned power while simultaneously exposing the glitchy fabrication through which that power is reproduced—a process at once mechanistic and naturalized. Reproductive defects are visible not only in the almost comic number of power changes staged by the play but also, I will suggest, in the emerging creative potential of Richard of Gloucester, whose moral and physical deformity manifests a host of glitches that plague the reproduction of hereditary monarchy. Second, kingship's claim to transcendence—to a mystical regal body that survives human mortality—is constructed always in relation to death. As Oliver puts it, "Life is haunted by technologies of death."[35] Kingship's perpetuity relies on its close proximity to death, if not its continual reproduction of death. Sovereign perpetuity or temporal transcendence is constructed through the staging of its opposite, a lurid mortality that itself functions as a prosthesis of kingship. Third, the historiographic medium through which claims of hereditary, mystified kingship are narrated is revealed to be fabricated and under constant negotiation. And fourth, because historical construction involves fabrication, history can be unmade and remade. While characters repeatedly turn to the past to stabilize the present and future, they reveal instead that the past is still under negotiation and therefore inadequate to secure the now, let alone the time to come.

Nearly all of these issues are staged in the long, tumultuous first scene of the play, which begins before an empty throne. The opening stage picture, featuring the central empty chair—a stage picture nearly identical to the one reproduced by Warhol—declares the drama's central conflict over who will occupy the seat of power in the wake of King Henry's defeat at the Battle of St. Albans. On returning to London, the Yorkist faction forcibly break into the throne room seeking to immediately seat the Duke of York. The case they make for his right is many-faceted, but a key component of that case is their assertion of the sovereign right to kill. York's opening account of the battle highlights the deaths of Lord Clifford and Lord Stafford, and his son Edward follows up with visual evidence of having delivered the Duke of Buckingham his death wound: "I cleft his beaver with a downright blow. / That this is true, father, behold his blood" (1.1.12–13). Edward's brandishing of the bloody sword provokes the Marquis of Montague to show the Earl of Wiltshire's blood on his sword (1.1.14). Their displays are trumped by young Richard, who holds the severed head of the Duke of Somerset aloft, saying to it, "Speak thou for me, and tell them what I did" (1.1.16). His father's playful answer to the head— "But is your grace dead, my lord of Somerset?"—at once conveys the Yorks' barbaric irreverence toward their enemies and announces a preoccupation of the play: When is the past dead enough for the future to begin (1.1.18)?[36] How many deaths—and whose, and what kind—does it take to securely occupy the throne? Or to pass it to one's heirs? Norfolk wishes that "all the line of John of Gaunt" would end up headless, and Richard replies, "Thus do I hope to shake King Henry's head" (1.1.19–20). While these wishes can be read as the simple Machiavellian drive to eliminate all rivals, they also suggest the Yorkists' deployment of particular forms of violence as a supplement to their claim to sovereignty.

Unlike the battlefield conquests of which Edward and Montague boast, signified by their display of bloody swords, Richard's postmortem beheading of Somerset mimics judicial decapitation, a form of state violence.[37] When Richard slays Somerset at the conclusion of *2 Henry VI*, he declares over the corpse, "Priests pray for enemies, but princes kill," identifying royal power as killing power (*2H6* 5.2.6).[38] Richard's decapitation of his enemy implies a sovereign prerogative carried out on behalf of his father, who praises the deed as superlative, declaring, "Richard hath best deserved of all my sons" (*3H6* 1.1.17). The Duke of Norfolk's subsequent wish that "Such hap" befall all of Gaunt's heirs and Richard's hope "to shake King Henry's head" express the desire for a Yorkist continuation of decapitations to eradicate treasonous counterclaims to the regal title. The Yorkist claim is articulated by Warwick's commentary on the state of the title, "Which now the house of Lancaster usurps" (1.1.23). Gesturing to the chair, Warwick declares, "this, the regal seat—possess it, York, / For this is thine, and not King Henry's heirs'" (1.1.26–27). As the scene unfolds and Henry finds York seated on the throne, York's declaration that he is Henry's sovereign verbally asserts what Somerset's head has silently attested: that York and his faction are exercising rightful sovereign power—specifically, the sovereign power of the death penalty (1.1.76).

Henry's refusal to invoke violence—"To make a shambles of the Parliament House," as he puts it—thus comes to signify his deposition from the throne, which he will formalize before the scene ends by bequeathing it to York's heirs

(1.1.71). In contrast to Warwick, who declares this scene the opening of "The Bloody Parliament" to establish York's claim, Henry takes up a pacifist position in defense of his title: "frowns, words, and threats / Shall be the war that Henry means to use" (1.1.39, 72–73). Henry's reluctance to assert his sovereign right to kill those who would usurp his authority suggests he is an imposter-king whose "title's weak," as he admits in an aside (1.1.135). Henry not only brooks York in his seat but brooks Somerset's head on a pike, a ghoulish effigy of Yorkist authority. Importantly, when Queen Margaret later reasserts Henry's right by killing York, she demands that his head be placed on York walls as a spectacle of Henry's claim. In both the play's opening scene and the postmortem fate of York, the display of decapitated heads conveys the willingness as well as the right to kill within the law. These heads are marionettes of sovereignty. They bespeak a regal authority that Henry himself refuses to exercise.

Derrida's suggestion that sovereignty is a model of temporality defined against other temporal models indicates how the sovereign production of death is connected to broader temporal and reproductive mechanisms. To plead his claim to the throne in the two factions' ensuing argument about its rightful occupant, Henry refers to various precedents that could establish unbroken continuity between his kingship and those of previous King Henrys. But he repeatedly encounters beginnings and endings—finitudes—that compromise the suggestion of timeless Henrician sovereignty. He first offers paternity as evidence of continuity—both the continuity of the Yorks' inferior position and the continuity of his title:

> Thy father was, as thou art, Duke of York;
> Thy grandfather, Roger Mortimer, Earl of March.
> I am the son of Henry the Fifth,
> Who made the Dauphin and the French to stoop
> And seized upon their towns and provinces. (1.1.105–109)

Henry posits himself and York as clones—as replicas of their dead fathers' titles and hierarchical arrangement. In the same breath that he articulates this claim through replication, however, he raises the specter of the failed or glitchy copy—of the son who is different, the clone who is not precisely identical. Henry attempts to claim authority as a faithful copy of his father, who bound the English together against their common enemy, the French. Warwick's reply, "Talk not of France, sith thou hast lost it all," reveals the problem for Henry of positing himself, via France, as a continuation of his father, since the conquest of France proved itself to be a temporary state not transmissible across generations (1.1.110). In his retort that "The Lord Protector Lost it, and not I," Henry not only admits that it was temporary but reveals a time when another ruled in his place—when English policy was dictated by a surrogate, the Lord Protector, who reversed the hallmark gains of his father's reign. Rather than securing his title by its continuity with the past, Henry's remarks expose both the ephemerality of his father's legacy and the ruptures in his claim of replicated, continuous rule between his father and himself. He raises the specter of bastardy, exposing how he is not like his father by pointing to the intervention of a surrogate between Henry V and Henry VI.

What Henry seeks to accomplish in this moment is to stabilize his claim to the crown by stabilizing a patrilineal origin. What he does instead is effectively destabilize both his direct lineage from Henry V and the regal claim that rests on it. In exposing how his ostensible genetic father cannot function as a fixed origin for his sovereignty, Henry's remarks reveal a set of irreconcilable assumptions, endemic to hereditary kingship, about how heirs are constituted. His wish to posit himself and York as precise replicas of their fathers articulates a fantasy of genetic reproduction as simple replication—replication without aberration, without differences between one generation and the next. This idea of what it is to be a son is much closer to the concept of cloning than to the ungovernable outcomes inherent in human sexual reproduction, in which the body of the mother contributes genetic material that inevitably renders the son different from the father. In addition, the figure of the mother introduces the possibility of bastardy, an anxiety that permeates Shakespeare's histories, such as in the figures of the two Talbots studied in chapter 3. Even without a promiscuous mother, Henry's case makes clear that it is possible to be derived from a father without inheriting the father's qualities. On the one hand, then, Henry's claim to sovereignty rests on a chimera of artificial reproduction in which offspring perfectly, automatically duplicate their fathers. On the other, his recourse to genealogy represents an attempt to naturalize artificial reproduction and thereby naturalize his claim. Through this logic, York cannot be king because that would entail an intrusion of artificial means, such as military aggression, into an institution that defines itself by natural succession.

Underlying Henry's irreconcilable idealization of both artificial and natural reproduction is an untenable distinction between the grown and the made. In her discussion of philosophical debates around cloning, Kelly Oliver, after Derrida, illustrates how the concept of children who are grown or naturally produced from their parents is already underwritten by artificial forms of reproduction, including the culturally generated notions of father and mother. She writes, "The mother, like the father, is a phantasm, a fiction, always substitutable, always already a supplement for an absent fantastic origin."[39] Cloning and other artificial reproductive technologies, such as artificial insemination, surrogacy, and genetic engineering, raise questions about the ethics of manufacturing children. Oliver argues that such questions elide the degree to which notions of the biological family—the family that is grown, not made—have always hinged on the cultural and even medical construction of roles and relations. Seeking to secure his claim by reference to his progenitor, Henry reveals how the "natural" link between father and son must be continually substantiated through artificial means like the defense of Henry V's conquests in France.[40] Failing to *make* the case, via military success, that he is Henry V's heir, Henry VI finds that his inheritance by birth is insufficient to underwrite his claim to be England's "natural king" (1.1.82).

Unable to stabilize a patrilineal origin in his father, Henry makes a second attempt to establish his claim by reaching further back in time:

> KING HENRY: My title's good, and better far than his.
> WARWICK: Prove it, Henry, and thou shalt be king.
> KING HENRY: Henry the Fourth by conquest got the crown.
> YORK: 'Twas by rebellion against his king.
> KING HENRY [*aside*]: I know not what to say—my title's weak. (1.1.131–35)

Henry's new tactic both repeats and exacerbates the problems of the old. Referring his claim to an earlier original, Henry IV, he reiterates the suggestion that his kingship is naturally grown—that his genetic provenance from prior Henries proves his sovereign title.[41] By referencing Henry IV's conquest of his predecessor, however, he also discloses a disruption in the ideal of hereditary kingship, naming a king whose reign was initiated by artificial rather than natural means. In his response, York exploits this glitch in the genetic line of succession, further problematizing Henry IV's claim by reference to the particular technologies of artificial reproduction by which he became Richard II's heir: rebellion and usurpation. York exposes the manufactured beginning point of a Lancastrian dynasty that has asserted a transcendent model of hereditary kingship—one generated naturally and divinely, with no contemporary beginning or end. He shows how the title was made, not grown, and therefore how it is fundamentally temporal and linguistic, not transcendent or natural.

In turning to Richard II's adoption of Henry IV as his heir, as he does in the next breath, Henry attempts to accommodate the rupture of the usurpation by recourse to a legal technology meant to mimic or copy the operations of hereditary succession. The ensuing exchange develops into the scene's most explicit statement of how transcendent kingship works. Responding to York's suggestion that Richard was forced to adopt Henry IV as his heir, Warwick asks a question less about the historical details of the event than the nature of Richard II's kingship: "Suppose, my lords, he did it unconstrained—/ Think you 'twere prejudicial to his crown?" (1.1.144–45). The decisive answer comes from one of Henry's supporters, the Duke of Exeter:

> EXETER: No, for he could not so resign his crown
>   But that the next heir should succeed and reign.
> KING HENRY: Are thou against us, Duke of Exeter?
> EXETER: His is the right, and therefore pardon me. (1.1.146–49)

Exeter's change of mind is rooted in a notion of kingship that is nontransferable by human means: Kingship cannot be made by entailing it on another, because it naturally inheres to the divinely anointed king and his biological heirs. As Exeter sees it, kingship is a property originating in the divine that exceeds human will or institutions; it passes from heir to heir without human intervention. In this way, the transmission of kingship operates by a kind of divine machinery that runs in the background according to its own rules, despite any human attempts to "play God" (Oliver's term) by redirecting succession to a mere replica or surrogate heir.[42] According to the kind of logic articulated by Kantorowicz's *The King's Two Bodies*, Exeter suggests that kingship cannot be manufactured but is an eternal property that conveys intact from one regal body to the next.[43]

Exeter's shift of support from Lancaster to York initiates a change of tide in the scene, one that culminates, ironically, in another attempt to resettle the crown through the legal adoption of an heir. But before the adoption agreement between Henry and York takes place, Warwick and Lord Clifford exchange telling threats of violence. Clifford vows to defend Henry's title "be [it] right or wrong" in revenge for the Yorks' killing of his father.[44] He sidesteps the disquisition on political theory that has just taken place, dismissing altogether the question of rightful possession that so impresses Exeter, and is persuaded by his wrongs alone to defend Henry's claim. Clifford's declaration admits none of kingship's transcendent or hereditary claims, instead positing Henry's regal title as a matter of political expedience and the defense of that title as retribution for personal injury. His justification of Henry's crown on these grounds thus competes with the transcendent model of sovereignty defended by Exeter. In taking up this position, Clifford presents one of the many instances in the play in which a mystified notion of kingship is closely juxtaposed with a frankly temporal one. The play's opening scene at once offers to stabilize divine kingship by restoring it to its "natural" hereditary claimant and evacuates it, through reference to revenge and adoption, of the transcendent properties that render sovereignty exceptional. Further, by affiliating kingship with revenge, Clifford offers to defend Henry's title through extralegal violence—precisely the opposite form of violence from the quasi-capital punishments the Yorkists have begun to carry out.

Warwick responds to Clifford by threatening violence against the Lancastrians, uncannily foreshadowing Edward's threat to decapitate him in act 5:

> Do right unto this princely Duke of York,
> Or I will fill the house with armed men
> And over the chair of state, where now he sits,
> Write up his title with usurping blood. (1.1.167–70)

By declaring the usurpation of York's rights, Warwick criminalizes the Lancastrian defense of Henry's title and posits himself as a punishing arm of rightful sovereignty. In his threat to inscribe York's kingship in the blood of Henry the usurper, he proposes to declare York's rights through a spectacular tableau of its prostheses: state-sponsored violence; the mortal blood of a pretender king; the written testimony of sovereign power; and the central prop in the Yorkist prosthstate, "the chair of state, where he now sits." With the exception of an explicit reference to decapitation, Warwick's threat contains all the elements that Edward's later speech will reprise, suggesting a stable vocabulary of sovereignty supplements shared by the play's two warring factions.

Additionally, Warwick's reference to "now"—a time-marker that will be echoed in Edward's hope that "Wind-changing Warwick now can change no more"—articulates the temporal mechanisms that supplement the Yorkist claim. If York occupies the throne *now* and those who would oppose him are usurpers, Warwick's threat makes claims about the present as well as the past and future. As the scene's vigorous debate about legitimacy makes clear, the question of who is king *now* is always also a question of who *was* king in the past and who will be in the future: If Henry VI is legitimate, Henry IV and Henry V were legitimate, and Henry's son, Prince Edward, will succeed. Henry VI's failure to occupy the throne *now* likewise has retroactive effects on the legitimacy of his predecessors as well as on Prince Edward's succession. Sovereignty not only claims a temporal dimension that transcends and is offset by human mortality; it also generates temporal effects, automatically—mechanistically—reconstituting past and future events.

Like the electric chair or the dust inscribed by Warwick's severed head, the prosthetic throne overwritten with Henry's blood would work as a time machine and a king machine—a technology for producing a sovereign "now" that eradicates irruptions, glitches, and discontinuities in the past and in the time to come. To inscribe the chair with mortals' blood, as Warwick proposes to do, is to manufacture the transcendent time of sovereignty. The relationship between the *now* of sovereignty and its past and future becomes explicit in the bargain struck between Henry and York in which York agrees to allow Henry to reign "as king" during his lifetime if he entails the title to York's heirs (1.1.172). This agreement cannot work by either the logic of continuous succession Henry draws on earlier in the scene or by the logic of a transcendent property that inheres in kingship and cannot be diverted by human means. Rather, the agreement is tantamount to an admission that Henry's own title—and therefore the future title of his son—is a bastard title, illegitimately held from illegitimate predecessors. This admission is unconsciously articulated by Prince Edward's question to his father, "If you be king, why should not I succeed?" (1.1.228). The fact that the prince will not succeed reveals that his father is not and has not been a legitimate king. As Peter Lake notes, however, the deal made by Henry and York also undermines the Yorkists' claim by heredity, for "if York is king by right, the crown is already his. And in that case, what is Henry doing giving York and his heirs something that already belongs to them? And by what right, then, is he retaining the crown until his death? And why on earth should the Yorkists allow him to retain it?"[45]

By leaving such questions open, the settlement between Henry and York unsettles more than it resolves, creating proleptic and retroactive effects. One of these effects is Henry's de facto death. As both he and Queen Margaret observe later in the scene—in a reprise of the sovereignty-or-death binary—Henry's confirmation of York as his heir is akin to suicide: "To entail him and his heirs unto the crown—/ What is it," Margaret asks, "but to make thy sepulchre / And creep into it far before thy time?" (1.1.236–38). By disinheriting Prince Edward, Henry has made the present the future, enacting his instant obsolescence and death. Henry recognizes in his actions this death as well as the death of his son: He foresees that York "Will coast my crown, and, like an empty eagle, / Tire on the flesh of me and of my son" (1.1.269–70). In replacing his son with York's heirs in the throne of the future, Henry kills his sovereign selves, the past sovereigns from whom he was generated and the sovereign-to-be who was to replicate him into the future. The temporal effects of Henry's act are expressed in several ensuing references to an undoing of the continuum that connects progenitor and heir. The Earl of Westmorland calls him a "faint-hearted and degenerate king," suggesting that Henry has undone generation itself (1.1.184). By failing to manifest what he inherited, he has reversed the process whereby he was generated and simultaneously degenerated his own son. The Earl of Northumberland curses Henry for his actions: "Be thou a prey unto the house of York, / And die in bands for this unmanly deed" (1.1.186–87). Like Westmorland's accusation of degeneracy, Northumberland's use of "unmanly" suggests Henry's self-undoing—his erasure of himself—and his failure in the principal imperative of virile aristocratic manhood: the reproduction of a legitimate heir. Henry's subsequent description of himself as "unnaturally . . . disinherit[ing]" his son further implies that his action is contrary to the very identity of a father, who by nature generates heirs.

These various names for Henry's action ratify a view of hereditary sovereignty as a work of nature that cannot be disrupted without cataclysmic effects to the orderly, linear unfolding of time itself. If this is the case, however—if in a few words a man can revise past, present, and future—Henry's actions also disclose the radically contingent, tenuous nature of sovereignty as a made thing vulnerable to mechanisms of unmaking. His act of legal disinheritance exposes the fragility of sovereignty and of linear time, but it also confounds the distinction between life and death, showing how, as Derrida observes, "death or nonexistence is already in the heart of the living present."[46] The throne presented in the opening scene of 3 Henry VI is an analogue to the electric chair studied by Warhol. It is a site intended to stabilize, perform, and reproduce authority through naturalized constructions of the past, the now, and the future. Like Warhol's electric chair, however, Shakespeare's "chair of state" instead discloses that authority as an invention constituted through a cooperation of organic and manufactured material. History—and even time itself—emerges as a prosthetic supplement to power, one that depends on the reproduction of both lives and deaths.

III. To Sit upon a Hill

Henry's soliloquy on the molehill in act 2, scene 5, after he is dismissed from the Battle of Wakefield by Margaret and Clifford, further develops these issues by dramatizing the relationship between kingship and temporality and exposing the temporal logic embedded in hereditary reproduction. Prior to this scene, the play establishes the molehill as a parodic throne where York, the would-be king in a paper crown, meets bitter death rather than sovereign transcendence. In keeping with the signification of this anti-throne, Henry's soliloquized fantasy of life as a "homely swain" is principally occupied with the alternative temporality that he attaches to "sit[ting] upon a hill" rather than in the chair of state (2.5.22–3). His first project in this other life would be to fashion himself a rude clock, to "carve out dials quaintly, point by point, / Thereby to see the minutes how they run" (2.5.24–5). After counting the number of minutes in an hour, hours in a day, and days in a year, Henry would use his sundial to determine "How many years a mortal man may live" (2.5.29).

The pastoral "now" described in Henry's meditation—"To sit upon a hill, as I do now"—is thus radically different from the static "now" constructed to supplement sovereignty (2.5.23). This "now" is in constant flux, changing from hour to hour, day to day, year to year. It is a "now" that is always being "passed over" in a progression toward death:

> So many hours must I tend my flock,
> So many hours must I take my rest,
> So many hours must I contemplate,
> So many hours must I sport myself,
> So many days my ewes have been with young,
> So many weeks ere the poor fools will ean,
> So many years ere I shall wear the fleece.
> So minutes, hours, days, weeks, months, and years,
> Passed over to the end they were created,
> Would bring white hairs unto a quiet grave. (2.5.231–40)

Contrary to John D. Cox and Eric Rasmussen's claim that Henry conjures "a timeless world of imagined bucolic perfection," Henry's wished-for life as a shepherd is one emphatically embedded in the flow of time.[47] His imagined escape from sovereignty is an embrace of sovereignty's other—an embrace of human mortality.

The scene punctuates this mortality by interrupting Henry's meditation with the tableau of the son who has accidentally killed his father in the battle and the father who has accidentally killed his son, the fathers and sons having been conscripted to opposing sides. This dramaturgically stylized episode further theorizes the relationship between father, son, and different time frames that were opened up by Henry's disinheritance of Prince Edward. Like Henry in his soliloquy on shepherd life, the first soldier who enters (the son who has killed his father) suggests the fundamental instability of "now" as a state open to change:

> This man, whom hand to hand I slew in fight,
> May be possessed with some store of crowns;
> And I, that haply take them from him now,
> May yet ere night yield both my life and them
> To some man else, as this dead man doth me. (2.5.56–60)

The death of his foe does not stabilize relations into static changelessness, as Edward imagines Warwick's decapitation would do. Rather, this death is situated in an ever-changing temporal flux that, even in the short term, might very well lead to the soldier's own death. He recognizes that the forward progress of time could result in a future copy of the scene he is currently acting but with a change of roles in which he is cast as the dead man. In this understanding of time's progress, scenes and actors may appear as clones of past ones but necessarily offer evidence of temporal difference, not sameness. In a possible future in which the soldier yields his life and money to someone "as this dead man doth [him]," he would be both a double of the dead man and a different dead man. That this dead man whom he may come to resemble turns out to be his own father suggests how the son is both like and unlike the father—both copy and not-copy. Embedded in the soldier's notion of repetition is therefore also an acknowledgment of failed repetition—of a Warholian "transmutation" in which the son-copy is not identical to his father-predecessor.[48] As scholars have long noted, the pun on "crowns" analogizes the soldier's plunder of the corpse to the war's broader dispute about who holds the crown. By connecting the possession of these two kinds of crowns, the soldier's meditation on the change implicit in temporal progress exposes the notion of sovereign and generational changelessness as an impossibility, a fantasy that elides death and difference—that hinges on a denial of "the irruption of the other."[49]

The soldier's subsequent unmasking of the corpse and recognition of it as that of his own father initiates an apostrophe to the period in which these events take place: "O, heavy times, begetting such events!" (2.5.63). In this expression, as in Henry's soliloquy, time again brings about death. Here, however, that change is described less as simply forward progress than as a generative process that mimics sexual reproduction. Time becomes pregnant or "heavy" and then "beget[s]" death in an image reminiscent of Queen Isabel's foreboding figurative pregnancy in *Richard II* (discussed in chapter 1). The interrelationship between procreation and death is articulated by the soldier: "I, who at his hands received my life, / Have by my hands of life bereaved him" (2.5.67–8). The curtailed chiastic structure of the lines and the echo between "received" and "bereaved" suggest the irony of giving life to death. While this irony is highlighted in the particular circumstances dramatized here, in which a son has killed a father, it is also merely a feature of human reproduction, where one generation is replaced by the next in a cycle of birth and death. The repetition of "hands" offers a particularly poignant compression of this dynamic. The son not only receives life at his father's hands but receives from them his own hands, which, in this scene, have become the means of the father's death by "hand to hand" combat (2.5.56). The hands represent at once the duplication of the father's body in the body of the son and the radical difference between father and son, between one set of hands and the other—a difference as stark as alive and dead, hands killing and hands killed. This sameness-yet-difference between the hands of the father and those of the son echoes a whole series of catastrophic discrepancies that reverberate across Shakespeare's histories: between Richard II and his adoptive heir, Henry IV; between Henry V and Henry VI; and between Henry VI and his adoptive Yorkist heir. All of these father-son pairs illustrate how the wish for continuity across generations is also underwritten with the father's erasure. Like the soldier who has killed his father, each of these "sons" will kill his father figure in one way or another.

The second soldier, the father who has killed his son, similarly describes the violence of "this miserable age" through the language of "beget[ting]":

> O, pity, God, this miserable age!
> What strategems, how fell, how butcherly,
> Erroneous, mutinous, and unnatural,
> This deadly quarrel daily doth beget!
> O boy, thy father gave thee life too soon,
> And hath bereft thee of thy life too late! (2.5.88–93)

In his declaration that this violence is "unnatural," the father who has slain his son echoes earlier criticism of Henry's adoption of a Yorkist heir, suggesting that both forms of filicide—disinheritance and killing—disturb the natural relationship between generations. This disturbance upsets temporal order itself, begetting events that occur "too soon" and "too late." As in the earlier scene of disinheritance, where Margaret accuses Henry of "mak[ing] [his] sepulchre / And creep[ing] into it far before [his] time," the father's undoing of his heir entails his own death:

> These arms of mine shall be thy winding sheet;
> My heart, sweet boy, shall be thy sepulchre.
> For from my heart thine image ne'er shall go.
> My sighing breast shall be thy funeral bell. (1.1.237–8; 2.5.114–15)

The father's imagery is even more morbid than Margaret's. He posits his body as a grave for his son, a burial place in which the son will return to his point of origin—an origin that has been retroactively rendered dead by filicide. Although the father gave life to the son in a biological relationship that makes the son's life conditional on the father's, the father's representation of his body as a tomb or cemetery illustrates the opposite—that the life of the father is conditional on the life of the son. A man who has killed his son is no longer a father. His paternal body becomes, instead, his son's burial ground. The two lives' interdependence complicates the very notion of inheritance at the heart of genetic reproduction, suggesting how the identity of fatherhood is contingent on the life of the son. This contingent structure exposes paternity, like sovereignty, as a made thing subject to unmaking—a naturalized institution that can nonetheless be unraveled by bad luck and the accidents of war.

The father's wish to bury his son within the grave of his own body echoes Henry's earlier fantasy of reproduction as cloning. The father imagines his son being absorbed into his body rather than that of the mother, from which the son emerged. It is the father who "gave life" to the son—albeit "too soon"— just as the son who killed his father "received [his] life" from the father's "hands" (2.5.92, 67). The mothers in these families are situated outside the essential procreative unit of father and son. They are marginalized to the role of extrinsic mourners who will passively bewail their losses "and ne'er be satisfied" (2.5.104, 106). In her bitter chastisement of Henry after he entails the crown to York, Margaret suggests that a mother—who "felt that pain" of childbirth and "nourished" her son "with [her] blood"—could not commit the unfilial acts of which these men are guilty (1.1.222–23). Lacking the bodily history shared by mothers and children, Margaret suggests, fathers like Henry undo themselves and their sons. In seeking to reestablish his paternity after the radical rupture of filicide, the father who has killed his son revises the corporeal history of his son's body by appropriating the role of the mother, integrating the son's body into his own. His erasure of the mother compensates for how this death has erased him as a father. In his image of incorporation, the father uses the son's corpse to supplement the fragile institution of paternity. The son he did not recognize is assimilated into his own body—into himself—in a gesture that asserts an essential physical bond in the face of that bond's catastrophic failure.

Although the molehill scene has often been denigrated as an example of Shakespeare's dramaturgic immaturity at this stage in his career, I have been suggesting, rather, that the scene offers an elegantly compressed rearticulation of the central concerns of the play—concerns dramatized in the turbulent confrontation of act 1, scene 1 and across the histories more generally. The molehill scene stages the contingent structures linking father and son, showing how death or erasure is embedded in the very operations of heredity, however persuasive the fantasy of paternal endurance through offspring may be. Although it is invoked as the stabilizing bedrock of patriarchy and sovereignty, paternity is largely invisible and can be unmade by accidents of fortune.[50] It is an institution constructed through both natural and artificial mechanisms, including, as here, the rhetorical mechanism of replacing the mother's womb with the father's hands in the account of reproduction. Thus reconstituted, corporeal intimacy between father and son works as a supplement to paternity, a supplement especially crucial in instances like those dramatized in this scene, in which the bond between father and son has become so theoretical as to render the two men not merely strangers but enemies. The molehill scene not only focalizes issues dramatized in the play's opening scene; it poses questions about the link between father and child that Shakespeare later develops beyond the chronicle play, such as in the Old Gobbo scene of *The Merchant of Venice* and through the intersecting plots of *King Lear*.

In its reflections on time, the scene also reiterates how paternity and sovereignty are underwritten by contingent temporal structures. Delivered from the anti-throne of the molehill, Henry's elaborate meditation on shepherds' time reflects the interdependence of sovereignty and mortality. Just as the electric chair constitutes sovereignty through the artificial production of death, Henry's hypothetical or counterfactual shepherd life—a life insistently bounded by mortality—highlights how the play's construction of sovereign time hinges on the production of its opposite, time passing toward death. To not be king is to enter into a temporal flow that leads inevitably to death—a death that Henry idealizes as an alternative to kingship, a state exempt from the passage of time that marks life as a shepherd. The temporal disorder articulated by the son who has killed his father and father who has killed his son discloses the tenuous linearity that organizes the hereditary relationships on which sovereignty depends.[51] If a son functions to extend the father's survival into the future, the son who has killed his father is an exemplar of this structure's failure—of the future killing the past, the future killing its own origins. Has the parricidal son rendered himself a bastard, a fatherless man, a man without a progenitor? Are his hands bastard hands? What are the implications of his act for his own identity, his sonness? These questions, percolating beneath the son's rumination on hands, are pursued explicitly in the temporal confusion described by the second soldier, whose wish to be his dead son's tomb demonstrates how events in the present at once project him into the future moment of his own death and automatically, retroactively reconfigure history, degenerating his son and unfathering himself by turning his son's origin point into a grave. In killing his son, the father, like Henry, has killed his own future and thereby his son's past—himself—in a series of events marked by the temporal disjuncture of "too soon" and "too late."

IV. No More My King

These temporal issues are taken up again in act 3, scene 1, in which Henry is arrested by a pair of gamekeepers who overhear him ruminating on his life as king. By referring to him as "the quondam king," the First Gamekeeper suggests that Henry's earlier wish in the molehill scene to exit the timelessness of sovereignty has been fulfilled: He is now moving through a temporal flow that marks his current state as different from his past one (3.1.23). When he is confronted by the gamekeepers, who attach him as an enemy to King Edward, Henry defends himself by a restatement of his prior claim to temporal and therefore sovereign continuity with the past: "My father and my grandfather were kings" (3.1.77). If Henry has a past, it cannot be differentiated from the present, he argues, because the terms of kingship render him identical to his predecessors and his sovereignty thereby transcendent and perpetual.

This model of sovereignty is not shared by the gamekeepers, however. In defending the Yorkist king's title, they ironically take up the position that Exeter abandoned in act 1, scene 1 in defense of the Yorkist claim. They suggest that the title can legitimately transfer from one king to the next through artificial means, outside of the naturalized terms of hereditary reproduction. "You are the king King Edward hath deposed," the Second Gamekeeper declares (3.1.69). In referring—with great syntactic economy, one word after the other—to the prior king and the current king, the Second Gamekeeper speaks what would have been a logical impossibility in the model of sovereignty articulated by Exeter. Henry seizes on this impossibility. When the First Gamekeeper declares that "we were subjects but while you were king," Henry asks, "Why, am I dead? Do I not breathe a man?" (3.1.80–81). Although Henry inherited the title as a consequence of Richard II's usurpation and murder, his confrontation with the gamekeepers echoes Richard's confrontation with Bolingbroke, in which Richard similarly chastises his former subjects for breaking their oath to him, points out the logical impossibility of the current circumstances, and presents his deposition from the "seat" as a death: "Long mayst thou live in Richard's seat to sit, / And soon lie Richard in an earthy pit" (R2 4.1.208–9). Unlike Richard, however, Henry has chosen his own figurative, untimely death by disinheriting Prince Edward in a de facto resignation of his title. In his scene with the gamekeepers, Henry is confronted with the full consequence of these multiple forms of degeneration. But the scene also suggests how the play has unmasked hereditary reproduction as an unstable foundation for paternity, let alone sovereignty. Henry is making an argument that the play has already repeatedly dismantled.

The full implications of this dismantling are staged two scenes later in Warwick's audience before another chair of state at the court of King Louis, where Warwick abandons the Yorkist Edward and pledges himself to his former enemies, Margaret and Henry. Margaret has traveled to France to seek aid from King Louis to reinstall Henry as king, but her suit is disrupted by the arrival of Warwick, who comes to negotiate a marriage between King Edward and Louis's sister, Lady Bona. As Arden editors John Cox and Eric Rasmussen note, in early productions of the play, the platform used for the throne in the opening scene was likely reused in both of the molehill scenes as well as in the scene at the French court, where King Louis sits on another throne.[52] Like the opening of the play and the events around the molehill in act 2, scene 5, the scene at the French court that is organized around the throne ruminates on the question of how succession and sovereignty are constituted and how events in the present at once affect the future and reconstruct history. Here is the first exchange between Warwick and the assembled supporters of Henry:

> WARWICK: Injurious Margaret.
> PRINCE EDWARD: And why not "Queen"?
> WARWICK: Because thy father Henry did usurp,
>   And thou no more are prince than she is queen.
> OXFORD: Then Warwick disannuls great John of Gaunt,
>   Which did subdue the greatest part of Spain;
>   And, after John of Gaunt, Henry the Fourth,
>   Whose wisdom was a mirror to the wisest;
>   And, after that wise prince, Henry the Fifth,
>   Who by his prowess conquered all France.
>   From these our Henry lineally descends.
> WARWICK: Oxford, how haps it in this smooth discourse
>   You told not how Henry the Sixth hath lost
>   All that which Henry the Fifth had gotten?
>   Methinks these peers of France should smile at that.
>   But for the rest, you tell a pedigree
>   Of threescore and two years—a silly time
>   To make prescription for a kingdom's worth. (*3H6* 3.3.78–94)

The Earl of Oxford's remarks articulate how Warwick's declaration in the present has implications for events that happened in the past. To declare Henry a usurper is to rewrite history—to cancel out great men and their political and military gains. Oxford is the first person in the play to defend the Lancastrian claim through Henry's descent from John of Gaunt; Henry's earlier genealogies went only as far back as Henry IV, because they were meant to demonstrate that kings beget kings. Oxford's genealogy takes a slightly different tack by suggesting, more generally, that great conquerors and thinkers beget great conquerors and thinkers. This argument exposes the same glitch that York pointed out in the opening scene, however—that Henry VI is not a true descendant of this line of greats, given the loss of France that occurred under his rule. Warwick accuses Oxford of leaving out salient details of history to create a "smooth discourse" in which "Henry lineally descends" from these great men. Additionally, he argues that the period covered by Oxford's gene-alogy is conveniently shortened and thereby inadequate to support Henry's claim. Both of these strategies for constructing sovereign claims—the bowd-lerization of historical details and the convenient foreshortening of the his-torical record—will return later in the scene.

When Warwick then proceeds to invite Oxford to "leave Henry, and call Edward king," Oxford's reasons for refusing to do so are reminiscent of the revenge argument Clifford makes in the opening scene (3.3.100). Oxford asks,

> Call him my king by whose injurious doom
> My elder brother, the Lord Aubrey Vere,
> Was done to death? And more than so, my father,
> Even in the downfall of his mellowed years,
> When nature brought him to the door of death?
> No, Warwick, no—while life upholds this arm,
> This arm upholds the house of Lancaster. (3.3.101–107)

Like Lord Clifford in act 1, scene 1 when pressed to weigh the legitimacy of Henry's claim, Oxford ultimately refers himself to the logic of revenge. He will defend the Lancastrian line to the death because of the insult and injury done to his noble family by King Edward. Although Warwick responds by swearing that he will likewise "uphold the house of York" till death, he, too, will be motivated by revenge to resettle his loyalties later in this same scene (3.3.108). When he receives the news that Edward has married Lady Grey, em-barrassing him before the French king just as he has secured Louis's vow to bestow his sister on Edward, Warwick declares Edward "No more my king, for he dishonours me" (3.3.184). Edward's title does not rest on a lineage of either unbroken genealogical succession or military conquest. It is contingent, in Warwick's estimation, on his current behavior—on a history extending back only a minute or two, when Edward embarrassed him before Louis. Warwick's revocation of Edward's crown initiates a revision of history:

> Did I forget that by the house of York
> My father came untimely to his death?
> Did I let pass th'abuse done to my niece?
> Did I impale him with the regal crown?
> Did I put Henry from his native right?
> And am I guerdoned at the last with shame?

Shame on himself, for my desert is honour.
And to repair my honor, lost for him,
I here renounce him and return to Henry. (3.3.186–94)

For Warwick, abandoning Edward and taking up arms on behalf of Henry is, in part, a project of remembering histories that he had suppressed—namely, his father's death in the Yorkist cause and Edward's attempted sexual assault of his niece. Warwick chastised Oxford for manipulating history to justify Henry's claim, but in his renunciation of the Yorkist, he discloses that his defense of Edward's right has similarly relied on historical revisionism and convenient forgetting.[53] Further, he suggests that how far back one must go in history "to make prescription of a kingdom's worth" varies from a minute or two to upwards of several generations. In this scene before the enthroned King Louis, the king of England emerges as a product not of hereditary right or even military might. England's king is a figure fabricated by his nobles through a combination of personal revenge motives and the manipulation of historical memory.

Warwick's turn from Edward both reveals and elides this fact. In now declaring Henry his king, he declares the title to be Henry's "native right," a formulation that obscures the degree to which the concept of a "native" king has been deconstructed by his own arguments and behavior as well as by the play's broader consideration of how kingship is made. In addition to "native right," Warwick invokes the notion of "planting": He declares that in joining forces with Margaret, he "will revenge his wrongs to Lady Bona / And replant Henry in his former state" (3.3.197–98). Metaphors of plants and planting recur several times in the play. Earlier in the scene, when Warwick is presenting Edward's love suit to Lady Bona, he claims, "Myself have often heard him say and swear / That this his love was an eternal plant, / Whereof the root was fixed in virtue's ground" (3.3.123–25). When this "eternal plant" with its "root . . . fixed" turns out very quickly to be neither eternal nor fixed, the metaphor of plants and roots that Warwick uses to suggest the organic, sacred, steadfast nature of Edward's love reveals itself as a rhetorical construct invented to secure political advantage. Warwick's use of root and plant metaphors in the scene before Louis echoes his use of "plant" at the very opening of the play to describe his king-making power. He declares before the empty throne that he will "plant Plantagenet, root him up who dares" (1.1.48).[54] The term "plant" suggests the natural or "native" right of those whom Warwick plants, implying that they are grown kings rather than made or artificially manufactured kings. But it also discloses Warwick's role in the process of naturalizing these kings. They are not growing on their own but are planted by him. He is an agent for installing and cultivating that which is not already in place and growing on its own.

After he abandons Edward's cause, Warwick becomes increasingly explicit in declaring himself a king-maker. Words like "native" and "plant" that sought to naturalize diverse sovereign claims give way to frank expressions of resettling the crown for revenge. His message to the post who returns to Edward is, "Tell him from me that he hath done me wrong, / And therefore I'll uncrown him ere't be long" (3.3.231–32). In his final lines of the scene—a short soliloquy to the audience—Warwick declares,

> I was the chief that raised him [Edward] to the crown,
> And I'll be chief to bring him down again.
> Not that I pity Henry's misery,
> But seek revenge on Edward's mockery. (3.3.262–65)

Warwick makes no pretense about native, hereditary, or organic kingship in these declarations. Like Clifford before him, he empties sovereignty of the transcendent claims made by figures like Exeter, presenting a king as an entirely artificial construct and himself as its artificer.

In the scene before Warwick is killed in battle—the scene with which this chapter began, when Edward threatens to decapitate him—Warwick insults Edward by reminding him of the power he has exercised throughout the play. "Wilt thou draw thy forces hence," he taunts, "Confess who set thee up and plucked thee down, / Call Warwick patron, and be penitent?" (5.1.25–27). He states to Edward's brother Richard, "'Twas I that gave the kingdom to thy brother" and announces that he now revokes the gift: "Warwick takes his gift again; / And Henry is my king, Warwick his subject" (5.1.34, 37–38). What Warwick articulates in his confrontation with Edward in act 5, scene 1 is the opposite of subjection. Having given Edward the crown, he was never Edward's subject. He was Edward's de facto king, exercising the right—like a sovereign wielding the death penalty or its pardon—to make or unmake, to spare or destroy. It is no accident that, at the turning point in the earlier Battle of Towton that temporarily wins the crown for Edward, Edward utters an apostrophe to Warwick that confusingly slips into an address to God:

> O Warwick, I do bend my knee with thine,
> And in this vow do chain my soul to thine.
> And, ere my knee rise from the earth's cold face,
> I throw my hands, mine eyes, my heart to Thee,
> Thou setter up and plucker down of kings,

Beseeching Thee, if with Thy will it stands
That to my foes this body must be prey . . . (2.3.33–39)

Without the capitalization of "Thee" that signals a shift in addressee in printed editions of the play—and even with the capitalization—Edward seems to be speaking to Warwick throughout this passage. Warwick "plays God," doing the work of fabricating sovereigns whose aura of naturalized, transcendent power is a product of marionettes or supplements.

In the face of Warwick's open declaration of a power that exceeds the king's, Edward threatens to decapitate him and to use Warwick's head to inscribe the dust with the sovereign "now" of Yorkist kingship. If Warwick has posited himself as the "setter up and puller down of kings" in a mimicry of the divine power to bestow sovereignty, Edward lays claim to a more rudimentary mimicry of the divine by threatening Warwick's execution. Importantly, neither Warwick's nor Edward's threat is fulfilled: Warwick fails to pull down Edward and reseat Henry, and he dies in battle before Edward can carry out the death penalty. Both men fail to approximate the operations of the divine. As I have been suggesting throughout this chapter, such failures are indicative of the prosthetic machinery that contrives sovereignty and sovereign time. Both men's divinity simulators are glitchy reproductive technologies. As such, they resonate with theoretical discourses on programmed forms of reproduction and their inherent glitches, such as Derrida's description of events that are "at once the effect of a machination and something that eludes machinelike calculation."[55]

V. Unexpected and Errant Outputs

The play's preoccupation with reproductive machinery and its in-built malfunction is summarized in the figure of Richard of Gloucester, who is described as an error or abomination in hereditary reproduction and, later in *Richard III*, as a mechanism for fulfilling providential design. Richard's double status as both a failed clone and an essential cog in the machinery of providence exposes how the mutually reinforcing ideologies of hereditary monarchy and divine providence rely at once on a fantasy of orderly reproduction and the effects of its unpredictable failure. The earliest reference in *3 Henry VI* to Richard's physical deformity occurs in Margaret's taunting speech to York before she and Clifford kill him.[56] She calls York's son Richard "that valiant crookback prodigy, / Dickie" (1.4.76–77). Clifford reuses Margaret's term, "crookback," a few scenes later, transforming it from an adjective into a noun:

"Ay, crookback, here I stand to answer thee" (2.2.96). Clifford treats Richard's deformity not simply as a feature of his character but as its defining quality. As Richard evolves into a more central figure in the later acts of *3 Henry VI*, his glitched body develops into an important component of the play's meditation on the successful reproduction of children and monarchs.

Richard responds to the insult about his crooked back by seeking to taint the resemblance between Margaret and Henry's son, Prince Edward, and his father. He suggests that Prince Edward is a failed reproduction of his father—an effeminately shrewish bastard who proves himself a true copy not of his father but of Margaret, in that he "hast [his] mother's tongue" (2.2.134). Margaret's retort denies Richard either paternal or maternal likeness: "thou art neither like thy sire nor dam, / But like a foul misshapen stigmatic, / Marked by the destinies to be avoided" (2.2.135–37). Her insult renders Richard's misshapen body parentless, outside the structure of hereditary resemblance that makes the child a reproduction of its parents. He is a double bastard, neither the mother's nor the father's child—a man with no discernible human origin. Margaret will later return to this claim in the cursing scene of *Richard III*:

> Thou elvish-marked, abortive, rooting hog,
> Thou that wast sealed in thy nativity
> The slave of nature and the son of hell,
> Thou slander of thy heavy mother's womb,
> Thou loathed issue of thy father's loins. (R3 1.3.225–29)

Rather than bearing marks of likeness to his parents, Richard bears the marks of a demonic progenitor. In both his physical and characterological deformity, he is a false impression of the maternal body from which he was derived, an impression his father regards not with loving pride or identification but with "loath[ing]." Richard represents a rupture in successful hereditary reproduction—an "abortive" or failed effort to embody a faithful, viable replica of either parent.

Henry echoes this reading of Richard's body in their final confrontation before Richard stabs him in the play's penultimate scene:

> Thy mother felt more than a mother's pain
> And yet brought forth less than a mother's hope—
> To wit, an undigested and deformed lump
> Not like the fruit of such a goodly tree. (3H6 5.6.49–52)

Henry lays particular emphasis on the discrepancy between Richard and his mother, not between Richard and his father. He thus claims for Richard, as Margaret did, a more radical kind of bastardy than one in which the supposed father has been supplanted by a substitute—a bastardy more radical even than the fatal breakdown of recognition between father and son dramatized in the molehill scene. As "an undigested and deformed lump," Richard fails to manifest so much as the basic outlines of an animal body, let alone a human body or the faithful corporeal copy of his parents. He is situated beyond the structure of human sexual reproduction, outside all norms of animal propagation. Richard makes similar claims about himself. In describing his body "Like to a chaos, or an unlicked bear whelp / That carries no impression like the dam," he describes himself according to a popular myth of bear reproduction (*3H6* 3.2.161–62). Importantly, however, he is an example of bear procreation that was not satisfactorily completed and therefore did not render him a bear. His mother bear, charged with the task of licking her offspring into a bear shape like her own, prematurely abandoned her maternal function, leaving him a "chaos"—a disordered, unshaped thing. Richard will reiterate this notion of himself as the product of an incomplete maternal process in the opening soliloquy of *Richard III*, in which he describes himself as "Deformed, unfinished, sent before my time / Into this breathing world scarce half made up" (*R3* 1.1.20–21).

Although the reproductive failure with which he charges his mother excludes him from the romantic dynamics that might make him a progenitor in his own right ("Why, love forswore me in my mother's womb"), Richard exploits his failed familial likeness to exempt himself from the rules governing familial relations and hereditary succession, a strategy that will be the main subject of chapter 5 (*3H6* 3.2.153). In disclaiming any familial likeness, Richard becomes a dangerously self-authoring subject:

> I had no father, I am like no father;
> I have no brother, I am like no brother;
> And this word, "love," which greybears call divine,
> Be resident in men like one another
> And not in me—I am myself alone. (*3H6* 5.6.80–84)

The filicidal and fratricidal plots that he pursues in *Richard III* are authorized by the disavowal of familial likeness that he articulates in *3 Henry VI*. He reads his body as a site of hereditary breakdown that releases him from the limitations imposed by filial and fraternal piety. Unbound by these limitations, Richard is also unbound by the structure of hereditary monarchical succession that rests on them. The chaos of his body leaves him untroubled—at least for

the moment—by the distinction between kingship that is grown through hereditary succession and kingship that is made through artificial means, such as
serial murder.[57]

The plays' descriptions of Richard's body—those advanced by his enemies
as well as those he advances himself—make positivist claims about what reproduction looks like when it goes wrong. In doing so, these descriptions im-
plicitly posit a model of normal, natural human reproduction against which
Richard's body is defined. In this model, children inherit multiple kinds of likeness from their parents, including basic bodily form, particular physical qualities, and a vaguer set of character traits—such as the capacity to love—that
prove their fidelity to a human parental origin. By suggesting that Richard runs
counter to this model, characters in both plays (including Richard himself) articulate an understanding of human reproduction that does not accommodate aberrations from the norm. Aberrations, they suggest, are evidence of
the unnatural—of a complete failure in human reproductive machinery. They
are proof of demonic intervention, for example, or of interrupted production
or abortion of the process. But as we have seen, one of the central projects of
3 Henry VI is the exposure of hereditary reproduction and the sovereign claims
built on it as delicate fictions produced through mechanisms like historical revisionism and capital punishment. Set in this broader context, Richard's deformity raises questions about how reproductive machinery runs. Is Richard's
body the result of a breakdown in the heredity machine or of mechanisms
built into it? Are the two mutually exclusive?

The phenomenon of the glitch helpfully addresses these questions. Since
its coinage in the early 1960s to describe effects produced by overloaded electrical equipment, the term "glitch" has evolved to describe errors of all kinds,
especially errors in electronic hardware and computer software. Most recently,
"glitch" has been taken up by media studies to name digital events, intentional
or accidental, that deviate from events the media is designed to produce but
that nonetheless occur within the parameters of their programming. Tim
Barker describes glitches as errors "internal to the machine" or as results "im-
manent to the machine's process" that appear as "unexpected and errant
outputs." Glitches expose what is possible within the designed algorithms of a
system; they "articulate a link to the field of potential . . . in order to generate
unforeseen, and perhaps unwanted, information."[58] Mark Nunes describes
glitches as "moments [when] an interstitial gap opens, an outside *within* the
logic of the system that threatens 'the good' of the system itself."[59] The glitch is
an other that is not other—an aberration that appears contrary to the mechanisms of a system but is, rather, a production of that very system. Such failures
are the central focus of practitioners of glitch art, who exploit errors in digital

systems to explore the potential or virtual possibilities built into those systems.[60] As Michael Betancourt explains, such artists do not invent the imagery they produce but discover it within the digital systems they manipulate. He writes, "The system already contains all the glitch imagery as potential results of the deterministic, iterative completeness fundamental to digital production."[61]

3 Henry VI represents Richard as a glitch in the full sense in which these theorists define the term. Although explanations for Richard posited by the play's characters seek to position him outside the workings of the human reproductive system, such explanations disclose the operations of that system and the range of outcomes it can produce. That Margaret, Clifford, Henry, and Richard have such a rich vocabulary for explaining Richard's aberration from his parents suggests that such aberrations occur within a recognizable set of potential outcomes. When they describe Richard's body, they are like computer systems rendering an error message: "While the error notice signals failure," Nunes notes, "it does so within the successful, efficient operation of a system."[62] Further, as this chapter has argued, *3 Henry VI* again and again undercuts the ideal of seamless, exact replication across generations, the ideal that underwrites hereditary sovereignty. In the vast discrepancy between Henry V and Henry VI, the play suggests how different one Henry can be from his supposed duplicate. In the intervention of the Lord Protector between these two Henrys, the play introduces surrogate fathers who disrupt the ideal of direct descent. In its discussions of the ineffectuality of legal adoption, followed by recourse to another legal adoption, the play points to an irreconcilable set of ideas about whether offspring must be grown or can be made. Through the episode with the father who has killed his son and the son who has killed his father, the play illustrates the fictitiousness of intergenerational likeness and the rhetorical contortions that must be pursued to reassert that likeness. And through the temporal disorder that arises from various forms of filicide and parricide, the play undercuts the notion of orderly linear inheritance that organizes intergenerational connections between past, present, and future. In short, by dramatizing a dizzying range of reproductive malfunctions, the play demonstrates that the machinery of human reproduction is characterized by imperfections that hinder the wished-for cloning of one generation into the next. These imperfections are not the other or the "outside" of the system, to borrow Nunes's term; they are the system itself.

Albeit more visually apparent than some of these other reproductive glitches, the aberration represented by Richard's body is thus one more example of reproductive machinery at work. The play presents Richard as the realization of one of the machine's many possible errors. As Barker puts it, "At any point in its process, a system is traversing potential errors and at any point, one may become actualized."[63] The play does not leave us to speculate about the "potential errors" built in to a family or monarchy defined by hereditary reproduction; it everywhere dramatizes both that potential and its realization, such as when sons and fathers accidentally kill each other because of failed recognition. Richard is a logical outcome of this potential. He is "an error coming into being as unformed and unforeseen *potential* is *actualized*"— that is, as the potential discrepancy between parent and offspring is realized in bodily form itself.[64] In Nunes's terms, "Error reveals not only a system's failure, but also its operational logic."[65] Richard visually represents the inherent discrepancies between parent and child that characterize the operational logic of hereditary reproduction.[66]

Warhol's electric chair paintings again usefully illustrate the relationship between the programmed operations of reproductive machinery and its potential glitches. As *3 Henry VI* makes clear, human reproduction is not a tidy cloning system, nor is hereditary monarchy seamless, organic, or transcendent. Similarly, the electric chair is not a bolt of lightning delivered through a transcendent judicial power that exceeds human bodies. It is and has always been a jerry-rigged counterfeit of that power—a contraption of human invention run by material wires and switches. These attributes of the electric chair become inescapably apparent when the machine glitches. Through the glitch, the fiction of a painless, instantaneous death is revealed to be the electrocution of one human being by others—a frying out of the circuitry of a human body that happens over time, not outside of time. Betancourt writes in his analysis of glitch art that the glitch makes us conscious of a process that the technology otherwise renders invisible through the aura of the digital, which erases traces of materiality and mystifies productivity into "the seemingly immaterial action of autonomous machinery."[67] This is precisely what Warhol's *Electric Chair* paintings accomplish. In this sense, Warhol is a predigital glitch artist, as are Richard and Shakespeare. All three exploit failures inherent in their technologies of interest—execution machines, photography, sovereignty, heredity, history—to unmask those technologies' ontological claims. Like a history play, a photograph, or a digital image glitched into discontinuous pixels, the smoking head of Ethel Rosenberg and the "crookback" body of Richard of Gloucester reveal their respective processes of reproduction to be messy, material, temporal, and imperfect.

As I have suggested, Richard capitalizes on the conspicuous nature of his difference to abandon the restrictions that familial likeness would impose on him. In this, he again illustrates properties of the glitch as it has been theorized by media studies. Just as glitch artists exploit the errors potential in digital technology to open up new avenues of creativity unplotted by the programmers of the machine, Richard-as-glitch-artist uses his difference to create a path to kingship that is not open to him according to the normal rules governing hereditary monarchy. In Barker's terms, "the potential for error marks the potential for the new and the unforeseen," such that "an error in itself may be creative." As a figure created by error, Richard uses that error creatively, "reconfigur[ing] and exploit[ing] the generative qualities of the unforeseen error" of his body to generate an avenue to the crown by means of serial murder rather than hereditary reproduction.[68] He exemplifies a defining feature of the glitch: "failure, glitch, and miscommunication provide creative openings and lines of flight that allow for a reconceptualization of what can (or cannot) be realized within existing social and cultural practices."[69]

While Richard's course to kingship is different from the one prescribed by the "existing social and cultural practices" that nominally organize hereditary monarchy, *3 Henry VI* demonstrates the degree to which this model of sovereignty, like the family defined by heredity, is another system or machine characterized by events that disrupt its orderly programming. Although Richard does not have a clear path to the title through the rules that organize English monarchy, the play discloses how that system is marked by its errors as much as by its adherence to order. The defense of kingship through the logic of revenge, for example, has no legitimate basis in the system of hereditary succession, and yet it goes relatively unchallenged as a motive for supporting or supplanting a king. Further, the characterization of Warwick—both by himself and others—as "king-maker" openly defines sovereignty as a fabricated institution. If Richard represents a glitch in that institution, he is again a glitch in the fullest sense, in that his fabricated rise to kingship exposes rather than disrupts or contradicts the "operational logic" of the king machine.[70]

In an interview conducted in 1963, the year Warhol began painting the electric chair, he famously claimed that he wanted to be a machine: "The reason I am painting this way is that I want to be a machine, and whatever I do and do machine-like is what I want to do."[71] If the machine at the center of his electric chair paintings is any indication of Warhol's notion of mechanistic production, what it meant to him to be like a machine was at once to clone and destroy, succeed and fail, enhance and degrade. Warhol saw in the "black dramaturgy" of the electric chair what Shakespeare found in the bloody wars over the English throne: political power fabricated through the naturalized mechanisms of synthetic reproduction and violent death, the prostheses of sovereignty consolidated in the chair of state.

CHAPTER 5

Fuck Off and Die
The Queercrip Reign of Richard III

> Thunder. Second Apparition, a Bloody Child.
> —*Macbeth*

I begin this chapter on *Richard III* by returning to Richard of Gloucester's two soliloquies in *3 Henry VI*. The earlier of these, after his older brother Edward has been crowned king (for the first time), opens with Richard's wish for Edward's demise:

> Would he were wasted, marrow, bones, and all,
> That from his loins no hopeful branch may spring
> To cross me from the golden time I look for.
> And yet, between my soul's desire and me—
> The lustful Edward's title buried—
> Is Clarence, Henry, and his son young Edward,
> And all the unlooked-for issue of their bodies,
> To take their rooms ere I can place myself.
> A cold premeditation for my purpose. (*3H6* 3.2.125–33)[1]

As he moves from imagining his brother's sterility—Edward "wasted, marrow, bones, and all"—to what would follow Edward's heirless death, Richard is confronted with the fact of his elder brother Clarence; the Lancastrian Henry and his son, who are still alive at this point in the play; and the untold number of their children who could hypothetically succeed them. Richard "look[s] for" a "golden time" in which he would be king, but what he sees ahead is a future ruled by the scions of other men, whose teeming procreative power would seem to trump his capacity to "place himself" on the throne through nonprocreative means. As the soliloquy unfolds into alternative futures that Richard might entertain in lieu of disappointed sovereignty, he suggests that his exclusion from dynastic succession is not a mere matter of birth order. It is a matter of his physical disability, which renders him impotent to procreate:

> Why, love foreswore me in my mother's womb,
> And, for I should not deal in her soft laws,
> She did corrupt frail nature with some bribe
> To shrink mine arm up like a withered shrub,
> To make an envious mountain on my back—
> Where sits deformity to mock my body—
> To shape my legs of an unequal size,
> To disproportion me in every part. (*3H6* 3.2.153–60)[2]

As a number of scholars have noted, Richard's image of himself is one of sexual impotence.[3] Because "every part" of his body is "disproportion[ed]," his "legs" are mis-sized, and his phallic "arm" is "shr[unken]" and "withered"—a "shrub" where a tree should be—Richard is excluded from the procreative exchange that would grant him a role as either a present lover or the father of future kings, as he imagines Clarence, Henry, and Henry's son may be. Although Richard has the power "to command, to check, to o'erbear such / As are of better person than [him]self," as he goes on to say, that power does not overturn the deeper hierarchy he describes, in which able-bodied men who are beneath him in social rank are nonetheless "better" than he is (*3H6* 3.2.166–67).[4]

Ostracized by virtue of his disability from either heterosexual procreativity or the sovereignty that hinges on it, Richard is left to seek the crown through the theatrical means for which his disabled status makes him especially suited. As Katherine Schaap Williams has argued, Richard exploits his ambiguous deformities "to reveal disability as a theatrical asset."[5] By embracing an image of himself as deformed, Richard is liberated to make the forms that fit his ambitions—to "frame [his] face to all occasions" (*3H6* 3.2.185). The shapes he takes are not dictated by a genealogy of predecessors, as I observe toward the end of chapter 4. Rather, they are borrowed from an adaptable medley of literary, theatrical, and animal models, such as the actor who "wet[s] [his] cheeks with artificial tears," the alluring mermaid, the deadly basilisk, the color-changing chameleon; Nestor, Ulysses, Sinon, Proteus, and Machiavelli (*3H6* 3.2.184–93).[6] If he cannot become king through the ableist, heteronormative system of hereditary succession, Richard will do so through alternative forms of reproduction: through theater and serial murder.

This chapter studies Richard as a queercrip figure who comes to power by a combination of mimicry and parody of the dominant culture that has abjected him. Although he has been shaped from birth by deformities that are presumed to foreclose the possibility of a royal future, Richard subverts the heterosexual, procreative, ableist structures into which he is born to create "the golden time [he] look[s] for" through alternative means. The construction of an alternative temporality to the one imposed on him is a key element of Richard's project. In the prophesy that the deposed King Henry delivers before Richard stabs him to death in the Tower toward the end of *3 Henry VI*, Henry warns him that old men, widows, orphans, fathers, and mothers "shall rue the hour that ever [he] wast born" (*3H6* 5.6.43). "The owl shrieked at thy birth—an evil sign," Henry intones. "The night-crow cried, aboding luckless time" (*3H6* 5.6.144–45). By turning Richard's birth into a litany of signs about the time to come, Henry's prophesy collapses Richard's birth into his adult murders, making Richard's body the sign of doom or death. In the prophetic logic that reads Richard's future as always already defined by the birth of his disabled body, Richard is excluded from the present and "cast . . . out of time," to borrow a formulation from crip theorist Alison Kafer.[7] Rather than rejecting the logic that Henry's prophesy imposes on him, Richard embraces it in the soliloquy that follows his stabbing of Henry, declaring that "since the heavens have shaped my body so, / Let hell make crooked my mind to answer it" (*3H6* 5.6.78–79). He announces his active intent to assume the deformed character that Henry and others have projected onto his disabled body. He will not only fulfill their expectations of him beyond their worst nightmares but also appropriate their own temporal tools, like prophecy, to do so. "For I will buzz abroad such prophecies / That Edward shall be fearful of his life," he declares, and from Edward's death will follow others, "one by one," in a form of reproduction that creates a sequence of dead people in lieu of a line of male heirs (*3H6* 5.6.87–91). If Richard is a cripple, determined by the body he was born with, then Richard will exploit what he has: he will crip succession, crip reproduction, crip time, crip sovereignty.

I. I'll Blast His Harvest

The verb "to crip" was introduced by Carrie Sandahl in a 2003 *GLQ* essay titled "Queering the Crip or Cripping the Queer?"[8] Rooted in the avant-garde practices of queer, disabled performance artists, Sandahl's notion of cripping is closely related to that of queering. "Crip" names the acts and utterances by which disabled performers appropriate pejorative categories—especially "cripple"—used by dominant, ableist culture to marginalize those with non-conformist bodies. Sandahl writes, "As outsiders, queers and crips refuse to minimize their differences by passing as either straight or able-bodied. Instead, they appropriate and rearticulate labels that the mainstream once used to silence or humiliate them."[9] When Richard stabs Henry and then continues the story Henry had begun about Richard's monstrous birth—

> The midwife wondered and the women cried
> "O, Jesus bless us, he is born with teeth!"—
> And so I was, which plainly signified
> That I should snarl and bite and play the dog (3H6 5.6.74–77)

—he "comes out crip" to the play's audience.[10] He rehearses the narrative circulated about his monstrous birth not to absorb the shame Henry attaches to him through that narrative but to empower himself to undo a world of Henrys by identifying with his own crip body. In doing so, Richard stages what Robert McRuer calls "the crip processes of refusal," transforming his body from a passive sign of the future inscribed with others' prophesies into a body through which he claims agency.[11] That agency develops, in part, through his manipulation of theatrical relations—through the discrepancy between the crip identity he articulates here and the "straight" performance of a "normate" brother, uncle, and lover elsewhere in the plays.[12] In the final scene of 3 Henry VI, for example, he declares his devotion to the house of York and kisses his new-born nephew for the court audience: "And that I love the tree from whence thou sprang'st / Witness the loving kiss I give the fruit" (3H6 5.7.31–34). He then likens his kiss to Judas's in an aside to the other audience he has established through the play's soliloquys. Richard makes a show of his filial loyalty—performing his allegiance to the institutions of sexual reproduction and hereditary succession—then turns to the play's audience to disclose the performative nature of that allegiance. In this way, Richard queers and crips the scene's celebration of the future represented by his nephew. The juxtaposition of the avuncular kiss with Richard's queercrip aside dramatizes, in Judith Butler's terms, his "refusal of the law in the form of the parodic inhabiting of conformity."[13] Like the queercrip performers Sandahl studies in "Queering the Crip or Cripping the Queer?" Richard enlists theatrical technology to "make [his] difference visible on [his] own terms."[14]

Sandahl's essay is a pioneering work in the discourse that has since come to be identified as crip theory, a radical branch of disability studies. In *Crip Theory*, the 2006 book that gave the field its name, McRuer writes that "crip theory . . .

should be understood as having a similar contestatory relationship to disability studies and identity that queer theory has to LGBT studies and identity."[15] Elsewhere, McRuer describes cripping as "processes that unsettle, unravel, and unmake" the assumptions of normativity underlying heterosexist and ableist culture.[16] Crip theory is heavily indebted to Lee Edelman's influential queer manifesto, *No Future* (2004), while it also critiques Edelman and other queer theorists for reproducing straight ableism's inattention to disability. Edelman argues that dominant, heterosexist culture is organized around the principle of "reproductive futurism," a compensatory structure that seeks to abrogate the lack constitutive of human identity by fantasizing future fullness that is perpetually deferred through the figure of the Child. In other words, heteropatriarchal culture—and therefore the domain of the political—is organized on the assumption that present good resides in the preservation of the future, represented by the Child. This value system ensures "the absolute privilege of heteronormativity by rendering unthinkable, by casting outside the political domain" anything that threatens reproductive futurism (such as queerness or, crip theorists add, disability as figured by ableism) or that posits an alternative political end (such as nonreproductive sexual pleasure). In this system, the figure of the Child thus functions both as the idealized issue of heterosexual coupling and the future promise that always retroactively "authenticates" a heterosexist social order. Edelman writes, "Th[e] Child remains the perpetual horizon of every acknowledged politics" and is a "fantasmatic beneficiary" of a system that "confirms the absolute value of reproductive futurism."[17]

Edelman's work theorizes queerness as oppositionality to the politics of futurism and the cult of the Child. He insists that queerness does not ratify an alternative politics, however, for to do so would be to reinscribe some version of social order. Rather, queerness poses a "radical challenge to the very value of the social itself." It is definitionally antisocial. Queerness = "queer negativity" that "marks the 'other' side of politics."[18] If politics is organized around reproductivity figured in the phantasmatic, always-deferred future of the Child, queerness names "the place of the social order's death drive"—a vitiating challenge to culture's assumption that the future is worth preserving and that the "the body politic must survive."[19] Queerness aggressively resists compulsory heteronormativity and reproductive futurism. Unapologetically unregenerate and unregenerating, queerness constitutes what Edelman famously summarizes as one big middle finger to the body politic: "Fuck the social order and the Child in whose name we're collectively terrorized."[20] This gesture of negation is precisely the one Richard makes in his asides during the closing scene of *3 Henry VI*, which takes place around the prosthetic chair of state where his brother, King Edward, is "Now . . . seated" (*3H6* 5.7.35).[21] The political moment of Edward's "now" is secured not only by the "blood of enemies"—the slaughter of Lancastrian fathers and sons whose defeat he catalogs in the scene's opening speech—but by the infant for whose future these killings were carried out:

> Young Ned, for thee, thine uncles and myself
> Have in our armours watched the winter's night
> Went all afoot in summer's scalding heat,
> That thou mightst repossess the crown in peace;
> And of our labours thou shalt reap the gain. (*3H6* 5.7.16–20)

Edward's address to his baby is immediately followed by an aside from Richard, who vows, "I'll blast his harvest" (*3H6* 5.7.21). Queering the consensus Edward asserts about the selfless, future-oriented motives for the war that he and his brothers have just won, Richard reveals that he has not fought for "Young Ned" or the future the child represents; he has not "watched the winter's night" so that Ned "shal[l] reap the gain." To Edward's reproductive futurism, Richard sneers, "Fuck you, and fuck your kid. Fuck off and die."

In positing Young Ned as the teleological realization of Yorkist rule, Edward rearticulates the cloning fantasy that I explored in chapter 4. Edward IV has begotten Edward V in a structure of repetition that Edelman observes to be inherent to—though disavowed by—reproductive futurism. With its emphasis on the "hetero," heterosexism celebrates difference while seeking to reproduce sameness. "Futurism," Edelman writes, "generates generational succession, temporality, and narrative sequence, not toward the end of enabling change, but, instead, of perpetuating sameness, of turning back time to assure repetition—or to assure a logic of resemblance."[22] Ned's kingship will not be a "possession" of the crown but a "repossession"—a mechanism that sutures the future to the past by creating continuity between an earlier rightful heir and the one to come. Richard's aside enunciates the queer threat to this generational, temporal, and narrative continuity. If "the figure of the Child enact[s] a logic of repetition that fixes identity through identification with the future of the social order," as Edelman observes, "the figure of the queer embod[ies] that order's traumatic encounter with its own inescapable failure."[23] That failure is death itself, a failure at once implicit in the need for a future Edward V and disavowed by the cloning fantasy he represents. As the queercrip uncle who kisses like Judas, Richard threatens the future embodied in this child and the Child, puncturing the politics staged in the play's final scene by marking his nephew as mortal. Richard's kiss is the kiss of death.[24]

This kiss—we might usefully call it a stigmatization—summarizes what, in Shakespeare's plays, is ominous not just about Richard's queerness but about his disability. In *Feminist, Queer, Crip*, which builds on Edelman's work, Alison Kafer describes how heteronormative, ableist culture treats the disabled body as a symbol of, essentially, death—as "the sign of the future of no future."[25] If a politics founded on reproductive futurism excludes queers, Kafer argues, it even more emphatically excludes the disabled, whose bodies must figure "a future to avoid" in a culture that fetishizes the promise of the (always white, always able-bodied) Child.[26] Kafer's use of "avoid" gestures toward the disabled body's function as a stigmatized, cautionary specter for ableist culture—something that must be actively evaded through means such as eugenics, selective abortion, and hoped-for medicinal cure.[27] Queen Margaret uses this very word when describing Richard's body in *3 Henry VI*, calling it "Marked by the destinies to be avoided / As venom toads or lizards' dreadful stings" (*3H6* 2.2.137–38). Margaret's comparison of Richard's deformity to animal poison suggests that his difference poses a danger to other, normate bodies—a danger that queercrip theory addresses. McRuer draws parallels between the homophobic marginalization of people with HIV/AIDS, especially during the first decades of the AIDS epidemic, and the abjection of the disabled. McRuer notes that a similar set of assumptions—"that AIDS is 'invariably fatal' and people with AIDS are in some ways already dead or better off dead—circulate around other people with disabilities, who find that their bodies are read in ways that only confirm the ableist notion that such bodies face 'imminent deterioration.'"[28] Disability may be catching, these ableist discourses suggest, and, like the skin spots indicative of Kaposi's sarcoma and therefore of AIDS, disability announces the body's mortality and makes the person who bears its marks into a kind of *muselmann*—someone whose future death is as good as already here and already now.[29] The association of disability with death is so prevalent in ableist politics that disability rights activists have taken up the slogan "Not Dead Yet" to confront the assumption that they are nothing more than future dead people or people who were never fully alive in the first place.[30] "Not Dead Yet" defies the implicit message that ableist, heterosexist politics broadcasts to the disabled—including, explicitly and repeatedly, to Richard: "Despair and die" (*R3* 5.5.74, 80, 81, 89, 94, 97, 103, 110, 117). Richard's "Fuck off and die" asides crip this message by turning it against the able bodies that bid him "despair and die."

Crip theory seeks to imagine a crip futurity, which is to say a future for disabled people that is not a future of despair and death-already or "a future of no future." In imagining crip futures, crip theory thereby envisions a present in which the disabled do not occupy the position of the already dead, the as-good-as-dead, or the once-dead who have been rescued by medicinal cure. I argue that Richard's rise to power is just such a present—that by theatricalizing his ability to stand in for death, Richard creates for himself a crip time in emphatic opposition to the ableist refrain that he is out of time or has no time because his birth is a sign of death. This refrain is explicit in Edward's articulation of a political order organized around reproductive futurism, an order that seeks to fold Richard's labor and time into a telos that effectively erases him by fetishizing the longevity of the Yorkist future represented by Young Ned. Richard's feigned agreement, in which he celebrates the tree and the fruit it bears, repeats this naturalization of Edward's temporal model. But in revealing to the audience that he will "blast [Young Ned's] harvest," Richard expresses his intent to crip straight time—to introduce into the orderly succession of planting, tending, and "reap[ing]" the equally natural forces of decay. The echo of "blast" in Richard's description of his arm in *Richard III*—it is "like a blasted sapling"—suggests that Richard's plan to "blast [Ned's] harvest" is an intent to reproduce his own disability in his nephew, propagating deformity or cripping the future (*R3* 3.4.69). In Joseph Campana's terms, "Richard is at once the monstrous child and the monstrous child-killer whose ruthless stratagems and vicious seductions violate temporal narratives of a future secured by the triumph of innocent youth."[31] In his intent to blast Ned's harvest, Richard announces that his queercrip rise to power does not offer an alternative model of longevity—for longevity, queer and crip theorists have argued, is an ableist, heteronormative value.[32] Rather, Richard illustrates a version of Edelman's "queer negativity," declining to articulate an alternative model of sociality and, instead, constructing an antisocial antifuture that embraces deformity and queercrip forms of reproduction.

Given the status of *Richard III* in the Western literary canon and biopolitical imaginary, it is no accident that queer and crip theories can be invoked to read the play. Indeed, McRuer has dubbed the play "Fuck the Disabled: The Prequel," with Richard in the part of "Tiny Tim's evil twin."[33] I want to complicate (or crip or queer) this mapping of theory onto prequel, however, by both looking forward and returning back to the figure of Andy Warhol, who not only precedes queer and crip theory but was the starting point—the post-predecessor—for this chapter's reading of Richard. Warhol's career exposes a queercrip kinship with Richard's—kinship defined not by linear time and the sexual reproduction of biological heirs but by exclusion from those normate structures. The resonance between Richard and Warhol therefore also exposes the limitations of ableist, heteronormative models of kinship, descent, development, and temporality that organize our politics, including the politics of academic disciplinarity and periodization. Both figures are queercrip artist-performers whose physical and social difference generates moribund progeny through nonprocreative and theatrical means. Their shared "Fuck off and die" stance toward straight, able-bodied culture stages forms of political and aesthetic subversion that undo both heteronormative claims to the future and the linear, genealogical model of temporality that those claims generate and ratify. If Richard III had a queer son, a crip son—a son who is also a father and brother, birthed otherwise from life and therefore death in a queercrip time at once before and after—his name would be Andy Warhol.

II. How Does It Feel to Be Dead?

Warhol was born Andrew Warhola in 1928 to a poor, immigrant Czech family in a two-room shack amid the pollution and squalor of industrial Pittsburgh. His mother spoke no English, and his father died when Andy was 13 after drinking poisoned water from a construction site. During elementary school, Andy became ill with rheumatic fever, a bacterial infection that thrives among impoverished populations. Soon after, he was diagnosed with a follow-on illness, Sydenham's chorea or Saint Vitus' dance, a disease of the nervous system that causes twitches and tremors. Biographers often attribute Warhol's precocious drawing skills to his two-year convalescence at home during this period. He emerged from this lengthy illness with extremely pale and markedly blotched skin that would, in his adulthood, be further blemished by chronic acne. Despite his health problems, unpromising appearance, disrupted schooling, and likely dyslexia, he went on to earn a B.A. in pictorial arts from Carnegie Technical Institute (later Carnegie Mellon University) in 1949 with money his father has assiduously saved for his education.[34] After graduation, he anglicized his last name to "Warhol" and moved to New York City to make a successful early career as an advertising artist. As he grew in reputation and transitioned out of advertising, he further obscured his working-class immigrant roots by telling few and sometimes conflicting stories about his past, preferring to respond to biographical questions by stating either "I come from nowhere" or "I come from another planet."[35]

Simon Watney has dubbed Warhol's planet of origin "Planet Queer" to summarize the alienation Warhol would have felt growing up gay, effeminate, artistic, odd-looking, and frail in working-class Pittsburgh in the 1930s and 1940s. But Warhol's difference was not confined to his childhood. Watney notes that his effeminate mannerisms would later exclude him from New York's fashionable, gay, midcentury artistic culture:

> To say as a child that you come from another planet is to speak from the narrative of comics and science fiction movies, which indeed describe people who are very pale and fair, who come from elsewhere, disguised

as earthlings. That strikes me as a not entirely inaccurate description of how queer Andrew felt. Thus when other fifties homosexuals such as Frank O'Hara and Truman Capote gave him the cold shoulder because, in their times, he was too "swishy," too much of a window dresser, something very profound was at stake. They had accepted a deal that was not available to Warhol. They had, if you will, dehomosexualized themselves, especially in their *social* role as artists or critics.[36]

By this account, Warhol was too queer to play it straight—too queer to pass—and his queerness posed challenges for his relationships with galleries, audiences, potential buyers, and fellow artists.[37] His "swishiness" was compounded with insecurities about his appearance—about his capacity to pass as normal-looking. Warhol's first lover, Carl Willers, said of him, "He had a lot of trouble with his skin and was for ever having eruptions of pimples almost like a teenager. He was very conscious of that. . . . He was acutely self-conscious. He thought he was totally unattractive, too short, too pudgy. He thought he was grotesque."[38] Additionally, Warhol was nearly bald by the age of 25. The extensive collection of wigs and toupees he would gradually come to own—and suffer mockery for in major print publications—were not initially attempts at theatrical zaniness, as they would later appear, but prostheses intended to compensate for a lack of hair that Warhol found mortifying. In the late 1960s, he began choosing gray and white wigs in particular to effect a kind of temporal drag—to look younger by artificially looking older.[39] "When you've got grey hair," he said, "every move you make seems 'young' and spry,' instead of just being normally active. It's like you're getting a new talent."[40]

As someone who carried with him a history of illness and marked physical disability—a history that included the "uncoordinated movements, muscular weakness, stumbling and falling, slurred speech, difficulty concentrating and writing, and emotional instability" that characterize Saint Vitus's dance—Warhol in his 20s and 30s might conservatively be categorized as a recovering disabled person.[41] In concert with his sense of inborn alterity, the shame he attached to his appearance cultivated in him a kind of freak or monster identity, particularly as he compared himself to the glamorous Hollywood stars and high-society celebrities he idolized.[42] This feeling of physical monstrosity was actualized after his near-murder in 1968, when he was 40 years old. Warhol was pronounced dead in the emergency room after Valerie Solanas, author of the *S.C.U.M. Manifesto*, shot him in the abdomen, damaging nine of his organs. Although he turned out to be Not Dead Yet after a lengthy and complex operation, Warhol suffered from the effects of the shooting for the rest of his life. Because his abdominal wall could not be fully repaired, he had to wear a surgical corset to support his bowels, and his torso was crisscrossed with Frankensteinian scars (see Figure 14). The death that was pronounced in 1968 finally came to pass in 1987, following gallbladder surgery. The surgery was significantly complicated by residual damage from the gunshot nearly 20 years before, which had marked him—in more ways than one—as a future dead person.

I want to suggest that Warhol's "hunkie roots," as biographer Victor Bockris calls his class background ("hunkie" being a pejorative term for Eastern European immigrants), combined with his childhood illness, his insecurities about his "grotesque" appearance, his swishy gayness, and the protracted and catastrophic effects of Solanas's attempted murder render Warhol a queercrip figure who has much in common with Richard III.[43] Like Richard, who "Torment[s] himself to catch the English crown" despite the accidents of his birth and the appearance of his body, Warhol had to overcome innate shyness, humble origins, and physical disadvantages to achieve his unlikely ambition: the celebrity that preoccupied him throughout his career—celebrity that he astutely perceived to carry a form of power equal to that of politicians (3H6 3.2.179).[44] As queercrips, Warhol and Richard develop homologous reproductive techniques that at once expose and subvert the politics of reproductive futurism. While cultivating public personae who outwardly perform what Rosemarie Garland-Thomson describes as "stigma management"—self-effacingly obscuring difference, as demanded by ableist culture—both develop means to subvert that culture and to propagate difference by queering and cripping reproduction.[45] For both figures, these means include embracing death as an alternative site of futurity in place of the cult of the Child. In the same way that Richard's kiss of death marks Young Ned's mortality, puncturing the utopic logic of reproductive futurism that posits the Child as the guarantor of longevity, many of Warhol's paintings disclose—if not enact—the moribundity of his subjects.

This moribundity is most explicit in Warhol's skull paintings from the mid-1970s (Figure 15). Ronnie Cutrone, Warhol's art assistant at the time, followed Warhol's instructions to photograph a human skull and the shadows it cast. From the options Cutrone offered him, Warhol chose for silk-screening the photo in which the shadow forms the shape of an infant's profile.[46] This photo became the template for numerous skull paintings that Warhol made over the next several years—paintings that represent the skull and the infant as doubles for one another. The skull paintings depict the complex temporal logic of the *memento mori* that I discuss in chapter 2, a logic by which the living person is admonished to recall, as though from the past, that death is in the future.[47] By alluding to the visual tradition of *memento mori* but selecting a

FIGURE 14. *Andy Warhol's Shooting Scars, The Factory* (1968). Photo by David Montgomery. Courtesy David Montgomery and Staley-Wise Gallery.

FIGURE 15.   *Skull* (1974), by Andy Warhol. Image and Artwork © 2021 The Andy Warhol Foundation for the Visual Arts, Inc./Licensed by ARS.

photo in which the skull precedes its infant shadow, Warhol suggests a cyclical temporality: Death gives way to infancy gives way to death in a ceaseless loop of beginnings and endings. Warhol's skull, like Edelman's later polemic, insists on the intrinsic morbidity of reproductive futurism and thereby resists the teleological, heteronormative mandate to idealize the future represented by the Child. That future, his skull paintings argue, is always already dead. Further, like all of Warhol's silk-screen paintings, the skull and its shadow are marked by imperfections in the printing process, such as the blue line that cuts into the infant's forehead where the ink—either through intention or accident—failed to transfer through to the canvas.[48] Warhol's trademark reproductive process generates glitchy babies—babies with cracked skulls. In much the way Richard "blast[s] [Young Ned's] harvest," Warhol's queer form of baby-making crips the future, proliferating the artist's own bodily disfigurement in his endlessly reproducible offspring.

Like the skull paintings, Warhol's portraits at once effect and reproduce death and deformity. Warhol's images of Marilyn Monroe, among the earliest paintings in his famed career as a celebrity portraitist, were inspired by the actress's suicide (Figure 16). The event that ostensibly marked the end of Monroe's life

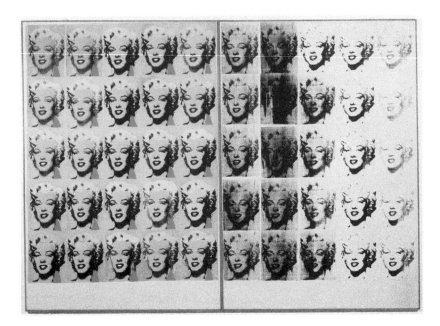

FIGURE 16. *Marilyn Diptych* (1962), by Andy Warhol. Image and Artwork © 2021 The Andy Warhol Foundation for the Visual Arts, Inc./Licensed by ARS. Marilyn Monroe™; Rights of Publicity and Persona Rights: The Estate of Marilyn Monroe LLC. marilynmonroe.com.

became, for Warhol, the beginning of an endlessly generative afterdeath of his production. Warhol and his assistants silk-screened an early publicity photo of Monroe over canvases pre-painted with eye shadow, skin, hair, and lip color to produce serial portraits of the star from a single source image. This production-line artistic process did not yield any two identical images. Each Marilyn is distinguished by its individual application of paint, its unique alignment and misalignment of painted and silk-screened elements, and the particular ink deposits left by an imperfectly repetitive silk-screening process. In their inevitable distortions, dislocations, and deformities, the resulting compositions are a study in both sameness and difference—a study in how the production of sameness is the production of difference. For Warhol, every clone is a failed clone, and every failed clone exposes the myriad fertile forms of failure—the queer and crip potential—built into the reproductive process.

In the first chapter of this book, I recounted Roland Barthes's argument for the deadening effects of photography: By representing a moment that has necessarily passed and translating the photographic subject into an object for view, the photograph is a mortifying technology that turns the present into the past, the living into the dead. The iconographic nature of Warhol's portraiture—his close framing of the subject on a blank background, for example—heightens photography's deadening effects. His subjects cease to be themselves and become, instead, "Warhols" through a reproductive process that propagates the persona of the artist at the expense of the subject's personhood. Jonathan Flatley writes:

> Jasper Johns is reported to have said to Holly Solomon on seeing Warhol's portrait of her, "Hi Holly, (kiss) how does it feel to be dead?" She gloated in reply, "Long after I'm dead, it will be hanging," acknowledging that the portrait renders her dead insofar as it turns her into an objet d'art, a "Warhol". . . . Like a visual elegy or epitaph, it preserves her best look for posterity.[49]

Warhol achieves fame as a kind of serial killer whose weapons of choice are technologies of asexual, serial reproduction: camera, copy machine, silkscreen, the Factory. (He was reputed to have had malignant effects on his entourage, who came to refer to him as "Drella," a portmanteau of Cinderella and Dracula.[50]) In defiance of reproductive futurism, which envisions no "long after" for queercrip Andy, the artist makes a future for himself through the deadening of others in images that survive not only their subjects but Warhol himself.

Richard similarly makes a future for himself through death—including, I suggest, his own. As in his final soliloquy in *3 Henry VI*, he opens *Richard III* by coming out crip to the new play's audience. He sneers at the heterosexual mating rituals that characterize peacetime at court, declaring that his disability makes him unsuitable to this "weak piping time of peace"—unsuitable to the "now" that is repeated three times in the first ten lines of the play *(R3* 1.1.24).[51] Richard has no place in the present, a present organized around straight courtship and straight sex, which he describes (not unlike Edelman) with disdain. In presenting himself as

> curtailed of this fair proportion,
> Cheated of feature by dissembling nature,
> Deformed, unfinished, sent before my time
> Into this breathing world scarce half made up (1.1.18–21),

Richard formulates his disability as a temporal problem, a common feature of discourses around the disabled body and one that will recur in the play. Kafer observes that "disability is often understood as a kind of disruption in the temporal field" and that the disabled body is frequently represented as "temporally disjointed."[52] In Richard's description, the rate of his body's early development was out of sync with his mother's progress from pregnancy to delivery, creating a disastrous asynchrony that resulted in anatomical deformity. Richard's soliloquy thus presents him doubly out of time. He describes himself as not only excluded from what is happening in the "now," a fact dramatized by the solitary monologue, but as the physical representation of chronological failure—of botched or glitched time. As the speech unfolds and Richard announces his intent to "prove a villain" through "plots," "inductions," and "prophesies," he suggests that he will address his temporal glitchiness by taking temporal devices in hand, cripping time and wresting conventional tools for charting the future to his own use. Importantly, as Williams has shown, he does not do this by disavowing his disabled body; rather, he treats that body as enabling.[53] For crip Richard, the disabled body and the inherited, ableist narratives around it become materials from which to generate a crip present and crip future that elude normate bodies.

By drawing attention to his disabled body in the play's opening gesture, Richard declines to perform "stigma management" for the play's audience, instead confronting us with the spectacle of his deformity and inviting us to notice it. As a crip performer staging his subversive identity, Richard translates his abjection from normate culture into the power to undo the happy, ableist world of nimble capering and lascivious pleasing that he has described. To accomplish this, however, Richard must develop a double self: a loyal, brotherly, avuncular persona that provides cover for the "subtle false and treacherous" intent that he discloses to the audience (1.1.37). The public-facing persona that mimes the imperatives of reproductive futurism is a consciously theatrical production—a character Richard puts on to hide his queercrip plot. In generating and occupying this persona, however, Richard enacts a kind of partial suicide. He must deaden his queercrip self—the self who identifies with his disability and derives agency from it—in order to perform servitude toward the normate culture that affords no place and no time for him. On the surface, he is "a packhorse in [King Edward's] great affairs"—a subhuman drudge of the political order that consigns him to subhuman drudgery (1.3.122). To perform this identity, he must submerge his ambitious aims. "Dive, thoughts, down to my soul," he warns when Clarence enters the scene (1.1.41).[54] If he is to succeed, he must disguise his "deep intent" by thrusting it below the surface (1.1.149).

As act 1 unfolds into Clarence's ominous dream and murder, the play draws harrowing associations between submersion and death. Clarence dreams that he has been pushed overboard by Richard while crossing the Channel from France and that he sees a vast underwater graveyard at the bottom of the ocean—"Ten thousand men that fishes gnawed upon" (1.4.25). In the eye sockets of their drowned skulls lie gleaming jewels. This dream is prophetic of both Richard's role in Clarence's death and Clarence's drowning in the malmsey butt at the end of the scene. The motif of deadly submersion that is carried across the first act of the play highlights the morbid stakes of Richard's "Dive, thoughts, down to my soul." The queercrip identity Richard declares in the play's opening soliloquy must be submerged by Richard himself in order for him to perform the public face of fraternal piety when his solitude is interrupted by Clarence's entrance.

This oppressive—even fatal—submersion of the queer and crip self is one of the defining features of closeted alterity, as LGBTQ and disabilities studies scholars have long observed, and it forms another point of contact between Richard and Warhol.[55] Although Warhol found it impossible to perform the kind of straight persona that gay artists like Frank O'Hara and Truman Capote pulled off, he developed a public face that effectively hid his politics, aesthetic judgments, and sex life from view. Although sexually active throughout adulthood, Warhol publicly claimed celibacy, and media interviews of him yielded little that was conclusive or illuminating, particularly about the political positions his work might be exploring.[56] As Graham Bader observes, "the most gripping element of his interviews is precisely the skill with which he avoids committing to a position on anything, much less the central political affairs of his day."[57] Warhol was notoriously deadpan, monosyllabic, and evasive when questioned about his art or that of others, preferring to say, "I like everything" rather than declare what he might or might not care for. It is as though Warhol the public figure emptied himself out of whatever content made Warhol the artist tick. Flatley suggests that Warhol understood this kind of self-emptying, self-deadening gesture to be an inescapable effect of having a public persona:

> Warhol saw that the poetics of publicity were also those of mourning. To become public or feel public was in many ways to acquire the sort of distance from oneself that comes with imagining oneself dead. The "self-negativity" that we experience by imagining ourselves as "public" might be seen as something like attending your own funeral.[58]

In generating public faces, figures like Warhol and Richard must submerge elements of themselves that have no place in normate culture and would therefore be compromised by exposure. In much the way that both figures reproduce disability and deformity by cripping reproduction, they develop queercrip reproductive practices—serial murder and serial portraiture—that translate living people into people who are deadened like themselves. They proliferate their deadness, spreading it to others.

III. A Marv'lous Proper Man

Both figures' public personae add up to elaborate drag shows, which is to say that in the construction of public faces, Richard and Warhol approach identity as manipulable and performative.[59] Self-conscious about how his body looked to others, Warhol put on a gray wig to make his movements appear more youthful; he made himself look older in order not to look old, treating age not as a matter of years lived but of superficial accessorizing. He declared himself celibate so as not to disclose that he was gay, as though sexuality, too, were a superficial characteristic that could be put on in one context and removed in another. Similarly, Richard becomes an energetic mimic of heterosexual masculinity as a subversive strategy for exposing it as performance. In his exchange with Clarence in the first scene of the play, as Clarence is being taken under arrest, Richard trots out a host of misogynist clichés that position himself, Clarence, Lord Hastings, and Edward against an antagonistic duo of sexually powerful women: Queen Elizabeth and Edward's mistress, Jane Shore, whom he describes as "mighty gossips in our monarchy" (1.1.83). Clarence has been sentenced to the Tower, Richard tells him, because "this it is when men are ruled by women" (1.1.62). After suggesting that the Queen was responsible for the imprisonment of Hastings, Richard warns, "We are not safe, Clarence; we are not safe" (1.1.70). Richard taps an available set of fears about women's emasculating control of men—fears rooted in heterosexual desire. Excluded from sex by virtue of his disability, Richard nonetheless puts on the identity of straight men who are brought into women's servitude by their desires—desires he shows no evidence of sharing.[60] Richard doubles down on this performance—this straight drag—when Brackenbury interrupts him and Clarence to forbid "private conference" between them (1.1.86). Richard answers,

> We speak no treason, man. We say the King
> Is wise and virtuous, and his noble Queen
> Well struck in years, fair, and not jealous.
> We say that Shore's wife hath a pretty foot,
> A cherry lip,
> A bonny eye, a passing pleasing tongue,
> And that the queen's kin are made gentlefolks.
> What say you, sir? Can you deny all this? (1.1.90–97)

Richard's skillful retort invites Brackenbury into locker-room talk—into a casual chat between bros about how their bro Edward is cheating on his old-bag wife with a "bonny," conventionally anatomized Mistress Shore. As Linda Charnes puts it, "Richard eclipses his 'difference' from the other men by invoking the 'differences' of gender" and becoming "one of the boys."[61] While not changing clothes, he "clothes his naked villainy," as he later puts it, in the performance of a straight man (1.3.334). For the straight drag he dons to trade misogynist worries with Clarence, Richard now substitutes another form of straight drag to obscure the content of the conversation with his brother, taking up the performative guise of a heterosexual man lustfully ogling the foot, lip, and eye of Edward's mistress.

Richard's straight drag reaches its flamboyant apex early in the play—in the second scene, when he improbably woos Lady Anne over the corpse of his murder victim, Henry. As scholars have long noted, Richard sues to Lady Anne through conventional heterosexual courtship tropes: "Your beauty slays me"; "Your beauty has driven me to extreme measures"; "I would die for you."[62] The formulaic, rhetorically rigid style of Anne's lament over the deaths of her husband and father-in-law finds an equally formulaic answer in Richard's performance of the clichés of heterosexual courtship. Given his disclosure of ulterior motives in the soliloquies that bookend his exchange with Anne, his adoption of courtship tropes amounts to an ostentatious drag show with Richard killing it in the lover role that he declared himself barred from only one scene earlier. What makes this an exceptional courtship scene is how Richard's crip performance as a straight lover literalizes—to absurdity—the romantic script he follows. In staging his courtship over Henry's dead body and then offering Anne his dagger and bared breast, Richard dramatizes the myriad dead ends represented by the very tropes he reproduces. He stages the morbidity of straight courtship's foundational metaphors of killing and dying—the morbid subtext of the heterosexual, normate romantic narrative that finds its raison d'etre in the production of children who will replace their moribund parents before dying and being replaced themselves.

In pushing straight courtship to its most macabre and absurd limit, Richard produces a flamboyant replica of norm love, one whose aesthetic underpinnings are shared by other queercrip artists and performers, including Warhol.[63] In the face of heteronormate culture's emphatic exclusion of Richard from the procreative coupling that underwrites its politics, Richard dramatizes the fictionality of distinctions between normal and defective by ridiculously, yet successfully, courting the woman most vehemently indisposed to him. His performance discloses the artifice of a romantic discourse that seeks to naturalize both heterosexuality in general and a particular version of male-female sexual relations. It is a discourse that can be successfully mimicked even by the most defective of suitors—even by a gimp in drag. For although Richard succeeds as a suitor, he never appears as other than unsuitable. In choosing to assail Anne in the presence of the "load" that is Henry's corpse (Anne's gloriously inert word), he stages and stars in a wooing scene of outlandishly bad taste (1.2.1, 29). The scene is remarkable for its "extravagance," a quality that Susan Sontag, in her influential essay "Notes on 'Camp,'" identifies as a "hallmark" of the camp aesthetic. "The essence of Camp is its love of the unnatural: of artifice and exaggeration," Sontag writes.[64] Richard's wooing is at once a form of drag—an ostentatious identity performance that culminates in the offer of his body for feminized penetration—and an exposure of the artificial, exaggerated, and unnatural discourse of heterosexual romance—an exposure of that discourse as camp. In McRuer's terms, the scene "position[s] heterosexuality, naturally linked to able-bodiedness, as a laughable ruse."[65] The engagement scene between a man and a woman of noble blood who will end up being the King and Queen of England is undercut by what Charnes has called Richard's "fabricat[ion] [of] sexual subjectivity as a usable fiction"—by the transparently theatrical guile of his performance, the series of lies and revised lies that unfold across the scene, and the sheer gaucheness of conducting romantic courtship in the presence of a bleeding corpse.[66] Richard's preposterous—and preposterously successful—courtship of Anne accomplishes camp's mission to "dethrone the serious." In the tradition of what Sontag calls "pure" camp, it is a scene that stages "a seriousness that fails."[67]

Like other areas of her thinking, Sontag's understanding of camp was influenced by Warhol, who is frequently cited as one of camp's most astute practitioners.[68] Across his career, Warhol generated camp productions of beauty, celebrity, tragedy, persona, and art itself. While his skull paintings meditate on the problem of mortality—a problem the paintings unflinchingly associate with human babies—they do so in gaudy, jarring colors that are indecently unsuited to their subject matter: blazing pinks, neon greens and yellows, purple, turquoise, bright blue. Electric chairs crackle in hues so hot they feel as if they could zap the viewer, an effect that at once transmits and diminishes their threat by decontextualizing and universalizing it. The famously beautiful and tragically deceased Marilyn Monroe is bedecked in tawdry lipstick and eye shadow, her skin cartoonishly pink, lavender, red, or green. A lurid press photo of a deadly car crash is so excessively and haphazardly silk-screened onto the canvas that only the title, *Green Burning Car I*, conveys the finished painting's subject matter. When the Ferus Gallery in Los Angeles presents a solo show of Warhol's work, the LA haut monde arrive to discover 32 paintings of Campbell's Soup cans. Twenty years later, Warhol is urinating on canvases covered in copper paint and selling them as works of abstraction—as "Oxidation Paintings." Everywhere in Warhol's oeuvre, we discover the artist covertly taking the piss in plain sight; we discover "a seriousness that fails." Like Richard, Warhol fabricates garish reproductions of the artifacts and discourses of normate culture. His camp aesthetics denaturalize, deauthenticate, and theatricalize those artifacts to expose them as the "industrially packaged and infinitely reproducible commodities" they have always been.[69]

Was ever public in this humor wooed? Was ever public in this humor won?

Richard's campy turn as a straight man in the throes of love ends with a soliloquy on drag. He may have convinced Anne of his worthiness, but he has not fooled himself. As if to dramatize this point, he proposes to dress his deformed body up as the "proper" body Anne has mistaken it for:

> And will she yet abase her eyes on me,
>
> . . .
>
> On me, whose all not equals Edward's moiety?
> On me, that halts and am misshapen thus?
> My dukedom to a beggarly *denier*,
> I do mistake my person all this while.
> Upon my life she finds, although I cannot,
> Myself to be a marv'lous proper man.
> I'll be at charges for a looking-glass
> And entertain a score or two of tailors
> To study fashions to adorn my body. (1.2.233–44)

Williams reads this moment as a declaration of Richard's newfound confidence in a body he now celebrates as "fi[t] for public view."[70] But Richard bluntly declares that he "cannot" share Anne's image of him as "a marv'lous proper man" and invokes the deictic "thus" to gesture toward a body he insists is "misshapen" and inadequate, unequal to "Edward's moiety." The passage is indeed confusing if we miss its mocking tone—if we miss Richard's misogynist critique of Anne and his contempt for the bogus hetero love scene she falls for. Richard's soliloquy invites us to share his view of his body as defective and not to be taken in by his performance of a "proper man," as Anne has just been.[71] In proposing to dress up behindhand for the part he has already successfully played, Richard shows the skillful drag artist to be less reliant on costume than on a convincing performance of the role. For Anne, Richard's exemplary rehearsal of that role transforms his "misshapen" body into the shape of legitimate masculinity. Richard does not quite share her view, however. His hyperbolic call for "a score or two of tailors" to bedeck a figure "that halts and is misshapen thus" is the crip-drag equivalent of putting lipstick on a pig—or, in this case, on a boar.

As the play moves into its busy middle scenes, Richard enlists other actors in camp reproductions of normate culture, expanding the subjects of his parodic performances beyond heterosexual romance to the genealogical and political systems built on it. Like his courtship of Anne, these absurdist scenes stage the artificiality of heteronormative logic by subjecting it to queercrip reproduction. Securing Buckingham's promise to "counterfeit the deep tragedian"—to copy a copy—Richard scripts a scene for Buckingham to play at Guildhall in which he will "Infer the bastardy of Edward's children" through various delegitimizing claims (3.5.5, 73). Some of these claims have nothing to do with Edward's children:

> Tell them how Edward put to death a citizen
> Only for saying he would make his son
> "Heir to the Crown"—meaning indeed, his house,
> Which by the sign therof was termed so. (3.5.74–77)

This first claim broadly suggests that Edward was given to a tyrannical mishandling of justice, and it hints that Edward may have harbored anxiety about challenges to his sons' legitimacy.[72] However, it does not "infer the bastardy of Edward's children," nor does the subsequent claim of Edward's "bestial appetite in charge of lust, / Which stretched unto [the] servants, daughters, wives" of London's citizens (3.5.79–80). On the contrary, the reference to Edward's sexual appetite infers the bastardy of his subjects' children rather than his own. Richard's mode of bastardizing his nephews is to translate all England into bastards. As an "anti-genealogical agent," to borrow a phrase from Vin Nardizzi, Richard overturns the whole logic of legitimacy by breeding illegitimate children—not through sex but through narrative reproductions of the past.[73] He ends his instructions to Buckingham by calling his own mother a whore, suggesting that she slept around while his father was in France. That his mother's alleged looseness might attaint Richard himself does not trouble his carpet-bombing strategy of legitimating himself by blowing up legitimacy.

In his appearance before the aldermen at Guildhall, Buckingham embellishes Richard's script, not only declaring Edward a bastard who looked nothing like his father but proposing that Richard is his father's true son in body and mind: "I did infer your lineaments—/ Being the right idea of your father / Both in your form and nobleness of mind" (3.7.12–14).[74] Much as Richard's script spreads bastardy across the English populace, Buckingham's claim of physical likeness between Richard and his father retroactively spreads deformity, turning York into a hunchback with a shriveled arm.[75] Rather than recuperating Richard from deformity, Buckingham's strategy proliferates it backward in time. Buckingham's account of his audience's mute response to this oration is a brilliant comic moment. He builds up to the great climax of "I bid them that did love their country's good / Cry 'God save Richard, England's royal king!'" only to puncture Richard's hopes with his deflating report that "They spake not a word" in reply (3.7.21–22, 24).[76] The reason for their muteness is fantastically Warholian: "the people were not used / To be spoke to but by the Recorder" (3.7.29–30). Buckingham only gets the response he requires—puny but sufficient—when his words are read from the Recorder's book by the Recorder—when they are filtered through a medium who reports to them secondhand what they have just heard firsthand. The people require a simulacrum to generate the emotional and political response that this entirely fraudulent spectacle is meant to fabricate.[77] Richard is not turning politics into fiction; he is exposing and capitalizing on its constitutive fictitiousness.

Richard's drag performance as Lady Anne's lover is topped only by his drag performance as a prayerful, humble, reluctant heir to the throne—a role that Buckingham expressly describes as cross-gender acting when he advises Richard to "Play the maid's part" (3.7.51).[78] Throughout the campy scene in which Buckingham sues to Richard to accept the crown—a scene Michael Torrey rightly describes as "outrageous"—Buckingham amplifies the staginess of the spectacle.[79] In addition to referring directly to the "props" and "ornaments" that make up the scene—the prayer book and priests that aid Richard's dramatization of piety—Buckingham stretches the limits of irony by swapping Richard's visible bodily deformity out for his nephews' noble health:

> Know then, it is your fault that you resign
> . . .
> The lineal glory of your royal house,
> To the corruption of a blemished stock,
> Whiles in the mildness of your sleepy thoughts—
> Which here we waken to our country's good—
> The noble isle doth want her proper limbs:
> Her face defaced with scars of infamy,
> Her royal stock graft with ignoble plants
> And almost shouldered in the swallowing gulf
> Of dark forgetfulness and deep oblivion. (3.7.117–129)

Buckingham aims to lull his audience into the "dark forgetfulness and deep oblivion" that he ascribes to England, inviting them to forget that they are looking at a "blemished" body that has repeatedly been associated with "corruption"—a body that "doth want her proper limbs," that is "ignoble" and "defaced with scars of infamy." Richard's hunched shoulder becomes England's deformity as the country is "almost shouldered in the swallowing gulf." By displacing Richard's deformity onto the princes and to England, Buckingham transposes Richard into a "royal" figure with "proper limbs."[80] Williams observes that "Buckingham reinscribes Richard's deformity upon the nation and casts Richard as the cure for its bodily lack," and Nardizzi usefully connects this moment specifically to early modern discourses around the crutch or prosthetic aid, arguing that "Richard presents himself as an unwilling but necessary prosthesis for England's bodily lack, whose amputations he has supervised, and as a salve for the wounds he has opened."[81] Even as Buckingham makes these remarks, Richard's deformed body is standing before the gathered audience. Buckingham invites his audience to forget the very body they are looking at—to see it as different than it appears. As Lindsey Row-Heyveld puts it, "Richard's body is a prop that he deploys in the performance of that body."[82] His stagy scene thus calls up the logic of theater, in which audiences temporarily suspend disbelief, taking what appears before them as something other than they know and see it to be. The stage depends on this misrecognition. Buckingham's staged misrecognition of Richard's prop-body is thus a staged scene about staginess, or what Sontag calls the "farthest extension, in sensibility, of the metaphor of life as theatre."[83] It is a camp extravaganza whose subject is the theatricality of politics, of the body, of identity.

Aided by Buckingham, Richard's queercrip performances have the effect of ironizing some of the core assumptions of ableist culture. By staging the competing ways that his body can signify—as at once "halting" and "proper," "ignoble" and "royal"—Richard's depictions of straight able-bodiedness challenge the notion of a stable norm against which abnormal bodies can be defined, subverting the assumption that bodily queerness is definitionally visible.[84] In this way, the scene illustrates David T. Mitchell's and Sharon L. Snyder's claim that in Western culture's representations of disability, "The prosthetic relation of body to word is exposed as an artificial contrivance."[85] Further, in much the way that Henry's disinheritance of Prince Edward in 3 Henry VI exposes the fictions underpinning dynastic coherence, Richard's and Buckingham's wholesale detonation of legitimacy subverts the very logic by which one king rightfully succeeds the next. Their rhetorical undoing of paternal origins through queercrip, iterative reproductions of history destabilizes not only the ideal of durable genealogy but the foundational notion of origin or originality.[86] In the same way that Warhol's purposely vacuous public persona frustrates his interviewers' search for an authentic identity bare of theatrical presentation, Richard's theatricalization of identity empties identity of all but theatricality.

Richard's subversive project is, like Warhol's, fundamentally queer and crip in that it challenges the normalizing claims of reproductive futurism by embracing death as a generative mechanism. Negating the heteronormative, ableist telos that excludes queers and crips from the present and future organized around the promise of the Child, both figures exploit the potential that death offers to open alternative temporal registers. By this moment in *Richard III*, Richard—with his company of assistants, his "Factory"—has effected the deaths of Clarence, Edward, Hastings, Vaughan, Dorset, and Gray, and the Princes' murders are but a few scenes away. In addition to negating the logic of reproductive futurism by proliferating bastardy, mimicking heterosexual courtship rituals, and evacuating hereditary legitimacy, Richard exposes the fragility of the whole project of the Child by simply killing people off in a form of antireproduction that produces dead people instead of heirs. In this way, Richard appears to negate the project of reproductive futurism by introducing death as its antithesis. However, Richard's queercrip interventions, like Warhol's, expose the morbidity implicit in straight ableism's fetishization of the able-bodied child. Recall that the final scene of *3 Henry VI* begins with Edward's list of the fathers and sons the Yorks have killed off—"mowed down," to be specific—in order to secure their claim:

> Once more we sit in England's royal throne,
> Repurchased with the blood of enemies.
> What valiant foemen, like to autumn's corn,
> Have we mowed down in tops of all their pride
> Three dukes of Somerset, threefold renowned
> For hardy and undoubted champions;
> Two Cliffords, as the father and the son;
> And two Northumberlands—two braver men
> Ne'er spurred their coursers at the trumpet's sound.
> With them, the two brave bears, Warwick and Montague,
> That in their chains fettered the kingly lion
> And made the forest tremble when they roared.
> Thus have we swept suspicion from our seat
> And made our footstool of security. (*3H6* 5.7.1–14)

Edward's "footstool of security" is a pile of corpses. The foundation on which he builds a future for "Young Ned" is a graveyard littered with the slaughtered heirs of noble blood. Richard's killings do not invert the logic of reproductive futurism by introducing death. They replicate its logic with only a degree of difference: Instead of killing distant Plantagenet fathers and sons, Richard kills those more closely related.[87] Further, although Richard has Young Ned murdered, the play hints at the bloodshed potentially averted by his death. In anticipation of his reign, Young Ned expresses his intent to "win our ancient right in France again"—to open a new era in the Hundred Years' War, which had already claimed the lives of between two and four million people (R3 3.1.92). Richard's bloody deed curtails a repetition of earlier bloody deeds valorized by heteronormate culture for the sake of "fame" (3.1.88). To create a Ricardian period—a queercrip present time otherwise unavailable to him—Richard turns the violence of normate culture against itself.[88] In doing so, he fulfills the "fate of the queer" as Edelman describes it, which is to "tak[e] seriously the place of the death drive [queers are] called on to figure." Richard's murderous parody of reproductive futurism argues "that the Child as futurity's emblem must die; that the future is mere repetition and just as lethal as the past."[89] His subversive performances stage, through failure, a serious critique of heteronormate violence by literalizing cultural associations between the queer, crippled body and death. They exemplify Jack Halberstam's "Queer Art of Failure," an art that "inhabits the darkness . . . [as] a crucial part of a queer aesthetic"—an art that "promises . . . to make a mess, to fuck shit up, to be loud, unruly, impolite, to breed resentment, to bash back, to speak up and out, to disrupt, assassinate, shock, and annihilate."[90]

IV. Shall They Last?

Richard sacrifices his queer aesthetic when he trades his crip body for the king's. As king, he represents the very locus of political order—the organizing principle of the social rather than a corporeal emblem of its failure or subversion. The scene of his faux-begrudging acceptance of the crown is the last one in the play in which he refers to his deformity. Thereafter, he inhabits the regal body, forfeiting the reproductive potential he claimed through queercrip identification with his deformity. His career as a queercrip performer is at an end for the moment, and the insurgent energies of his camp theatrics give way to insecurity and paranoia. Not coincidentally, this new role thrusts him into the structure of reproductive futurism and thereby into the temporal logic of ableist prophesies that exclude him from legitimate succession and provoke fears about his own mortality.

Richard opens the scene following his coronation with a concern about the future: "shall we wear these glories for a day? / Or shall they last, and we rejoice in them?" (4.2.6–7). These anxieties about securing the future of his kingship organize the remaining events of the play. Richard's anti-hereditary campaign for the crown has audaciously queered and cripped the discourse of legitimacy. As king, however, his first concern is that he may not be legitimate—that legitimacy is more than a discursive or theatrical construct:

> KING RICHARD: Why, Buckingham, I say I would be king.
> BUCKINGHAM: Why, so you are, my thrice-renowned liege.
> KING RICHARD: Ha? Am I king? 'Tis so. But Edward lives.
> BUCKINGHAM: True, noble prince.
> KING RICHARD: O bitter consequence,
>   That Edward still should live "true noble prince." (4.2.13–18)

Richard's camp production of legitimate succession here gives way to the fear that he is up against an ontological truth that cannot be fabricated—the fear of a "true noble prince" who is a product of hereditary succession, the form of reproduction that conventionally generates "true" princes and kings. While Richard may "wish the bastards dead," as he goes on to tell Buckingham, it is precisely because he knows their bastardy to be fabricated that the "true noble prince[s]" must die (4.2.19). His wish for their deaths discloses a belief in the efficacy of heteronormative social structures to generate something that his queercrip mind and body cannot. In short, it discloses Richard's own internalized ableism and heteronormativity.

Although he is not a direct hereditary successor in the way Edward's sons are, the Earl of Richmond likewise presents a threat to Richard, because Richmond is linked to reproductive and temporal mechanisms that Richard can only counterfeit. Richard appears to have forgotten the lessons of *3 Henry VI*, which discloses these mechanisms, I argued in chapter 4, to themselves be forms of counterfeiting. The news delivered by Lord Stanley that the "Marquis Dorset . . . is fled / To Richmond" provokes Richard to invent the rumor of Anne's "grievous" illness to clear the way for his intended marriage to young Elizabeth (4.2.49–50, 53). After then giving orders to his henchman Tyrrell for the princes' assassination, Richard ruminates at length on Richmond despite Buckingham's multiple interruptions on the subject of the promised earldom of Hereford:

> BUCKINGHAM: What says your highness to my just request?
> KING RICHARD: I do remember me, Henry the Sixth
>   Did prophesy that Richmond should be king,
>   When Richmond was a little peevish boy.
>   A king . . . perhaps . . . perhaps.
> BUCKINGHAM: My lord?
> KING RICHARD: How chance the prophet could not at that time
>   Have told me, I being by, that I should kill him?

BUCKINGHAM: My lord, your promise for the earldom.
KING RICHARD: Richmond? When last I was at Exeter,
　　The Mayor in courtesy showed me the castle,
　　And called it "Ruge-mount"—at which name I started,
　　Because a bard of Ireland told me once
　　I should not live long after I saw "Richmond." (4.2.97–109)

The prophetic attention attracted by the boy Richmond was markedly differ-ent from that paid to young Richard, whose dental precocity was interpreted as a sign of a violent future—of a "future of no future," to return to Kafer's formulation.[91] The fact that Henry VI is the person who prophesied Rich-mond's future kingship positions Richmond as his heir in an oracular form of reproduction that generates a successor for Henry—a substitute for his dead son, Prince Edward—only moments before Richard stabs Henry to death. Richard's rumination over this prophesy prompts his recollection of another prophesy uttered by a nameless "bard of Ireland" who linked Richmond to Richard's death. The growing threat of Richmond's return to England is thus also a threat of Richard's foretold demise. Forces gathering to advance the future of the Child or destined heir, here figured in Richmond, dovetail with ableist prophesies that read Richard's body as a sign of death. The convergence of prophesies that guarantee a future for Richmond and none for Richard leave him unsettled by the temporal questions that frame the scene: How long will I be king? How much time do I have? "What's o'clock?" (4.2.111, 113).

As the corporeal site of political order rather than its embodied antithesis, King Richard frantically seeks to reproduce the very structure of familial like-ness and inheritance that he renounced in *3 Henry VI* when he declared him-self fatherless, brotherless, and like no one but himself ("I had no father, I am like not father; / I have no brother, I am like no brother / . . . / I am myself alone" [*3H6* 5.6.80–84]). Cut off from the queercrip forms of reproduction that characterized his rise to power, Richard attempts to participate in the normate operations of hereditary sovereignty by marrying Edward's daughter, Eliza-beth. "I must be married to my brother's daughter," he resolves, "Or else my kingdom stands on brittle glass" (*R3* 4.2.62–63). Although his theatrical and morbid reproductions of straight culture succeeded in delivering him the king-dom, he here discloses a lack of faith in their sufficiency to guarantee its future—a future he can only imagine securing through the mechanisms of heterosexual coupling. After bastardizing Edward and his children, Richard (paradoxically) attempts to marry Edward's daughter in order to shore up his title. When Queen Elizabeth impedes this plan by unrelentingly insisting on the fact of her dead sons, Richard promises to return them to her through her daughter:

> QUEEN ELIZABETH: Yet thou didst kill my children.
> RICHARD: But in your daughter's womb I bury them,
>   Where, in that nest of spicery, they will breed
>   Selves of themselves, to your recomfiture. (4.4.353–56)

The Richard who had previously disclaimed any familial bonds here inscribes himself into a reproductive process at once morbid, intensely incestuous, and perfect. In his proposal for Queen Elizabeth's "recomfiture," the nephews Richard killed are transformed into his own sperm to be implanted, dead, in the tomb of his niece's uterus.[92] In positing himself as the progenitor of his own nephews, Richard suggests he is not merely like the brother he had disowned but that he is genetically indistinguishable from his brother—that he can fill Edward's genetic place in a procreative process that would regenerate Edward's sons. Richard will function as a clone of Edward in a transaction that will clone the dead princes. That this regeneration would happen inside his niece's womb multiplies his already-incestuous marriage proposal, placing the bride's uncle, father, and dead brothers inside her body. As Richard's promise develops into its final turn, "they will breed / Selves of themselves," it becomes unclear whether he is even a necessary party in the cloning fantasy that would regenerate Queen Elizabeth's dead sons, apart from his role in burying them—dead—in his niece's womb. Neither he nor his niece has an apparent genetic function in the breeding process he imagines this burial to initiate, a process through which the boys reproduce themselves, either asexually or homosexually, out of their own corpses. Their sister's womb would become at once a grave, a petri dish, and a time machine—a final resting place for the princes and the site where they will clone themselves to survive into the future, indistinguishable from the boys whom Richard killed in the past.

From his earlier incarnation as a glitched, unlicked lump-son who disavowed any likeness to his father and brothers, Richard has come around to inventing an intensely endogamous, incestuous form of reproduction that would not only guarantee the exact replication of Yorkist heirs but bring the dead ones back to life. His procreative fantasy seeks to literalize the ideals of reproductive futurism and hereditary sovereignty by which kingship is reproduced from heir to heir through a form of identical replication that eliminates biological, corporeal, temperamental, and temporal difference. With his niece as a supplement to his dubious regal claim, Richard would use his dead nephews to generate the time of sovereignty, a time without end in which the regal Yorkist body is reproduced so perfectly that it effectively never changes or dies. Richard's incestuous cloning experiment reasserts what Edelman calls "the absolute privilege of heteronormativity" and, concomitantly, "the absolute value of reproductive futurism" by positing the children of his proposed marriage as the kingdom's only salvation.[93] At the same time, however, his reproductive plans lay bare these systems' queer-crip underpinnings by literalizing their core morbidity, exposing the incestuous implications of idealized endogamy, and declaring his radically disabled nephews Not Dead Yet. Even in his most urgent performance of a straight, able-bodied man—the performance on which his very sovereignty depends—Richard cannot quite pass as a heteronorm. In unfolding the perfect fantasy of endogamous reproduction and sovereign perpetuity, he ends up queering and cripping both, enlisting the dead to unsettle distinctions between straight and queer, able and disabled, fertile and impotent, living and deceased, past and future.

V. His Last Major Body of Work

Richmond's betrothal to Elizabeth and his defeat of Richard in the final scene of the play announce a heteronormate victory over the crippled and the queer, one always already triumphalized by the past and future reign of the Tudor Queen Elizabeth I.[94] And yet, as critics have long observed, the sheer dramatic magnetism of Shakespeare's character exceeds the play's providential arc. Furthermore, Richard's career is not yet over. It continues to unfold in forms that expose the limits of our current theoretical vocabulary, at once transcending what José Esteban Muñoz calls Edelman's "political nihilism" and mortifying the queer utopia that Muñoz offers in its place.[95] This transcendence is itself a queercrip mechanism, one that the figure of Andy Warhol retrospectively anticipates. During the last decade of his life, Warhol carried a 35-millimeter camera with him everywhere he went, shooting about a roll of black-and-white film per day. The resulting images, about 130,000 collected on 3,600 photographic contact sheets, were not released by the Andy Warhol Foundation until 2014, when they were acquired by the Cantor Arts Center of Stanford University. In addition to providing insight into aspects of Warhol's social life and artistic process, the contact sheets represent what Peggy Phelan describes as "laten[t]" works by Andy Warhol.[96] They make possible the production of new Warhols—or, more precisely, works of art that are at once Warhols and not-Warhols, given that any prints made from them would both postdate Warhol himself and definitionally represent images that Warhol chose *not* to use. The contact sheets make possible the production of queercrip Warhol offspring—works with an insistently incomplete, simulacral, differential relationship to what they document. They are forsaken works abandoned at birth as deficient; moribund works generated out of the death-effects of photographic technology; posthumous works of a dead man; bastard works at once by and not by Warhol.

Phelan writes, "The contact sheets comprise Warhol's last major body of work, which has been largely unseen until now, some thirty years after his death. These past three decades might be seen as a kind of developing ink, as if the exposures were slumbering in a very slow chemical bath, and the conditions of visibility did not allow us to see them until now."[97] The 30 years during which Warhol's photographs lay "slumbering" in "developing ink" seem a short space of time compared with the more than five centuries that Richard III's skeleton lay undisturbed in the buried ruins of the Greyfriars church in Leicester, his grave a "developing ink" awaiting the archaeological, osteopathological, and genetic technologies—"the conditions of visibility"—that made it possible to identify the remains as Richard's when they were exhumed in 2012. Like the release of Warhol's contact sheets, the discovery of Richard's remains has made possible a new generation of Richards the Third that both are and are not Richard, such as the bust commissioned by the Richard III Society and produced from CT scans of his skull; a re-creation of the gravesite and skeleton center stage in the 2016 Rupert Goold/Ralph Fiennes production of the play at the Almeida Theatre; and the prosthetic spine prominently displayed by a shirtless Benedict Cumberbatch in the opening soliloquy of the *Richard III* episode of *The Hollow Crown*—to name but a few.[98] What would it mean to consider these offspring—propagated from a skeleton, no less—as Richard's "last major body of work"?

It would mean that Richard the Third is Not Dead Yet. It would mean that Richard errs in seeking longevity through sexual reproduction when his longevity is paradoxically constituted through the radical difference and disability of death. It would mean that his "last major body of work" is only his latest major body of work and that his body will continue to do work that we cannot yet foresee. It would mean that there is a future for the queer and the crip, one that transcends the death drive at the center of Edelman's queer theory to reconstitute the very ontologies of living and dead. It would mean that Richard himself is the fantastical, resurrected future he imagines germinating in his niece's womb.

Deformed, mortal, illegitimate: The king is dead; long live the king.

Postscript

Lazarus Again

I flew from Philadelphia to Portland, Oregon, on January 13, 2016, to visit a friend who was recovering from cancer. It was a Wednesday. David Bowie had died of cancer three days earlier. Two days before that, on his 69th birthday, he had released his final album, *Blackstar*.[1]

On the Friday *Blackstar* came out, Sony Music released a video for the single "Lazarus" that came to be viewed in the wake of the news on Monday morning as a harbinger of Bowie's imminent death.[2] The video depicts multiple Bowies. One lies prone in a hospital bed, singing, clutching at a blanket, and levitating slightly. His eyes are covered by a bandage wrapped around his head, buttons marking his pupils. This Bowie is himself suggestively double: an animate doll and a singing corpse, shrouded, with weighted eyes. The eeriness of this dead-undead figure is amplified by the presence of a young woman who emerges in the opening shot from a large, coffinlike armoire in the corner of the hospital room. She later appears underneath the bed, reaching up from around its side toward the Bowie who lies in it singing,

Look up here, I'm in heaven
I've got scars that can't be seen
I've got drama can't be stolen
Everybody knows me now.

As the video progresses, a second singing Bowie appears as if also out of the armoire, wearing a black knit unitard marked by diagonal blue streaks—the reproduction of a costume from a photo shoot for his 1976 album *Station to Station*.[3] After trading lines of the third verse with the Bowie in the bed, this second Bowie sits down at a desk in the room, fountain pen in hand, making histrionic gestures of anxiety. With an expression of inspiration, he then begins to write in the weathered manuscript book before him. He scribbles so frenetically that the words run off the page and down the front of the desk as the bed-ridden Bowie reaches the climax of the song:

This way or no way
You know I'll be free
Just like that bluebird
Ain't that just like me?

On the desk sits a bejeweled skull, one associated in an earlier *Blackstar* short film with a recurring alter ego from Bowie's oeuvre, Major Tom.[4] The video ends with the writer-Bowie retreating, in the awkward manner of a superannuated robot, backward into the armoire and closing the door.

The first time I saw this video was the evening I arrived in Portland, when my friend took me to see a Bowie retrospective at the historic Clinton Street Theater. The film—more than two hours of concert clips, videos, and interviews—culminated in a screening of "Lazarus" that left me crying so hard that I could not stand when the house lights came up. I had always loved David Bowie, and I was saddened by his death. But what triggered my cataclysm of grief was not the loss of him. It was the courage manifested by that video: the courage of a dying artist to represent himself as dead—to act out the scene of an end that was not an abstraction for him but an approaching surety.[5] In "Lazarus," he had said what we all know but mostly try not to think about: "I am dying. I will be dead." When I cried for "Lazarus," I cried as much for my own inevitable death as for the clarity he showed in figuring his.

Like Richard II's meditation on his corpse, Bowie's reflection on his dead self reproduces him through forms that transcend the deathbed—forms like the scribbling writer, the mysterious and urgent manuscript, the video itself and its controlling artistic vision, all of which survive the man with buttons for eyes. Even as he constructs his dead self, Bowie is generating afterdeaths—afterdeaths that resonate with those of Warhol, Richard II, Falstaff's Lazaran conscripts, Richard III, and many of the other figures who inhabit this book, including the one in its haunting cover photograph by David Maisel.[6] "Lazarus" is the title of not only a song from *Blackstar* but Bowie's late-career musical, which was in its debut off-Broadway run when he died, his artistic creation restaged and replayed again and again even as his body was cremated and his ashes scattered over Bali.[7] As a musician, performer, virtuoso of camp, actor, painter, art collector, denizen of the past, Starman of the future, and—above all, he once asserted—as a writer, Bowie hovers at the site of disciplinary and temporal crossings this book has explored. His impersonation of Hamlet talking to a skull in live performances of "Cracked Actor" in the 1970s and 1980s unfolds almost inexorably into the aged writer who appears in "Lazarus," the skull of an alter ego before him, an undead double in the bed at his side.[8]

When I returned from Portland, I began relistening to Bowie's catalog. My son Adam, who was five years old at the time, fell in love with him. Teachers and relatives expressed surprise about his fascination with a throwback artist from the last century, but Bowie seemed to me a child's irresistible hero: the zany costumes, hair, and makeup; the one-man cast of characters; the songs about a man from outer space. "If David Bowie is dead," my son asked one day, "is Ziggy Stardust also dead?" "No," I assured him. "Ziggy Stardust is a character. A character doesn't die the way a person dies."

By first grade, he had become so enamored that he wanted to be Bowie for Halloween. I bought a Lycra bodysuit and decorated it with carefully stenciled lightning bolts. We spray-painted a pair of black boots metallic red. I studied tutorials on replicating Bowie's *Aladdin Sane* makeup and scoured the Internet for a bright red rocker wig that would fit a boy of six. I don't know that I have ever seen my son look more fiercely alive than he did in that costume. It is an odd feeling to see your child happy and confident in the guise of a dead man you have been mourning.

Over the years that I have worked on this book, my son has been experimenting with his own version of how to do things with dead people. When he had to choose a historical figure for his second-grade Notable People project, he ended up with Shakespeare, though only after first proposing Bowie, about whom his teacher determined there was insufficient age-appropriate literature. Per the assignment, he dressed up for the Notable People Convention and memorized biographical facts, which he delivered like an actor from his elementary-school stage: "My name is William Shakespeare. I wrote 38 plays in the sixteenth and seventeenth centuries. All of them are still studied and performed today." For Halloween the next year he was Andy Warhol, whom he had first encountered in a song about the artist on Bowie's 1971 album *Hunky Dory*. He was intrigued when I told him that I had once seen footage of Bowie visiting Warhol's studio and that Bowie had played Warhol in a movie. One afternoon he noticed, in a book lying open on my desk, a

photo of Warhol in a black leather jacket holding a camera. The Halloween costume was a fait accompli.

It was not until I began drafting this postscript that it occurred to me that I have photographs of my son as David Bowie, William Shakespeare, and Andy Warhol.[9] In the process of writing a book that attempts to do Shakespeare criticism differently, I had been reproducing in my own life the structure of the Child—the structure, Edelman observes, of sameness. These photos of my

son are photos of myself—of my work and obsessions replicated across the body of the next generation. They are the past reproduced in the future: my child as a series of dead men. Because I can see these others in the photos— see myself and see the dead—there is an element of melancholy in them for me. And yet they are also photos of the dead living again—of the dead more alive than ever through the happy wish of this boy. In impersonating the past, my son is generating himself. These are photographs of his becoming. And they are photographs of his love for me.

I dedicate this book to Adam, though not without sadness and a twinge of superstitious angst. He earnestly wanted this dedication—wanted, I think, what he sought when he dressed up as Shakespeare and Warhol: to have a place

in the work that has occupied me for as long as he can remember. I tried to explain how morbid it would be for me to dedicate a book about dead people to my child, but he was not to be dissuaded. He cannot yet see the shadow of mortality this token casts over our love. He cannot know that the shadow has been with us from our beginning: that death is love's double, love's ghost. Or perhaps this is something I tell myself because I would rather not see what he knows.

We bought for the Warhol costume a vintage, 1980s-era Polaroid camera and some film. At nearly two dollars per exposure, the Polaroid makes for an expensive prop. Since its Halloween debut, I have occasionally replenished my son's supply of film, always with the advice that he use it judiciously. He doesn't, of course. He uses all of it at a go, documenting banal scenes of our everyday life as though he had at his disposal Warhol's roll of film per day. I adore these Polaroids. They capture not what my child looks like dressed as someone else but what it is for him to look at our life, through the antique technology of his Warholian camera, as himself.

I close with one of his Polaroids, a shot he took of me working on this book. In doing so, I perform, Barthes would argue, a self-embalming gesture. But I am happy to suffer this little death. It opens here a magic box where the eyes of the future touch the eyes of my son.

Notes

Introduction

1. Giorgio Agamben, "Bartleby, or On Contingency," in *Potentialities: Collected Essays in Philosophy*, trans. Daniel Heller-Roazen (Stanford, CA: Stanford University Press, 1999), 243–74, 257.

2. "National Portrait Gallery Finds Relics of an English King in its Basement," National Portrait Gallery press release, November 16, 2010. Arthur Penrhyn Stanley, Dean of Westminster and member of the Society of Antiquaries, reported that Richard's tomb was opened in 1871 for cleaning. See Arthur Penrhyn Stanley, "On an Examination of the Tombs of Richard II. and Henry III. in Westminster Abbey," *Archaeologia* 12 (June 26, 1873), 309–27, 311.

3. Mark Brown, "Richard II Relics Found in National Portrait Gallery Archive," *The Guardian*, November 16, 2010, https://www.theguardian.com/artanddesign/2010/nov/16/richard-second-national-portrait-gallery.

4. Quotations of Shakespeare's plays are from William Shakespeare, *The Oxford Shakespeare: The Complete Works*, ed. Stanley Wells and Gary Taylor (Oxford: Clarendon, 1988), cited parenthetically. Philip Schwyzer traces a similarly "weird posthumous history" of the corpse of King Henry VI, which, like that of Richard II, was disinterred, moved, and reburied (as Richard III's has also been). See Philip Schwyzer, *Shakespeare and the Remains of Richard III* (Oxford: Oxford University Press, 2013), 12. In a claim that has resonances with my observations here about the Richard who returns through the cigarette box, Schwyzer remarks that "Richard III has not ceased to be our contemporary" (*Shakespeare and the Remains*, 9).

5. Available documents related to the 1871 opening of Richard's tomb note that a number of objects found in the tomb appeared to have been added, over time, through a series of side holes that remained open from Richard's interment at Westminster Abbey in 1413 until the holes were closed up some time in the eighteenth century. Through these holes, some of Richard's bones also appear to have been stolen, though his skeleton was mostly intact (Stanley, "On an Examination of the Tombs," 311). The complete list of objects found in the tomb that is included as Appendix B in Stanley's account does not delineate between those judged to be original and those added through the holes later, though the objects were separated into two different boxes that were re-enclosed in the tomb in 1871, one marked "Accompaniments of the interment of King Richard II. and his Queen" and the other marked "Later insertions into the tomb of King Richard the Second" (Stanley, 316, 326–27). Presumably, the items collected by Scharf fall into the first category and were kept as souvenirs for precisely that reason. The complete list

of objects includes marbles, buttons, coins, and other random items that are more clearly detritus that was not placed in Richard's coffin either when he was first buried or when his remains were moved to Westminster Abbey. Neither the documents of the Society of Antiquaries nor those of Westminster Abbey indicate whether anything was added to Richard's coffin when it was moved in 1413 under the orders of Henry V.

6. Jacques Derrida, *Archive Fever: A Freudian Impression*, trans. Eric Prenowitz (Chicago: University of Chicago Press, 1995), 68–70. See also Alexander Nagel and Christopher S. Wood, *Anachronic Renaissance* (New York: Zone Books, 2010), in which the authors' observations about the work of art echo Derrida's claims about the archive, suggesting that it gestures backward to prior artifacts or origins and also forward to future viewers "who will activate and reactivate it as a meaningful event" (9). For an extended meditation on the Derridean archive in relation to imaging technologies, including atomic radiation, see Akira Mizuta Lippit, *Atomic Light (Shadow Optics)* (Minneapolis: University of Minnesota Press, 2005).

7. In describing the souvenir as composed for a future encounter such as the one narrated by Adamiec, I contradict the influential discussion of the souvenir in Susan Stewart's *On Longing: Narratives of the Miniature, the Gigantic, the Souvenir, the Collection* (Durham, NC: Duke University Press, 1993). She writes, "It is an object arising of the necessarily insatiable demands of nostalgia. The souvenir generates a narrative which reaches only 'behind,' spiraling in a continually inward movement rather than outward toward the future" (135). Stewart is concerned mainly with the souvenirs of childhood and tourism, and her psychoanalytic framework emphasizes the loss of an original experience for which the souvenir can only substitute. But Adamiec describes the experience of having made contact with history itself. The discrepancy between Adamiec's experience and Stewart's description arises out of the Scharf souvenir's mutations into an archive through the National Portrait Gallery's acts of preserving and cataloging it. I interrogate claims about the nostalgic loss of an original—shared alike by psychoanalysis, performance theory, and criticism on the history plays—in chapters 3 and 4 of this book and in my earlier work; see Alice Dailey, "The Talbot Remains: Historical Drama and the Performative Archive," *Shakespeare Bulletin* 35, no. 3 (2017): 373–87. For a discussion of what constitutes an archive, see Zachary Lesser, *Ghosts, Holes, Rips and Scrapes: Shakespeare in 1619, Bibliography in the Longue Durée* (Philadelphia: University of Pennsylvania Press, 2021), 23–25.

8. In a note dated March 8, 1872, Professor George Busk, a Fellow of the Royal Society, wrote to Scharf about volume measurements taken of the interior of Richard's skull. Reporting that the skull is smaller, by volume, than those of either early or contemporary Britons, Busk concludes that "King Richard the Second was not distinguished by the size of his brain. What its quality may have been is quite another question" (Stanley, "On an Examination of the Tombs," 325). Richard's 1871 disinterment also revealed that he was not killed by a blow to the head, as both the chronicles and Shakespeare's play imply (Stanley, 315).

9. Schwyzer observes a similar phenomenon in connection to remains that have been uncertainly identified as those of the two princes whom Richard III is reputed to have killed in the Tower, remarking that the representation of their deaths in Shakespeare's play "seems to precede reality, and writing somehow calls matter into being" (*Shakespeare and the Remains*, 51).

10. Productions of *Richard III* that feature replicas of the exhumed spine include those by the Folger Shakespeare Theater, directed by Robert Richmond (2014), and the Almeida Theater, directed by Ruper Goold (2016), as well as the *Richard III* episode of *The Hollow Crown*, directed by Dominic Cooke (2016).

11. Margreta de Grazia, "Anachronism," in *Cultural Reformations: Medieval and Renaissance in Literary History*, ed. Brian Cummings and James Simpson (Oxford: Oxford University Press, 2010), 13–32, 13.

12. Nagel and Wood, *Anachronic Renaissance*, 13. Rita Felski lodges a related complaint about historicist understandings of literary artifacts in particular in "Context Stinks!" *New Literary History* 42, no. 4 (2011): 573–91.

13. Rebecca Schneider, *Performing Remains: Art and War in Times of Theatrical Reenactment* (New York: Routledge, 2011), 98, italics original. My thinking about intermediality and anachronicity is influenced by Schneider and, in addition, by Rebecca Bushnell's discussion of video games as theater and performance in *Tragic Time in Drama, Film, and Videogames: The Future in the Instant* (London: Palgrave Macmillan, 2016). For a consideration of theater as "a 'technology' that represents 'technologies,'" see W. B. Worthen, *Shakespeare, Technicity, Theatre* (Cambridge: Cambridge University Press, 2020), especially the introduction, which draws useful distinctions between technology, technicity, mediation, and mediatization.

14. Jonathan Gil Harris, *Untimely Matter in the Time of Shakespeare* (Philadelphia: University of Pennsylvania Press, 2009), 1–19; David Scott Kastan, *Shakespeare and the Shapes of Time* (Hanover: University Press of New Hampshire, 1982), 1–33; Matthew D. Wagner, *Shakespeare, Theatre, and Time* (New York: Routledge, 2012), 1–11, 34–67; Gilles Deleuze, *The Fold: Leibniz and the Baroque*, trans. Tom Conley (Minneapolis: University of Minnesota Press, 1993), 3–13; and Michel Serres with Bruno Latour, *Conversations on Science, Culture, and Time*, trans. Roxanne Lapidus (Ann Arbor: University of Michigan Press, 1995), 60. The epigraph for this book is taken from Serres (with Latour), 43.

15. Early modernists working in the area of political theology have registered important reservations about new historicist uses of the concept of the king's two bodies and its particularly well-known formulation by Ernst Kantorowicz. See, for example, David Norbrook, "The Emperor's New Body? *Richard II*, Ernst Kantorowicz, and the Politics of Shakespeare Criticism," *Textual Practice* 10, no. 2 (1996), 329–57; Julia Reinhard Lupton, *Thinking with Shakespeare: Essays on Politics and Life* (Chicago: University of Chicago Press, 2011); Graham Hammill and Julia Reinhard Lupton, eds., *Political Theology and Early Modernity* (Chicago: University of Chicago Press, 2012); and Jennifer R. Rust, *The Body in Mystery: The Political Theology of the Corpus Mysticum in the Literature of Reformation England* (Evanston, IL: Northwestern University Press, 2014).

16. Phyllis Rackin, *Stages of History: Shakespeare's English Chronicles* (Ithaca, NY: Cornell University Press, 1990). Linda Charnes notes that the concept of nostalgia that has informed editorial and scholarly engagement with the history plays, especially *Henry V*, is itself an anachronism. An understanding of nostalgia as sentimental longing for the past did not develop until the late eighteenth century. See Linda Charnes, "Reading for the Wormholes: Micro-Periods from the Future," *Early Modern Culture: An Electronic Seminar* 6 (2007): para. 8–10, accessed June 12, 2017, http://emc.eserver.org/1-6/charnes.html (site discontinued). See also Svetlana Boym, *The Future of Nostalgia* (New York: Basic Books, 2001); and Kevis Goodman, "Romantic Poetry and the Science of Nostalgia,"

in *The Cambridge Companion to British Romantic Poetry*, ed. James Chandler and Maureen N. McLane (Cambridge: Cambridge University Press, 2008), 195–216.

17. Rackin, *Stages of History*, 154–55; Brian Walsh, "'Unkind Division': The Double Absence of Performing History in *1 Henry VI*," *Shakespeare Quarterly* 55, no. 2 (2004): 119–47, 123, 146–47; and Walsh, *Shakespeare, the Queen's Men, and the Elizabethan Performance of History* (Cambridge: Cambridge University Press, 2009). I am here revisiting the challenges I pose to such readings in "The Talbot Remains," which also thinks in depth about Derrida's *Archive Fever* in relation to Shakespeare's history plays, focusing on Lord Talbot in particular.

18. J. L. Austin, *How to Do Things with Words* (New York: Clarendon, 1962).

19. Madhavi Menon suggests the utility of the Shakespearean text for engaging and disrupting contemporary theory, specifically queer theory. See "Queer Shakes," her introduction to *Shakesqueer: A Queer Companion to the Complete Works of Shakespeare*, ed. Madhavi Menon (Durham, NC: Duke University Press, 2011), 1–27, esp. 3. For a useful reflection on the notion of theory being "Shaken" (Menon's term) by the works of Shakespeare, see Stephen Guy-Bray, *Shakespeare and Queer Representation* (New York: Routledge, 2021), 2–3.

20. On Scharf's habits and obsessions, see National Portrait Gallery, "The Gallery's First Director George Scharf Had a Fascination for the Macabre," Facebook, October 31, 2019, https://www.facebook.com/nationalportraitgallery/videos/423585408341063. Warhol collected artifacts from his daily life in boxes he titled *Time Capsules*, which are the subject of a considerable, if sometimes perplexed, scholarly literature.

21. Derrida, *Archive Fever*, 4n1.

22. Roland Barthes, *Camera Lucida: Reflections on Photography*, trans. Richard Howard (New York: Hill and Wang, 1980), 95.

23. *The Oxford Shakespeare* uses play titles from the First Quartos of *2 Henry VI* and *3 Henry VI*, published in 1594 and 1595, respectively. Those titles are *The First Part of the Contention of the Two Famous Houses of York and Lancaster with the Death of the Good Duke Humphrey* and *The True Tragedy of Richard, Duke of York, and the Good King Henry the Sixth*. Following the convention established by the First Folio (1623) of referring to these two plays as second and third parts of *Henry VI*, I refer to them as *2 Henry VI* and *3 Henry VI*.

1. Little, Little Graves

1. Unless otherwise noted, all quotations of Shakespeare's plays are from William Shakespeare, *The Oxford Shakespeare: The Complete Works*, ed. Stanley Wells and Gary Taylor (Oxford: Clarendon, 1988), cited parenthetically. For a useful comparison of the deposition scene of *Richard II* with the procedures for Richard's abdication in Holinshed's *Chronicles*, see Maggie Vinter, *Last Acts: The Art of Dying on the Early Modern Stage* (New York: Fordham University Press, 2019), 103–4.

2. I here follow the 1608 Quarto, which repeats "Was this the face" in all three iterations, in contrast to the First Quarto and First Folio, which have "Is this the face" in the third iteration. See *The tragedie of King Richard the second As it hath been publickly acted by the Right Honourable the Lord Chamberlaine his seuantes. By William Shake-speare* (London, 1608), sig. H3.

3. A-text of Christopher Marlowe, *Doctor Faustus: A Two-Text Edition*, ed. David Scott Kastan (New York: Norton, 2005), 5.1.90. On the relationship between *Richard II* and Marlowe, see Paul Menzer, "cf., Marlowe," in *Richard II: New Critical Essays*, ed. Jeremy Lopez (New York: Routledge, 2012), 117–34.

4. Ernst H. Kantorowicz, *The King's Two Bodies: A Study in Medieval Political Theology* (Princeton, NJ: Princeton University Press, 1957), 195–96. On the historicity of Kantorowicz's own discussion of the king's two bodies and subsequent distortions generated in old and new historicism that relies on him, see David Norbrook, "The Emperor's New Body? *Richard II*, Ernst Kantorowicz, and the Politics of Shakespeare Criticism," *Textual Practice* 10, no. 2 (1996), 329–57. On the idiosyncrasies of Kantorowicz's concept of the king's two bodies, particularly in relation to one of his principal sources, Henri de Lubac's 1944 *Corpus Mysticum*, see Jennifer R. Rust, *The Body in Mystery: The Political Theology of the 'Corpus Mysticum' in the Literature of Reformation England* (Evanston, IL: Northwestern University Press, 2014).

5. Kantorowicz, *The King's Two Bodies*, 26.

6. Victoria Kahn, "Political Theology and Fiction in *The King's Two Bodies*," *Representations* 106, no. 1 (2009), 77–101, 87. In the same issue of *Representations*, which assesses the legacy of Kantorowicz, Richard Halpern observes that the book's conversation between the concept of the king's two bodies and the aesthetics of *Richard II* works in both directions: *Richard II* provides "a compendium of intellectual strategies" for Kantorowicz's "poetic" yet "bureaucratic tome." See Richard Halpern, "The King's Two Buckets: Kantorowicz, *Richard II*, and Fiscal *Trauerspiel*," *Representations* 106, no. 1 (Spring 2009), 67–76, 74. Norbrook notes how the king's two bodies has "often been seen as a keystone of Elizabethan theories of language and representation" and thereby as a concept of semiotic unity ("The Emperor's New Body?," 329).

7. Roland Barthes, *Camera Lucida: Reflections on Photography*, trans. Richard Howard (New York: Hill and Wang, 1980), 95–96.

8. Barthes, *Camera Lucida*, 31–32.

9. Seminal studies of Shakespeare and the iconographic tradition include John Doebler, *Shakespeare's Speaking Pictures: Studies in Iconic Imagery* (Albuquerque: New Mexico University Press, 1974); M. H. Fleischer, *The Iconography of the English History Play* (Salzburg: Institut für Englische Sprache und Literatur, 1974); and James Siemon, *Shakespearean Iconoclasm* (Berkeley: University of California Press, 1985). Pertinent criticism on *Richard II* and the visual arts includes Ernest B. Gilman on painting in "*Richard II* and the Perspectives of History," *Renaissance Drama* 17 (1976), 85–115, esp. 105–10; Phyllis Rackin on temporality and pageantry in *Stages of History: Shakespeare's English Chronicles* (Ithaca, NY: Cornell University Press, 1990), 119–20; and Carol Banks and Graham Holderness, "'Mine Eye Hath Play'd the Painter,'" in *Shakespeare and the Visual Arts*, Shakespeare Yearbook, ed. Holger Klein and James L. Harner, vol. 11 (Lewiston, NY: Edwin Mellen Press, 2000), 454–73. For a discussion of static tableaux in historical drama and their implications for theories of history, see Philip Lorenz, "'In the Course and Process of Time': Rupture, Reflection and Repetition in *Henry VIII*," in *Temporality, Genre and Experience in the Age of Shakespeare: Forms of Time*, ed. Lauren Shohet (London: Arden, 2018), 61–80. For an account of stage productions that have represented Richard iconographically, see Jeremy Lopez, "Introduction," in *Richard II: New Critical Essays*, ed. Jeremy Lopez (New York: Routledge, 2012), 1–48, esp. 7–10.

The BBC's *Richard II* episode of *The Hollow Crown* draws sustained visual parallels between Richard's tragedy and iconography of the Crucifixion and St. Sebastian.

10. Jonathan Gil Harris, *Untimely Matter in the Time of Shakespeare* (Philadelphia: University of Pennsylvania Press, 2009), 2. For a bibliography related to temporal models that have been influential in early modern studies, see my Introduction to this book, n14. Mark Netzloff invokes Michel Serres's and Bruno Latour's theories of time in "Insurgent Time: *Richard II* and the Periodization of Sovereignty," in *Richard II: New Critical Essays*, ed. Jeremy Lopez (New York: Routledge, 2012), 202–22.

11. Rebecca Schneider, *Performing Remains: Art and War in Times of Reenactment* (New York: Routledge, 2011), 161.

12. In this chapter, as throughout this book, I contest the assumption that "rethinking or even challenging historical periodization inevitably requires the use of historical periods," as articulated by Kristen Poole and Owen Williams, eds., *Early Modern Histories of Time: The Periodizations of Sixteenth- and Seventeenth-Century England* (Philadelphia: University of Pennsylvania Press, 2019), 1–17, 10.

13. Barthes, *Camera Lucida*, 10–12.

14. See especially chapters 3 and 5 in this book.

15. Barthes, *Camera Lucida*, 14.

16. Barthes, *Camera Lucida*, 12, 14.

17. Barthes, *Camera Lucida*, 14.

18. Samuel Daniel, *The First Four Books of the Civil Wars between the Two Houses of Lancaster and York* (1595). Quoted in William Shakespeare, *The Tragedy of Richard the Second*, ed. Charles R. Forker, Arden Third Series (London: Bloomsbury, 2002), 281n.

19. Scott McMillin, "Shakespeare's Richard II: Eyes of Sorrow, Eyes of Desire," *Shakespeare Quarterly* 35, no. 1 (1984), 40–52, 41–42.

20. Bushy's reference to "perspectives" has attracted significant critical commentary, much of it contextualizing his remarks alongside sixteenth-century developments in optics and painting, particularly the exemplary anamorphic skull in Hans Holbein's *The Ambassadors*. See, for example, Marjorie Garber, *Shakespeare After All* (New York: Pantheon, 2004), 266–67; Gilman, "*Richard II* and the Perspectives of History," 93–105; Christopher Pye, *The Regnal Phantasm: Shakespeare and the Politics of Spectacle* (New York: Routledge, 1990), 89–91; and Matthew D. Wagner, *Shakespeare, Theatre, and Time* (New York: Routledge, 2012), 41–43.

21. Peggy Phelan, "Haunted Stages: Performance and the Photographic Effect," in Jennifer Blessing and Nat Trotman, *Haunted: Contemporary Photography/Video/Performance* (New York: Guggenheim Foundation, 2010), 50–63, 52.

22. Musee d'Orsay, "Oscar Gustave Rejlander, *The First Negative*," curator notes, accessed February 8, 2021, https://www.musee-orsay.fr/fr/oeuvres/first-negative -164048?S=2&cHash=b42cb0c65a&tx_commentaire_pi1%5BpidLi%5D=847&tx _commentaire_pi1%5Bfrom%5D=844.

23. Musee d'Orsay, "Oscar Gustave Rejlander." See also Lori Pauli, ed., *Acting the Part: Photography as Theatre* (New York: Merrell, 2006), 26; and Jean-Christophe Bailly, *The Instant and Its Shadow: A Story of Photography*, trans. Samuel E. Martin (New York: Fordham University Press, 2020).

24. Barthes, *Camera Lucida*, 79.

25. Bailly, *The Instant and Its Shadow*, 6.

26. Kantorowicz, *The King's Two Bodies*, 338.

27. Pye, *The Regnal Phantasm*, 93.

28. Barthes, *Camera Lucida*, 96.

29. Sigmund Freud, "The Uncanny," in *On Creativity and the Unconscious*, ed. Benjamin Nelson, trans. Alix Strachey (New York: Harper and Brothers, 1958), 122–61, 123–24.

30. Charles R. Forker, ed., *The Tragedy of Richard the Second*, Arden Third Series (London: Bloomsbury, 2002), 3.2.150n; and Andrew Gurr, ed., *King Richard II* (Cambridge: Cambridge University Press, 2003), 3.2.155n.

31. Barthes, *Camera Lucida*, 14.

32. Vinter, *Last Acts*, 91. See also Andrew Griffin, *Untimely Deaths in Renaissance Drama: Biography, History, Catastrophe* (Toronto: University of Toronto Press, 2020). Griffin observes that "Richard continues to live as a spectral agent in Shakespeare's later history plays" (35). See also Marjorie Garber, *Shakespeare's Ghost Writers: Literature as Uncanny Causality* (New York: Routledge, 1987), 20–21.

33. See Pye, *The Regnal Phantasm*, 94, 100.

34. Barthes, *Camera Lucida*, 96.

35. Vinter, *Last Acts*, 92. Vinter adds, citing Zenón Luis-Martínez, that the phrase "hollow crown" is suggestive of both the actual crown and a skull. This reading resonates with my discussion of Sir George Scharf's drawing of Richard's skull in the Introduction. See Vinter (93) and Zenón Luis-Martínez, "Shakespeare's Historical Drama as *Trauerspiel: Richard II* and After," *ELH* 75, no. 3 (2008), 673–705, 689.

36. *Henry V*, in Shakespeare, *The Oxford Shakespeare*.

37. On Richard's role as a dramatist, see McMillin, "Shakespeare's Richard II: Eyes of Sorrow."

38. On Richard's development into an object of the gaze, see Richard Ashby, "'Pierced to the soul': The Politics of the Gaze in *Richard II*," *Shakespeare* 11, no. 2 (2015), 201–13. Ashby's discussion hinges on a Lacanian difference between the eye and the gaze, especially Lacan's suggestion that the gaze translates subjects into objects. See Jacques Lacan, "Of the Gaze as *Objet Petit a*" in *The Four Fundamental Concepts of Psycho-Analysis*, trans. Alan Sheridan (London: Penguin, 1979), 67–119.

39. See "camera, n.," *OED Online*, July 2018, Oxford University Press.

40. See, for example, Katie Warfield, "Digital Subjectivities and Selfies: The Model, the Self-Conscious Thespian, and the #realme," *International Journal of the Image* 6, no. 2 (2015), 1–16. On the motif of mirror images within the tradition of photographic self-portraiture, see Alec Mackenzie, "The Age of the Selfie," *Royal Photographic Society (RPS) Journal* 154, no. 5 (2014), 288–93, especially his mention of the *Invisible* series by Laura Williams (293).

41. In reading Richard's image as a selfie, I seek to complicate the claim that he wants to disappear, advanced by McMillin, "Shakespeare's Richard II: Eyes of Sorrow," 49; Lopez, "Introduction," 14, 16, and 35; and Donovan Sherman, "'What More Remains?': Messianic Performance in *Richard II*," *Shakespeare Quarterly* 65, no. 1 (Spring 2014), 22–48.

42. On the authority of photographic captioning, see Susan Sontag, *On Photography* (New York: Picador, 1973), 107–10.

43. On the significance of the deictic gesture of epitaphs, see Scott L. Newstok, *Quoting Death in Early Modern England: The Poetics of Epitaphs beyond the Tomb* (New

York: Palgrave, 2009), chap. 1. For a discussion of the history plays' epitaphic gestures, broadly conceived, see Emily Shortslef, "Acting as an Epitaph: Performing Commemoration in the Shakespearean History Play," *Critical Survey* 22, no. 2 (2010), 11–24.

44. William Camden, *Annales* (1625), 1.26, quoted in Newstok, *Quoting Death in Early Modern England*, 66.

45. Newstok, *Quoting Death in Early Modern England*, 63.

46. On the crime of imagining the king's death, see John Bellamy, *The Tudor Law of Treason: An Introduction* (London: Routledge & Kegan Paul, 1979), 30–33; Karen Cunningham, *Imaginary Betrayals: Subjectivity and the Discourses of Treason in Early Modern England* (Philadelphia: University of Pennsylvania Press, 2002),1–22; and Rebecca Lemon, *Treason by Words: Literature, Law, and Rebellion in Shakespeare's England* (Ithaca, NY: Cornell University Press, 2006), 1–10.

47. I thus disagree with H. Austin Whitver's assertion that Richard's imagined tomb "becomes an icon of monarchical insufficiency" and that by picturing his own death, he "create[s] a static identity." See H. Austin Whitver, "Materiality of Memory in Shakespeare's Second Tetralogy," *SEL* 56, no. 2 (2016), 285–306, esp. 289, 291.

48. Schneider, *Performing Remains*, 162.

49. Schneider, *Performing Remains*, 22.

50. Schneider, *Performing Remains*, 162.

51. Daniel Sack, *After Live: Possibility, Potentiality, and the Future of Performance* (Ann Arbor, University of Michigan Press, 2015), 6.

52. Sack, *After Live*, 18, 81.

53. Sontag, *On Photography*, 154.

54. Barthes, *Camera Lucida*, 76, 78.

55. Debora Shuger notes that "the mirrors pictured in Renaissance texts are, in fact, often paintings. The concepts frequently seem interchangeable." Her survey of how mirrors are imagined in texts from the period concludes that mirroring is rarely "used as a paradigm for reflexive self-consciousness" and notes Richard's use as an exception. See Debora Shuger, "The 'I' of the Beholder: Renaissance Mirrors and the Reflexive Mind," in *Renaissance Culture and the Everyday*, ed. Patricia Fumerton and Simon Hunt (Philadelphia: University of Pennsylvania Press, 1999), 21–41, esp. 30–31. On Renaissance mirror technologies, see also Rayna Kalas, *Frame, Glass, Verse: The Technology of Poetic Invention in the English Renaissance* (Ithaca, NY: Cornell University Press, 2007), chap. 4.

56. Barthes, *Camera Lucida*, 77, 76.

57. In his study of literary uses of the mirror, Herbert Grabes notes that mirror images are often associated with "a personified Death, who may also appear in the mirror." See Herbert Grabes, *The Mutable Glass: Mirror-imagery in Titles and Texts of the Middle Ages and English Renaissance*, trans. Gordon Collier (New York: Cambridge University Press, 1982), 119. The linings of some mirrors, called *miroirs de mort*, were painted with a death's head.

58. Sontag, *On Photography*, 71.

59. Sontag, *On Photography*, 24. Sontag reassesses some of her conclusions about photography dulling ethical action in *Regarding the Pain of Others* (New York: Picador, 2003), chap. 7.

60. Sontag, *On Photography*, 80, 67.

61. Sontag, *On Photography*, 67.

62. In describing Richard as generating nostalgia for a self he is rendering as past, my claim here is related but slightly different from J. K. Barret's notion of "anticipatory nostalgia," by which she means "looking forward to looking back" or imagining a future in which the past will be worth looking back on or "worth remembering." By contrast, Richard looks forward *in order to* look back. He constructs a future self in order to look back at his present self, who becomes past. See J. K. Barret, *Untold Futures: Time and Literary Culture in Renaissance England* (Ithaca, NY: Cornell University Press, 2016), 21, 4, 166, and chap. 4 more generally. Barret's book pays particularly useful attention to how aesthetic elements of early modern literature construct temporal possibility.

63. Grabes, *The Mutable Glass*, 111.

64. Reading the play in the context of influential Senecan notions of selfhood, Jonathan P. Lamb likewise concludes, contra Kantorowicz, that Richard's rhetorical division into multiple selves signals self-possession rather than fragmentation, a claim that resonates with my argument here. See Jonathan P. Lamb, "The Stylistic Self in *Richard II*," *Medieval and Renaissance Drama in England* 28 (2015), 123–51.

65. On the display of Richard in his coffin in Shakespeare's play and Holinshed's *Chronicles*, see Jeremy Lopez, "Eating Richard II," *Shakespeare Studies* 36 (2008), 207–28, esp. 214–15.

66. "Sonnet 55," in Shakespeare, *The Oxford Shakespeare*, 757, line 11.

67. Noting the historical event of Richard's reburial and Henry V's reference to this event in *Henry V*, Griffin suggestively observes that the persistent Richard "require[es] more than one burial" (Griffin, *Untimely Deaths*, 35–36).

2. Haunted Histories

1. Unless otherwise noted, all quotations of Shakespeare's plays are from William Shakespeare, *The Oxford Shakespeare: The Complete Works*, ed. Stanley Wells and Gary Taylor (Oxford: Clarendon, 1988), cited parenthetically.

2. Biblical quotations are from the Geneva Bible.

3. Thomas Nashe, *Piers Penniless His Supplication to the Devil*, in *The Works of Thomas Nashe*, ed. Ronald B. McKerrow, revised by F. P. Wilson, vol. 1 (Oxford: Basil Blackwell, 1958), 137–246, 212. See also Alice Dailey, "The Talbot Remains: Historical Drama and the Performative Archive," *Shakespeare Bulletin* 35, no. 3 (2017): 373–87, 374–76, where I discuss this passage from Nashe at greater length. On the likelihood of the passage being a description of Shakespeare's *1 Henry VI*, see Edward Burns, ed., *King Henry IV, Part I*, Arden Third Series (London: Bloomsbury, 2000), 1–6.

4. Marvin Carlson, *The Haunted Stage: The Theatre as Memory Machine* (Ann Arbor: University of Michigan Press, 2001), 1; quoting Herbert Blau, *The Eye of Prey* (Bloomington: Indiana University Press, 1987), 173, italics in the original. I treat Carlson's specific notion of theatrical "ghosting" more fully in an essay on Michael Boyd's 2008 staging of Shakespeare's eight English chronicle plays at the Royal Shakespeare Company (RSC), an event that significantly influenced my thinking in this book. See Alice Dailey, "The RSC's 'Glorious Moment' and the Making of Shakespearean History," *Shakespeare Survey* 63 (2010): 184–97.

5. Rebecca Schneider, *Performing Remains: Art and War in Times of Theatrical Reenactment* (New York: Routledge, 2011), 109, italics in the original.

6. Roland Barthes, *Camera Lucida: Reflections on Photography*, trans. Richard Howard (New York: Hill and Wang, 1980), 14.

7. Derrida's translator, Peggy Kamuf, writes, "A common term for a ghost or specter, the *revenant* is literally that which comes back." See Jacques Derrida, *Specters of Marx: The State of the Debt, the Work of Mourning and the New International*, trans. Peggy Kamuf (New York: Routledge, 1993), 224n1. On the specter and deconstruction, Derrida writes, "The spectral logic is *de facto* a deconstructive logic. It is in the element of haunting that deconstruction finds the place most hospitable to it, at the heart of the living present, in the quickest heartbeat of the philosophical." See Jacques Derrida and Bernard Stiegler, "Spectrographies," in *Echographies of Television: Filmed Interviews*, trans. Jennifer Bajorek (Cambridge: Polity Press, 2002), 117. See also Peter Buse and Andrew Scott, "Introduction: A Future for Haunting," in *Ghosts: Deconstruction, Psychoanalysis, History*, ed. Peter Buse and Andrew Scott (New York: Palgrave, 1999), 1–20.

8. Derrida, *Specters*, 166, italics and ellipsis in original.

9. Derrida, *Specters*, 63.

10. Derrida, *Specters*, 96.

11. Stephen Greenblatt, *Shakespearean Negotiations: The Circulation of Social Energy in Renaissance England* (Berkeley: University of California Press, 1988), 1.

12. Derrida, *Specters*, 12.

13. Buse and Scott, "Introduction: A Future for Haunting," 14.

14. For a summary and bibliography of New Historicist readings of the *Henry IV* plays as well as responses to those readings, see Giorgio Melchiori, ed., *The Second Part of King Henry IV* (Cambridge: Cambridge University Press, 2007), 58–60.

15. For a useful discussion of Mumler in the context of Derridean hauntology, see the concluding chapter, "Spooked Theories: Deconstruction, Psychoanalysis, and the Specters of Mumler," in Louis Kaplan, *The Strange Case of William Mumler Spirit Photographer* (Minneapolis: University of Minnesota Press, 2008), 211–56.

16. Crista Cloutier, "Mumler's Ghosts," in *The Perfect Medium: Photography and the Occult*, ed. Clément Chéroux et al. (New Haven, CT: Yale University Press, 2004), 20–28, 20. Molly McGarry usefully describes spiritualism as "the faith that this world and the next were merely two stages in an unbroken process." See Molly McGarry, *Ghosts of Futures Past: Spiritualism and the Cultural Politics of Nineteenth-Century America* (Berkeley: University of California Press, 2008), 9.

17. Tom Gunning, "Phantom Images and Modern Manifestations: Spirit Photography, Magic Theater, Trick Films, and Photography's Uncanny," in *Fugitive Images: From Photography to Video*, ed. Patrice Petro (Bloomington: Indiana University Press, 1995): 42–71.

18. McGarry, *Ghosts of Futures Past*, 18, italics mine.

19. Paola Cortés-Rocca notes how portraits like that of Mary Todd Lincoln frame the primary subject awkwardly, leaving significant empty space above her head. The ghosts "know the rules of the genre well enough to stand behind [the subjects] and to occupy the empty spaces that had been left and which, without their presence, would have been absolutely useless." See Paola Cortés-Rocca, "Ghost in the Machine: Photographs of Specters in the Nineteenth Century," *Mosaic: An Interdisciplinary Critical Journal* 38, no. 1 (2005): 151–68, 157.

20. On such controversies, see Cloutier, "Mumler's Ghosts"; Cortés-Rocca, "Ghost in the Machine"; Gunning, "Phantom Images"; and Andreas Fischer, "'A Photographer

of Marvels': Frederick Hudson and the Beginnings of Spirit Photography in Europe," in *The Perfect Medium: Photography and the Occult*, ed. Clément Chéroux et al. (New Haven, CT: Yale University Press, 2004), 29–43.

21. Gunning, "Phantom Images"; and Fischer, "'A Photographer of Marvels.'"

22. Fischer, "'A Photographer of Marvels,'" 32.

23. Gunning, "Phantom Images," 65–66.

24. William Crookes, the inventor of the Crookes tube, was a scientist as well as an ardent spiritualist. He served as president of both the British Royal Society and the Society for Psychical Research, organizations that we would now consider antithetical to one another. He is a useful example of how scientific study and spiritualist belief frequently overlapped in the period. See Gunning, "Phantom Images," 54–56; and McGarry, *Ghosts of Futures Past*, 106–7, 128–29.

25. Corey Keller, "Sight Unseen: Picturing the Invisible," in *Brought to Light: Photography and the Invisible, 1840–1900*, ed. Corey Keller (New Haven, CT: Yale University Press, 2008), 19–35, 33.

26. Allen W. Grove, "Röntgen's Ghosts: Photography, X-Rays, and the Victorian Imagination," *Literature and Medicine* 16, no. 2 (1997): 141–73, 142.

27. Derrida, *Specters*, 217.

28. Nicholas Abraham, "Notes on the Phantom: A Complement to Freud's Metapsychology," in *The Shell and the Kernel: Renewals of Psychoanalysis*, by Nicholas Abraham and Maria Torok, trans. Nicholas T. Rand (Chicago: University of Chicago Press, 1994), 171–76, 175, italics in the original. The psychoanalytic work of Abraham and Torok was brought to international attention by Derrida. On the distinction between their concept of the specter and Derrida's, see Colin Davis, *Haunted Subjects: Deconstruction, Psychoanalysis, and the Return of the Dead* (New York: Palgrave, 2007), esp. chap. 1. For Freud's discussion of the concepts of the *heimlich* and *unheimlich*, see Sigmund Freud, "The Uncanny," in *On Creativity and the Unconscious*, ed. Benjamin Nelson, trans. Alix Strachey (New York: Harper and Row, 1958), 122–61, esp. 1–4. On the concept of the *unheimlich* in Derrida's hauntology, see Buse and Scott, "Introduction: A Future for Haunting."

29. Derrida, *Specters*, 166.

30. Derrida, *Specters*, 169, 136, 176–77.

31. Derrida, *Specters*, 131.

32. Martin Friedman, "Foreword," in *Vanishing Presence*, ed. Martin Friedman et al., (Minneapolis: Walker Art Center/Rizzoli, 1989), 6–7. Linda Benedict-Jones and Max Kozloff explicitly link Michals's use of double exposure to earlier spirit photography. See Linda Benedict-Jones, "Duane Michals: Storyteller," in *Storyteller: The Photographs of Duane Michals*, ed. Linda Benedict-Jones (New York: DelMonico Books, 2014), 18–57, 42; and Max Kozloff, *Duane Michals: Now Becoming Then* (Altadena, CA: Twin Palms, 1990), 15v. Kozloff's introductory essay in *Now Becoming Then* is unpaginated and alternates black and white pages. I have assigned it conventional recto/verso page numbers.

33. Michals explores this final question more overtly in *The Man in the Room* (1975). Kozloff writes of Michals's double exposures, "Each symbolizes that the protagonist or the viewer is looking into the scene from across a mortal divide. Too bad that Michals doesn't always clarify which side of that divide they find themselves on" (Kozloff, *Now Becoming Then*, 9v).

34. Derrida, *Specters*, 5.

35. Buse and Scott, "Introduction: A Future for Haunting," 12.

36. Buse and Scott, "Introduction: A Future for Haunting," 1.

37. Duane Michals, "This Is a Real Dream (1974): Duane Michals Interviewed by William Jenkins," in *Storyteller: The Photographs of Duane Michals*, ed. Linda Benedict-Jones (New York: DelMonico Books, 2015), 84–88, 86.

38. Derrida, *Specters*, xviii; italics in the original.

39. On Michals as a theatrical photographer, particularly by contrast to the Western tradition's treatment of photography as a documentary medium, see Michals, "This is a Real Dream"; and Kozloff, *Now Becoming Then*, 5r–v. Elsewhere, Kozloff notes that Michals has been "frequently and rightly accused of a literary bent." See Max Kozloff, "The Etherealized Figure and the Dream of Wisdom," in *Vanishing Presence*, ed. Martin Friedman et al. (Minneapolis: Walker Art Center / Rizzoli, 1989), 30–61, 56. Benedict-Jones compares Michals's sequences to Alexander Gardener's photographs of the execution of the Lincoln conspirators, who include Lewis Payne (see chapter 1), and to the famous staged photograph of a death scene, *Fading Away* (1858), by nineteenth-century British photographer Henry Peach Robinson; see Benedict-Jones, "Duane Michals: Storyteller," 24, 26. Kozloff includes nineteenth-century Swedish photomontagist Oscar Gustave Rejlander (also discussed in chapter 1) as another precursor to Michals (Kozloff, *Now Becoming Then*, 3v). For Michals's thoughts on photography as a mode of invention rather than documentation, see Duane Michals, "Duane Michals Speaks with Enrica Viganò," in *Storyteller: The Photographs of Duane Michals*, ed. Linda Benedict-Jones (New York: DelMonico Books, 2015), 116–21, esp. 118.

40. Clément Chéroux, "Ghost Dialectics: Spirit Photography in Entertainment and Belief," in *The Perfect Medium: Photography and the Occult*, ed. Clément Chéroux et al. (New Haven, CT: Yale University Press, 2004), 45–71, 53.

41. Gunning, "Phantom Images," 51; Cortés-Rocca, "Ghost in the Machine," 151. For the history of this usage of the word "extra," see "extra, n., 2," *OED Online*, June 2020, Oxford University Press.

42. Cloutier, "Mumler's Ghosts," 21.

43. Tom Gunning, "Invisible Worlds, Visible Media," in *Brought to Light: Photography and the Invisible, 1840–1900*, ed. Corey Keller (New Haven, CT: Yale University Press, 2008), 51–63, 60. Gunning notes that "nearly every major illusionist of the nineteenth century offered a 'fake Spiritualist' show aimed at debunking rivals by presenting the same phenomena as illusions, exposing the means pretend séances used to achieve their effects" (60). See also Gunning, "Phantom Images." Steven Connor describes the séance as both a "laboratory" and a "stage," suggesting how scientific investigation and entertainment overlapped in spiritualist practice. See Steven Connor, "The Machine in the Ghost: Spiritualism, Technology and the 'Direct Voice,'" in *Ghosts: Deconstruction, Psychoanalysis, History*, ed. Peter Buse and Andrew Scott (New York: Palgrave, 1999), 203–25, 204.

44. Gunning, "Invisible Worlds," 52. Gunning goes on to remark that "although [cinema and X-ray] may strike us as antithetical, they were occasionally fused in the public imagination. Some early journalistic accounts even claimed that cinematic images were produced using X-rays" (53). I would argue that the contemporary practice of displaying X-rays on a computer monitor or other illuminated screen retains aspects of the X-ray's history as a cinematic spectacle.

45. Derrida, *Specters*, xx, 14, italics in the original.

46. Kozloff, *Now Becoming Then*, 11r, 5v.

47. Derrida, *Specters*, xix.

48. Derrida, *Specters*, 10, 11.

49. For an influential discussion of how theater of the period complicates distinctions between real and represented royalty, see David Scott Kastan, "Proud Majesty Made a Subject: Shakespeare and the Spectacle of Rule," *Shakespeare Quarterly* 37, no. 4 (1986): 459–75. More recently, Vimala Pasupathi has argued that the motif of soldiers dressed in the king's coats suggests how the military has a "metonymic association with the body of the ruling monarch." See Vimala C. Pasupathi, "Coats and Conduct: The Materials of Military Obligation in Shakespeare's *Henry IV* and *Henry V*," *Modern Philology* 109, no. 3 (2012): 326–51, 333. Barbara Hodgdon expresses both of these positions in her observation that "having others march in the King's armor represents the King's body both as powerfully doubled and redoubled in his subjects and as an empty lie." See Barbara Hodgdon, *The End Crowns All: Closure and Contradiction in Shakespeare's History* (Princeton, NJ: Princeton University Press, 1991), 158.

50. Douglas uses "bought" again after killing Blunt: "A borrowed title hast thou bought too dear" (*1H4* 5.3.23).

51. Kiernan Ryan's description of this scene, which "breeds a multiplicity of sovereigns," usefully links the theatrical production of Henry doubles to reproduction or breeding. See Kiernan Ryan, "The Future of History: *1* and *2 Henry IV*," in *Shakespeare's History Plays*, ed. R. J. C. Watt (New York: Longman, 2002), 147–68, 158.

52. Hodgdon, *The End Crowns All*, 159. Hodgdon also observes that the couplet that concludes Hal's epitaph on Hotspur and Falstaff (5.4.108–9) cues a sense of the play ending.

53. Susan Zimmerman, *The Early Modern Corpse and Shakespeare's Theatre* (Edinburgh: Edinburgh University Press, 2005), 12.

54. Carlson, *The Haunted Stage*, 7.

55. David Scott Kastan, ed. *King Henry IV, Part 1*, Arden Third Series (London: Bloomsbury, 2002), 64.

56. Jean Baudrillard, *Simulacra and Simulation*, trans. Sheila Faria Glaser (Ann Arbor: University of Michigan Press, 1994), 1, italics in the original.

57. Baudrillard, *Simulacra and Simulation*, 6.

58. Kastan, *King Henry IV, Part 1*, 5.4.121–2n.

59. This episode occurs in *The Aeneid*, Book 2.

60. John Kerrigan, "*Henry IV* and the Death of Old Double (1990)," in *On Shakespeare and Early Modern Literature: Essays* (Oxford: Oxford University Press, 2001), 66–88, 77.

61. The links between Falstaff and the historical figure of Sir John Oldcastle, the name that the character had in its early performances, have been a subject of much critical discussion. Kastan tellingly describes "Oldcastle" as "a name which, even erased, continues to haunt the play" as "the ghostly Oldcastle, who has not quite been exorcized" (Kastan, *King Henry IV, Part 1*, 52, 55) and further discusses the renaming of Oldcastle to Falstaff (51–62); see also David Scott Kastan, *Shakespeare after Theory* (New York: Routledge, 1999), 93–108. On the implications of Shakespeare's original naming of the character after Sir John Oldcastle, a Lollard martyr, see Kristen Poole, *Radical Religion from Shakespeare to Milton* (Cambridge: Cambridge University Press, 2000), 16–44; and

Jonathan Baldo, *Memory in Shakespeare's Histories: Stages of Forgetting in Early Modern England* (New York: Routledge, 2012), 51–72. Evan Choate usefully relates editorial attempts to resolve the identity of Falstaff/Oldcastle to the Henriad's purposive destabilizing of historical origins. See Evan Choate, "Staged History and Alternative Sir Johns," *Shakespeare Quarterly* 70, no. 3 (2019): 207–229.

62. See, for example, Herbert Weil and Judith Weil, eds., *The First Part of King Henry IV*, New Cambridge Shakespeare (Cambridge: Cambridge University Press, 1997), 5.4.133n.; A. R. Humphreys, ed., *King Henry IV, Part I*, Arden First Series (London: Methuen, 1960) 5.4.137n; and Kastan, *King Henry IV, Part 1*, 5.4.138n. In addition to a number of other readings of this line, Baldo connects the "duplicity" of Falstaff's response—its double meaning—to the character's doubleness as both Falstaff and Old-castle, with Oldcastle "peek[ing] out from behind the massive girth of Falstaff, reminding us of the palimpsest-like quality of the character" (Baldo, *Memory in Shakespeare's Histories*, 56).

63. Mumler's portrait of the Lincolns also resonates intriguingly with the tableau reproduced in these two moments from *2 Henry VI* and *1 Henry IV*, in which a dead person is draped over the back of a living one. Like Falstaff, Mrs. Lincoln appears in the Mumler portrait as a ghostly double of her living self, the death-effects of the photographic form revealing her inhabitation with her own specter. Resting on her shoulders, like Hotspur on Falstaff's back, is another specter who is both other and self, both past and past's future.

64. By one count, there are 64 occurrences of "death," "die," and their cognates in *2 Henry IV*, more than in any other play of the second tetralogy. See Rebecca Warren-Heys, "Death and Memory in Shakespeare's *2 Henry IV*," *HARTS & Minds: The Journal of Humanities and Arts* 1, no. 3 (2013–14): 1–15, 2.

65. The quotation is from Meredith Evans, "Rumor, the Breath of Kings, and the Body of Law in *2 Henry IV*," *Shakespeare Quarterly* 60, no. 1 (2009): 1–24, 5. The claim about Rumour's challenge to the reliability of historical narratives is made, for example, by Loren M. Blinde, "Rumored History in Shakespeare's *2 Henry IV*," *English Literary Renaissance* 38, no. 1 (2008): 34–54.

66. On the duplication of "Bardolph" among the characters' names, see Melchiori, *The Second Part of King Henry IV*, 15–16; and Choate, "Staged History," who argues that confusion between the earlier Bardolph and this "alt-Bardolph" is exactly the point (220).

67. Baldo, *Memory in Shakespeare's Histories*, suggests that Morton's name is a pun on *"la mort"* (98).

68. See Ryan, "The Future of History." Although he does not discuss this scene of the play, Ryan observes that the characters of *2 Henry IV* "afford us a proleptic glimpse through their eyes of the future in the past" (162). I would argue that such a future-in-the-past is observed by the characters themselves.

69. James C. Bulman, ed., *King Henry IV, Part Two*, Arden Third Series (London: Bloomsbury, 2016), 1–2, quoting Stephen Booth, "Shakespeare in the San Francisco Bay Area," *Shakespeare Quarterly* 29, no. 2 (1978), 267–78, 270. In his criticism of these attitudes toward *2 Henry IV*, Jonathan Crewe complains that they treat the play as "a diminished repetition," a phrase that resonates with the spectral double. See Jonathan

Crewe, "Reforming Prince Hal: The Sovereign Inheritor in *2 Henry IV*," *Renaissance Drama* 21 (1990): 225–42, 227.

70. Richard David, "Shakespeare's History Plays—Epic or Drama?," *Shakespeare Survey* 6 (1953): 129–39, 137.

71. Bulman, *King Henry IV, Part Two*, 3, 18.

72. Harry Berger Jr., "On the Continuity of the *Henriad*: A Critique of Some Literary and Theatrical Approaches," in *Shakespeare Left and Right*, ed. Ivo Kamps (New York: Routledge, 1991), 225–40, 236.

73. Bulman, *King Henry IV, Part Two*, 3–16.

74. Bulman, 59. See also Baldo, *Memory in Shakespeare's Histories*, chap. 3.

75. Derrida, *Specters*, 6.

76. Nicholas Grene, *Shakespeare's Serial History Plays* (Cambridge: Cambridge University Press, 2002), 212.

77. Melchiori, *The Second Part of King Henry IV*, 18. For Melchiori, this treatment of Falstaff is one of several elements that give *Part Two* "the imprint of a moral Interlude" and make it "a reconsideration of the subject matter and leading themes of *Part One* in a Morality key" (19, 25). I find this to be a problematic oversimplification of the arc of the play—one that does not sufficiently acknowledge all that is troubling about Prince Harry's reformation and ascent.

78. Charles Spencer, "Delicate Debauchery," *The Telegraph*, April 21, 2000; and Matt Wolf, "Sly yet Sweet Falstaff in 'Henry IV, 1 and 2,'" *New York Times*, May 11, 2005, cited in Bulman, *King Henry IV, Part Two*, 44.

79. Kerrigan, "*Henry IV* and the Death of Old Double (1990)," 71–73. Kerrigan compares this passage to *Hamlet*'s preoccupation with how "the past returns" and notes that "'double' could mean 'ghost' or 'apparition'" (72). He observes that "'Old,' 'death,' 'doubling' suffuse the lexis of *2 Henry IV*" (73).

80. Crewe, "Reforming Prince Hal," 233.

81. Naomi Conn Liebler, "'And Is Old Double Dead?': Nation and Nostalgia in *Henry IV Part 2*," *Shakespeare Survey* 63 (2010): 78–88, 81.

82. Jacques Derrida, *Archive Fever: A Freudian Impression*, trans. Eric Prenowitz (Chicago: University of Chicago Press, 1995), 37.

83. Phyllis Rackin, *Stages of History: Shakespeare's English Chronicles* (Ithaca, NY: Cornell University Press, 1990), 85; Graham Holderness, *Shakespeare Recycled: The Making of Historical Drama* (Hertfordshire: Harvester Wheatsheaf, 1992), 102. Such claims have suffused criticism on the history plays since the early 1990s.

84. McGarry, *Ghosts of Futures Past*.

85. Derrida, *Specters*, 10, 11, italics in the original.

86. On the play's suggestion of a "'natural' relationship between name and identity in this scene, see Patricia Cahill, *Unto the Breach: Martial Formations, Historical Trauma, and the Early Modern Stage* (Oxford: Oxford University Press, 2008), 89.

87. Bulman, *King Henry IV, Part Two*, 85.

88. For a list of scenes in the Quarto edition of *Part Two* that include ghost characters, see Bulman, *King Henry IV, Part Two*, 3.2n54.1. On ghost characters in Shakespeare, see Kristian Smidt, "Shakespeare's Absent Characters," *English Studies* 61, no. 5 (1980): 397–407.

89. Freud, Derrida, and Michals all discuss *déjà vu* in connection with the appearance of the spectral other. See Freud, "The Uncanny"; Derrida, *Specters*, 15; and Kozloff, *Now Becoming Then*, 15v. See also Ryan, "The Future of History"; Ryan observes that *2 Henry IV* "is riddled with double-takes" and "backtracking devices" (160, 161).

90. See Kastan, *King Henry IV*, 5.1.126n.

91. Eugenia Parry Janis intriguingly connects the shadow figures created by long photographic exposures to "sleepwalkers." See Eugenia Parry Janis, "The Bug in Amber and the Dance of Life," in *Vanishing Presence*, ed. Martin Friedman et al. (Minneapolis: Walker Art Center/Rizzoli, 1989), 8–29, 18.

92. Bulman, *King Henry IV, Part Two*, 122.

93. For a fuller discussion of what he calls "psychologized politics or a politicized psychology" in this and other scenes in *Part Two*, see Crewe, "Reforming Prince Hal," 229.

94. See William Shakespeare, *The Famous Victories of Henry the Fifth*, London, 1598. In this principal dramatic source for *2 Henry IV*, the Prince's final visit with his ailing father is explicitly parricidal; he enters the scene *"with a dagger in his hand"* (6.0). Quoted in Bulman, *King Henry IV, Part Two*, 128–29. I take up the repeated erasure of mothers, evident here in Henry IV's suggestion that he is the person who "gave [Hal] life," in chapter 4.

95. See Baldo, *Memory in Shakespeare's Histories*, who argues that Falstaff "grandly embodies" the "spirit of revisionism" (53, and again on 78). In suggesting that Prince Harry picks up his revisionism skills from Falstaff, I am dissociating revisionism from the specific body of Falstaff.

96. Ernst H. Kantorowicz, *The King's Two Bodies: A Study in Mediaeval Political Theology* (Princeton, NJ: Princeton University Press, 1957), 394, quoted in Evans, "Rumor, the Breath of Kings," 2–3.

97. Michael Hattaway illustrates the critical habit of mapping the doctrine of the king's two bodies onto representations of royalty in his problematic claim that Falstaff represents "the material body" of kingship. See Michael Hattaway, "The Shakespearean History Play," in *The Cambridge Companion to Shakespeare's History Plays*, ed. Michael Hattaway (Cambridge: Cambridge University Press, 2002), 3–24, 22.

98. Derrida, *Specters*, 166, italics in the original. Jonathan Goldberg observes that Harry's replacement of his father is a repetition of his earlier replacement of another Harry, Hotspur, at the end of *1 Henry IV*. See Jonathan Goldberg, *Sodometries: Renaissance Texts, Modern Sexualities* (Stanford, CA: Stanford University Press, 1992), 151. Remarking on the same moment of replacement after Hotspur's death, Stephen Greenblatt suggestively notes that "Hal hides with his 'favors' (that is, a scarf or other emblem, but the word *favor* also has in the sixteenth century the sense of 'face') the dead Hotspur's 'mangled face (5.4.96), as if to mark the completion of the exchange" (Greenblatt, *Shakespearean Negotiations*, 46).

99. Although focused on issues of gender, class, and sexuality, Goldberg argues that Henry V's gestures of reformation at the end of *2 Henry IV* are "the predations of the engrossing arriviste that write themselves as civilized restraint" (Goldberg, *Sodometries*, 172). In addition to Falstaff, who is one of the principal objects of Henry V's predation in Goldberg's reading, I would add Henry IV.

100. In observing how Henry V increases or multiplies over these final scenes of *Part Two*, I echo Goldberg's uneasiness, though on different grounds, with readings that identify Falstaff with feminine increase, such as Valerie Traub's "Prince Hal's Falstaff: Posi-

tioning Psychoanalysis and the Female Reproductive Body," *Shakespeare Quarterly* 40, no. 4 (1989): 456–74. See Goldberg, *Sodometries*, chap. 5, "Desiring Hal," esp. 173–75.

3. Dummies and Doppelgängers

1. For a reading of the style of Bedford and Gloucester's speeches, see Michael Hattaway, ed., *The First Part of King Henry VI* (Cambridge: Cambridge University Press, 1990), 5–6.

2. Unless otherwise noted, all quotations of Shakespeare's plays are from William Shakespeare, *The Oxford Shakespeare: The Complete Works*, ed. Stanley Wells and Gary Taylor (Oxford: Clarendon, 1988), cited parenthetically.

3. Bert O. States, "Death as a Fictitious Event," *The Hudson Review* 53, no. 3 (2000): 423–32, 423–24. For a discussion of when Henry's coffin is removed from the stage, see Edward Burns, ed., *King Henry VI, Part 1*, Arden Third Series (London: Bloomsbury, 2000), 95–96. Building on the work of Katherine Park, Susan Zimmerman argues that early modern English beliefs in a liminal state between aliveness and deadness inform theatrical representations of corpses. See Susan Zimmerman, *The Early Modern Corpse and Shakespeare's Theatre* (Edinburgh: Edinburgh University Press, 2005), chap. 4; Katherine Park, "The Criminal and the Saintly Body: Autopsy and Dissection in Renaissance Italy," *Renaissance Quarterly* 47, no. 1 (1994): 1–33; and Park, "The Life of the Corpse: Division and Dissection in Later Medieval Europe," *Journal of the History of Medicine and Allied Sciences* 50, no. 1 (1994): 111–32, especially Park's observation that the corpse of a recently deceased person was regarded as "active, sensitive, or semianimate, possessed of a gradually fading life" (115).

4. On the "untimeliness" and causes of Henry V's death, see Andrew Griffin, *Untimely Deaths in Renaissance Drama: Biography, History, Catastrophe* (Toronto: University of Toronto Press, 2020), 5.

5. Phyllis Rackin, *Stages of History: Shakespeare's English Chronicles* (Ithaca, NY: Cornell University Press, 1990), 84, 85.

6. Peggy Phelan, *Unmarked: The Politics of Performance* (New York: Routledge, 1996), 146; and Herbert Blau, *The Audience* (Baltimore: Johns Hopkins University Press, 1990), 365–66. Performance theory's identification of performance with disappearance is well documented. Usefully succinct summaries appear in Rebecca Schneider, *Performing Remains: Art and War in Times of Theatrical Reenactment* (New York: Routledge, 2011), 91–96; and Diana Taylor, *The Archive and the Repertoire: Performing Cultural Memory in the Americas* (Durham, NC: Duke University Press, 2003), 5–7. Schneider's work posits an influential set of claims, contrary to the disappearance thesis, that I take up at length in other sections of this project and in a separate essay on *1 Henry VI*; see Alice Dailey, "The Talbot Remains: Historical Drama and the Performative Archive," *Shakespeare Bulletin* 35, no. 3 (2017): 373–87. Alice Rayner, *Ghosts: Death's Double and the Phenomena of Theatre* (Minneapolis: University of Minnesota Press, 2006), also presents an important corrective to the present-absent binary, arguing that "any point at which dualistic, oppositional thought is invoked but then breaks down might be said to be theatrical" (xii).

7. Joseph Roach, *Cities of the Dead: Circum-Atlantic Performance* (New York: Columbia University Press, 1996), 3.

8. Roach, *Cities of the Dead*, 6, 3.

9. Brian Walsh, "'Unkind Division': The Double Absence of Performing History in *1 Henry VI*." *Shakespeare Quarterly* 55, no. 2 (2004): 119–47, 146–47. See also Burns's claim that "the play is a play of desire, the desire of the audience to fill the void with some imaginative confirmation" (Burns, *King Henry VI, Part 1*, 89), and the play's emphasis on loss as discussed in Jean E. Howard and Phyllis Rackin, *Engendering a Nation: A Feminist Account of Shakespeare's English Histories* (New York: Routledge, 1997), chap. 5. For a useful summary of critical attitudes toward the *Henry VI* plays, especially those of new historicists and cultural materialists, see Neema Parvini, *Shakespeare's History Plays: Rethinking Historicism* (Edinburgh: Edinburgh University Press, 2012), 122–25.

10. Roach offers an especially spectacular example of the dead surrogating the living, though with markedly different emphasis. In discussing the function of Aztec rituals of human sacrifice in performatively reconstituting the community and its god, he describes the practice of flaying sacrificial victims who have been given the god's name and then wearing the skin as a costume. His focus is on sacrificial "expenditure, surrogation, and continuity" (Roach, *Cities of the Dead*, 148).

11. The image is 90.125 inches by 164.125 inches, or slightly larger than 7.5 feet by 13 feet.

12. Quoted in Frank Möller, "The Looking/Not Looking Dilemma," *Review of International Studies* 35, no. 4 (2009): 781–94, 782.

13. Susan Sontag, *Regarding the Pain of Others* (New York: Picador, 2003), 124.

14. Sontag, *Regarding*, 125–26.

15. As in chapter 1's meditation on the future-looking gesture of the still photo, my thinking about stillness is informed by Schneider's discussion of "remains" as both what has been left behind and what "remain[s] before . . . as both *ahead of* and *prior to*" (Schneider, *Performing Remains*, 22).

16. Christopher Pye, *The Regal Phantasm: Shakespeare and the Politics of Spectacle* (New York: Routledge, 1990), 19–20.

17. Madhavi Menon, "Queer Shakes," in *Shakesqueer: A Queer Companion to the Complete Works of Shakespeare*, ed. Madhavi Menon (Durham, NC: Duke University Press, 2011), 1–27, 6. I take up the issue of queer temporality more fully in chapter 5.

18. See Carolyn Dinshaw, Lee Edelman, Roderick A. Ferguson, Carla Freccero, Jack [Judith] Halberstam, Annamarie Jagose, Christopher Nealon, and Hoang Tan Nguyen, "Theorizing Queer Temporalities: A Roundtable Discussion," *GLQ* 13, no. 2–3 (2007): 177–95, 184; and Carla Freccero, Madhavi Menon, and Valerie Traub, "Historicism and Unhistoricism in Queer Studies," *PMLA* 128, no. 3 (2013): 781–86, 781. Although scholars have noted other kinds of repetition in the play—such as the sequence of funerals, its implicit comparisons of character (Henry V versus Henry VI, for example), and verse parallelisms that link episodes—the play's proliferation of doubles for Talbot has gone unremarked. See, for example, Hattaway, *The First Part of King Henry VI*, 9–11. Burns discusses Joan's double nature as *pucelle* and *puzel* but does not observe the representation of Talbot via doubles, a fact that is especially striking when he is discussing Joan and Talbot together (Burns, *King Henry VI, Part 1*, 23–47, esp. 37–38). Similarly, Marjorie Garber, *Shakespeare After All* (New York: Pantheon, 2004), remarks on the "patterns of symmetry, echo, inversion, and opposition" in the *Henry VI* plays but does not remark on the many doubles of Talbot in *1 Henry VI* (94).

19. Stanley Cavell, "The Avoidance of Love: A Reading of *King Lear*" in *Must We Mean What We Say?* (New York: Cambridge University Press, 2002), 267–353, 333.

20. For a useful discussion of the convention of a darkened theater audience and the theatrical exchange of attention between actors and audience, particularly in a subject-object relationship, see Erika Fischer-Lichte, *The Transformative Power of Performance: A New Aesthetics*, trans. Saskya Iris Jain (London: Routledge, 2008), chap. 3, "Shared Bodies, Shared Spaces: The Bodily Co-Presence of Actors and Spectators."

21. Cavell, "The Avoidance of Love," 307n16, in reference to the work of Fried.

22. Michael Fried, "Art and Objecthood," in *Art and Objecthood: Essays and Reviews* (Chicago: University of Chicago Press, 1998), 148–72, 155.

23. Fried, "Art and Objecthood," 154, 155.

24. Fried, "Art and Objecthood," 160, 156. W. J. T. Mitchell explores the seeming aliveness of images in *What Do Pictures Want?* (Chicago: University of Chicago Press, 2005), asking, "Why do [people] behave as if pictures were alive, as if works of art had minds of their own, as if images had a power to influence human beings, demanding things from us, persuading, seducing, and leading us astray?" (7). Mitchell refers to the "unconscious ventriloquism" of images, suggesting that "they present not just a surface but a *face* that faces the beholder" (29, 30). On the sentience of objects, see also Victoria Nelson, *The Secret Life of Puppets* (Cambridge, MA: Harvard University Press, 2001). My thinking about sentient objects was stimulated by an essay by Jonathan Lethem in the printed collection of David Maisel's *History's Shadow* from which this book's cover image is taken. See Jonathan Lethem, "X, Curator," in *History's Shadow*, by David Maisel (Portland, OR: Nazraeli Press, 2011), unpaginated.

25. Daniel Sack, *After Live: Possibility, Potentiality, and the Future of Performance* (Ann Arbor: University of Michigan Press, 2015), 61–62, 95.

26. Sack, *After Live*, 61, 122.

27. Sack, *After Live*, 9, 62. Sack adapts the term "potentiality" from Giorgio Agamben, *Potentialities: Collected Essays in Philosophy*, trans. Daniel Heller-Roazen (Stanford, CA: Stanford University Press, 1999).

28. Sack, *After Live*, 94.

29. Sack, *After Live*, 107.

30. Sack, *After Live*, 61.

31. Sack, *After Live*, 121. Elaine Freedgood makes an analogous claim, arguing, "We all believe, in one way or another, in the agency, return, and presence of the dead. Whether it is in the form of history, the unconscious, mourning, melancholia, the commodity fetish, the heirloom, the will, the grave, or the family photo album, the dead clearly make meaning in and of our lives." See Elaine Freedgood, "Ghostly Reference," *Representations* 125, no. 1 (2014): 40–53, esp. 40.

32. On history plays as sites for imagining the hypothetical, a concept related to the subjunctive, see Marissa Nicosia, "'To Plant Me in Mine Own Inheritance': Prolepsis and Pretenders in John Ford's *Perkin Warbeck*," *Studies in Philology* 115, no. 3 (2018): 580–97.

33. Phelan, *Unmarked*, 27.

34. Sack, *After Live*, 82, 79.

35. Cavell, "The Avoidance of Love," 297.

36. Cavell, "The Avoidance of Love," 336.

37. Laurie Ellinghausen usefully traces the centrality of shame to the production of heroic masculinity in the history plays, especially the *Henry VI* plays, in "'Shame and Eternal Shame': The Dynamics of Historical Trauma in Shakespeare's Early Histories," *Exemplaria* 20, no. 3 (2008): 264–82.

38. Fried, "Art and Objecthood." See also Michael Fried, *Absorption and Theatricality: Painting and Beholder in the Age of Diderot* (Chicago: University of Chicago Press, 1988); *Courbet's Realism* (Chicago: University of Chicago Press, 1990); *Manet's Modernism: or, The Face of Painting in the 1860s* (Chicago: University of Chicago Press, 1996); *Why Photography Matters as Art as Never Before* (New Haven, CT: Yale University Press, 2008).

39. Fried, *Why Photography Matters*, 102.

40. Fried, *Why Photography Matters*, 41, quoting Martin Schwander. See "Jeff Wall in Conversation with Martin Schwander," in *Selected Essays and Interviews* (New York: Museum of Modern Art, 2007), 229–38, 230. In this interview, Wall refers to but also complicates Fried's thesis about absorption and theatricality, arguing that both representational forms "are modes of performance" (230).

41. Sontag, *Regarding*, 124.

42. Fried, *Why Photography Matters*, 34.

43. Maurice Hunt, "The Politics of Vision in Shakespeare's *1 Henry VI*," *South Central Review* 19, no. 1 (2002), 76–101, 80.

44. For a discussion of the extensive use of eyes in *1 Henry VI*, see A. C. Hamilton, *The Early Shakespeare* (San Marino, CA: Huntington Library, 1967), 12–13.

45. Hunt, "The Politics of Vision," 83. Hunt goes on to apply this notion of giving voice to non-sentient objects in ways that become diffuse and largely metaphorical, arguing, for example, that the various figurative meanings ascribed to red and white roses in the Temple Garden scene are ventriloquistic. However, at no point in that scene do the characters project voices onto the roses. Rather, York describes them as "dumb significants," or nonspeaking signifiers (2.4.26).

46. Cavell, "The Avoidance of Love," 306.

47. This "English Henry" could plausibly be Henry VI, but at this point in the play, he has neither appeared onstage nor been crowned king, and the defense of France is described by Exeter in the opening scene as the fulfillment of an oath to the dead Henry V (1.1.162–64). As Andrew Leggatt notes in *Shakespeare's Political Drama: The History Plays and Roman Plays* (New York: Routledge, 1988), the first half of the play "is set in a kingless world" (1).

48. Sack, *After Live*, 61.

49. See also 2.3.23, 4.2.16, and 4.7.78.

50. On the mirror as an exemplar, see Herbert Grabes, *The Mutable Glass: Mirror-imagery in Titles and Texts of the Middle Ages and the English Renaissance*, trans. Gordon Collier (Cambridge: Cambridge University Press, 1982), 48–56.

51. States, "Death as a Fictitious Event," 427.

52. Jacques Derrida, *"Peines de mort,"* quoted and translated by Carla Freccero, *Queer/Early/Modern* (Durham, NC: Duke University Press, 2006), 88.

53. Freccero, *Queer*, 88.

54. Sack, *After Live*, 121, referring specifically to Louise Bourgeois's sculpture *Velvet Eyes* (1984).

55. Roach, *Cities of the Dead*, 2.

56. Roach, *Cities of the Dead*, 6.

57. Sack, *After Live*, 121, 82.

58. The other character in Shakespeare's histories who is notable for using this form of self-address is "the Douglas" of *Henry IV, Parts One* and *Two*, who is a likewise largely a figure of reputation: "I am the Douglas, fatal to all those / That wear those colours on them" (*1H4 5.4.25–26*).

59. Gregory M. Colón Semenza situates this reference to sport among the *Henry VI* plays' broader concern about the degradation and emasculation of warfare in "Sport, War, and Contest in Shakespeare's *Henry VI*," *Renaissance Quarterly* 54, no. 4 (2001): 1251–72.

60. Rackin, *Stages of History*, 151–55.

61. In thinking about *2 Henry IV* as a queer play, Stephen Guy-Bray observes, "The idea that identities of all sorts are fluid and determined by performance has become one of the central concepts of much queer theory." I find this statement applicable to Talbot, whose identity is repeatedly theatricalized through others. See Stephen Guy-Bray, "*Henry VI, Part 2*: The Gayest Play Ever," in *Shakesqueer: A Queer Companion to the Complete Works of Shakespeare*, ed. Madhavi Menon (Durham, NC: Duke University Press, 2011), 139–45, esp. 139–40.

62. Otto Rank, "Introduction by Harry Tucker Jr.," in *The Double: A Psychoanalytic Study*, trans. and ed. Harry Tucker Jr. (Chapel Hill: University of North Carolina Press, 1971), xiii–xxii, xiv.

63. Otto Rank, "The Double as Immortal Self," in *Beyond Psychology* (New York: Dover, 1941), 62–101, 76.

64. See, for example, Burns, *King Henry VI, Part 1*, 61; and Hattaway, *The First Part of King Henry VI*, 27. Hattaway is drawing on Keith Thomas, *Religion and the Decline of Magic: Studies in Popular Beliefs in Sixteenth and Seventeenth Century England* (New York: Oxford, 1971), 513–14.

65. Otto Rank, *The Double: A Psychoanalytic Study*, trans. and ed. Harry Tucker Jr. (Chapel Hill, University of North Carolina Press, 1971).

66. Rank, "The Double as Immortal Self," 100.

67. Roland Barthes, *Camera Lucida: Reflections on Photography*, trans. Richard Howard (New York: Hill and Wang, 1980), 1.

68. Barthes, *Camera Lucida*, 11–12.

69. Barthes, *Camera Lucida*, 14. Siegfried Kracauer made a similar set of observations in his earlier 1927 essay "Photography," observations that resonate with the figure of the doppelgänger. He writes that "it is not the person who appears in his or her photograph, but the sum of what can be deducted from him or her. It annihilates the person by portraying him or her, and were person and portrayal to converge, the person would cease to exist." See Siegfried Kracauer, "Photography," trans. Thomas Y. Levin, *Critical Inquiry* 19, no. 3 (1993): 421–36, 431.

70. Rank links images, shadows, and mirrors, noting "the equivalence of the mirror and shadow as images, both of which appear to the ego as its likeness" (Rank, *The Double: A Psychoanalytic Study*, 10).

71. Rank, "The Double as Immortal Self," 76.

72. Rank, "The Double as Immortal Self," 81–82. See also Harry Tucker Jr.'s "Introduction" in Rank, *The Double: Psychoanalytic Study*, xvi–xxi.

73. Hattaway, *The First Part of King Henry VI*, 30.

74. For an earlier iteration of this claim, see Dailey, "The Talbot Remains," 384. In arguing that Talbot dramatizes himself through this staged spectacle, I contest Howard and Rackin's characterization of the scene as "an antitheatrical joke" (Howard and Rackin, *Engendering a Nation*, 60).

75. Alexander Leggatt observes that the couplets make the Talbots seem "boxed in"; see Leggatt, "The Death of John Talbot," in *Shakespeare's English Histories: A Quest for Form and Genre*, ed. John W. Velz (Binghamton: MRTS, 1996), 11–30, 18.

76. Garber notes how "the play simplifies the opposition between 'legitimate' and 'bastard,'" by omitting the fact that Talbot's illegitimate son, Henry Talbot, died in this same battle (Garber, *Shakespeare After All*, 98). For a study of Shakespeare's adaptation of his source materials for the first tetralogy, see Dominique Goy-Blanquet, *Shakespeare's Early History Plays: From Chronicle to Stage* (Oxford: Oxford University Press, 2003).

77. Mario DiGangi observes that "John's death might indicate that the project of reproductive futurism, of 'fighting for the children,' has been jeopardized by the masculine ethos of military honor that requires children to fight." See Mario DiGangi, "Henry VI, Part 1: 'Wounded Alpha Bad Boy Soldier,'" in *Shakesqueer: A Queer Companion to the Complete Works of Shakespeare*, ed. Madhavi Menon (Durham, NC: Duke University Press, 2011), 130–38, 133. (The issues of reproductive futurism and child-killing are the central interest of my study of *Richard III* in chapter 5.) DiGangi also usefully points out the "intensely emotive interaction of male bodies" in *1 Henry VI*, a formulation that suggests the fundamental queerness of Talbot's many doublings with other men (132).

78. Leggatt, "The Death of John Talbot," 14. Rank notes among "primitive peoples" a superstition that resonates with how the Talbots' likeness ensures death, a superstition about children resembling their parents too closely: "Should a child strikingly resemble its father, the latter must soon die, since the child has adopted his image or silhouette" (Rank, *The Double: A Psychoanalytic Study*, 53), 1.

79. Thomas Nashe, *Piers Penniless His Supplication to the Devil*, in *The Works of Thomas Nashe*, ed. Ronald B. McKerrow, revised by F. P. Wilson, vol. 1 (Oxford: Basil Blackwell, 1958), 137–246, 212.

80. Nashe, *Piers Penniless*, 212.

81. In describing these titles as proliferating Talbots, I contest Hattaway's characterization of Lucy's catalog of Talbot titles as marking the end of the chivalric order Talbot represented (Hattaway, *The First Part of King Henry VI*, 30).

82. In observing how *Henry V* ends in a summary of what the *Henry VI* plays have already dramatized, Patricia Parker draws attention to what she calls the "preposterous ordering" of the histories; see Patricia Parker, *Shakespeare from the Margins: Language, Culture, Context* (Chicago: University of Chicago Press, 1996), esp. chap. 1, 37. Her discussion demonstrates the degree to which the plays, particularly of the first tetralogy, posit a recursive rather than linear model of history. Garber also notes the importance of *1 Henry VI*'s nonlinear situatedness in the first tetralogy, identifying it as a "prequel" to Parts 1 and 2 (Garber, *Shakespeare After All*, 93). Menon refers to the compositional order of the plays as "Shakespeare's queer ordering of history" (Menon, "Queer Shakes," 24).

4. The King Machine

1. Unless otherwise noted, all quotations of Shakespeare's plays are from William Shakespeare, *The Oxford Shakespeare: The Complete Works*, ed. Stanley Wells and Gary Taylor (Oxford: Clarendon, 1988), cited parenthetically.

2. Michel Foucault, *Discipline and Punish: The Birth of the Prison*, trans. Alan Sheridan (New York: Vintage, 1995), 47, 43.

3. Jacques Derrida, *The Beast and the Sovereign*, trans. Geoffrey Bennington, vol. 1 (Chicago: University of Chicago Press, 2009), 1:187.

4. Derrida, *Beast*, 1:187.

5. I was introduced to the binary of "grown vs. made" by Kelly Oliver, *Technologies of Life and Death: From Cloning to Capital Punishment* (New York: Fordham University Press, 2013), chap. 1. Oliver notes that this is a common formulation in philosophy and bioethics.

6. Oliver, *Technologies*, 90.

7. Jacques Derrida, *The Death Penalty*, trans. Peggy Kamuf, vol. 1 (Chicago: University of Chicago Press, 2014), 1:22.

8. Derrida, *Death Penalty*, 1:258–59.

9. Derrida, *Death Penalty*, 1:258.

10. See also Richard's battlefield declaration, recounted by his father, that the Yorkists will achieve either "A crown or else a glorious tomb! / A scepter or an earthly sepulchre!" (1.4.17–18).

11. The earliest reference in the first tetralogy to Warwick as "king-maker" occurs in *2 Henry VI* when Warwick tells York, "My heart assures me that the Earl of Warwick / Shall one day make the Duke of York a king" (*2H6* 2.2.78–79).

12. Gwynne Fulton, "Phantasmatics: Sovereignty and the Image of Death in Derrida's First *Death Penalty* Seminar," *Mosaic: An Interdisciplinary Critical Journal* 48, no. 3 (2015): 75–94, 92.

13. Jacques Derrida and Elisabeth Roudinesco, *For What Tomorrow . . .* , trans. Jeff Fort (Stanford, CA: Stanford University Press, 2004), 49.

14. Oliver, *Technologies*, 3.

15. Derrida and Roudinesco, *For What Tomorrow*, 49.

16. Michael Hattaway, ed., *The Third Part of King Henry VI* (Cambridge: Cambridge University Press, 1990), 30.

17. David Wills, *Killing Times: The Temporal Technology of the Death Penalty* (New York: Fordham University Press, 2019), 9.

18. A total of 614 people were executed in the Sing Sing chair between its introduction in 1888 and its retirement in 1963. Capital punishment was abolished in the state of New York in 2004.

19. Heiner Bastian, "Death and Disaster in the Work of Andy Warhol: A Day Like Any Other," in *Andy Warhol: Death and Disaster*, ed. Ingrid Mössinger (Berlin: Kerber Verlag, 2014), 15–33, 20.

20. Derrida, *Death Penalty*, 1:222. Derrida is quoting a description of the guillotine by its inventor, Joseph Ignace Guillotin. Wills cites the development of the trap door in hangings as a precursor to the mechanized instantaneity sought by the guillotine and electric chair (Wills, *Killing Times*, 59). See also Kelly Oliver, "See Topsy 'Ride the

Lightning': The Scopic Machinery of Death," *Southern Journal of Philosophy* 50, no. 1 (2012): 74–94.

21. Derrida, *Death Penalty*, 1.220, 281. Hal Foster has called the electric chair "a kind of modern crucifix." See Hal Foster, "Death in America," *October* 75 (Winter 1996): 36–59, 56.

22. Wills, *Killing Times*, 82. Wills points to a problem described with particular acuity in Augustine's *Confessions*: "If we can think of some bit of time which cannot be divided into even the smallest instantaneous moments, that alone is what we can call 'present.' And this time flies so quickly from future into past that it is an interval with no duration. If it has duration, it is divisible into past and future. But the present occupies no space." See Saint Augustine, *Confessions*, trans. Henry Chadwick (Oxford: Oxford University Press, 1991), 11.20 (232); quoted in J. K. Barret, *Untold Futures: Time and Literary Culture in Renaissance England* (Ithaca, NY: Cornell University Press, 2016), 165–66.

23. On the permanently unpardoned and unpardonable state of the victim of capital punishment, see Derrida, *Death Penalty*, 1:45–46.

24. The most horrifically efficient example of "corpse production" remains the Nazi concentration camps. Giorgio Agamben—following Martin Heidegger, Hannah Arendt, and others—argues that such mechanisms degrade death itself, such that "extermination victims . . . did not truly die, but were rather only pieces produced in a process of an assembly line production." See Giorgio Agamben, *Remnants of Auschwitz: The Witness and the Archive*, trans. Daniel Heller-Roazen (New York: Zone Books, 1999), 72–76, esp. 73. On images of execution machines as harbingers of future killings, see Maria Pia Di Bella, "Observing Executions: From Spectator to Witness," in *Representations of Pain in Art and Visual Culture*, ed. Maria Pia Di Bella and James Elkins (New York: Routledge, 2013), 170–85, 182. For a discussion of empty chairs as memorials of the dead, see Alice Rayner, *Ghosts: Death's Double and the Phenomena of Theatre* (Minneapolis: University of Minnesota Press, 2006), 110–36, chap. 4, "Empty Chairs: The Memorial Double."

25. Bennett Capers notes that the "SILENCE" sign addresses this audience, which functions as "a spectator and a witness." See Bennett Capers, "On Andy Warhol's *Electric Chair*," *California Law Review* 94, no. 1 (2006): 243–60, 251. On the public's function as an "authorizing audience, unseeing and unseen, but present nonetheless," see Austin Sarat, *When the State Kills: Capital Punishment and the American Condition* (Princeton, NJ: Princeton University Press, 2001), 205. On the distinction between spectators and witnesses of capital punishment, see Di Bella, "Observing Executions."

26. See "glitch, n.," *OED Online*, September 2019, Oxford University Press.

27. In addition to eyewitness accounts, opponents of the electric chair have also used "sound portraits"—audio recordings of executions—as legal evidence against the claim of instantaneous death (Fulton, "Phantasmatics," 90).

28. On the "inefficiency" of the electric chair, especially in Ethel Rosenberg's execution, see Capers, "On Andy Warhol's *Electric Chair*," 250. Wills notes that the guillotine was likewise subject to malfunctions that resulted in botched executions (Wills, *Killing Times*, 76–78).

29. On photography's documentation of the visible world, see Susan Sontag, *On Photography* (New York: Picador, 1973), 154; and Roland Barthes, *Camera Lucida: Reflections on Photography*, trans. Richard Howard (New York: Hill and Wang, 1980), 76–77.

30. Fulton, "Phantasmatics," 90. For a history of photography's ambition to capture the illusive "instant," see Phillip Prodger, *Time Stands Still: Muybridge and the Instantaneous Photography Movement* (New York: Oxford University Press, 2003), esp. "In the Blink of an Eye: The Rise of the Instantaneous Photography Movement, 1839–78" (24–111). See also Tom Gunning's essay in Prodger's book, "Never Seen This Picture Before: Muybridge in Multiplicity" (222–72), which describes how Eadweard Muybridge's photographs of galloping horses revealed movement—and therefore action in time—not visible to the naked eye. On the idea of instantaneity in the development of cinema, particularly with regard to the concept of the afterimage, see Mary Ann Doane, *The Emergence of Cinematic Time: Modernity, Contingency, the Archive* (Cambridge, MA: Harvard University Press, 2002), chaps. 1 and 3. On the documentation of the moment of death in photography, film, video, and digital media, see Jennifer Malkowski, *Dying in Full Detail: Mortality and Digital Documentary* (Durham, NC: Duke University Press, 2017).

31. Fulton, "Phantasmatics," 82 and Wills, *Killing Times*, 74–83. For a reverse analogy, in which a camera's shudder is likened to a guillotine, see Prodger, *Time Stands Still*, 89.

32. For a discussion of images and cloning, see W. J. T. Mitchell, *What Do Pictures Want?* (Chicago: University of Chicago Press, 2005), chap. 1.

33. Peggy Phelan, "The Same: Reflections on Andy Warhol and Ronald Reagan," *Umbr(a): A Journal of the Unconscious* 1 (2002): 65–70, 66.

34. Derrida, *Beast*, 1:27, 1:28.

35. Oliver, *Technologies*, 16.

36. On the difficulty of pinpointing a precise moment of death for a capital punishment victim, see Derrida, *Death Penalty*, 1:237–41; and Fulton, "Phantasmatics," 90.

37. On why capital punishment often focuses on the human head, see Derrida, *Death Penalty*, 1:42, and Julian Pitt-Rivers, *The Fate of Shechem, or the Politics of Sex: Essays in the Anthropology of the Mediterranean* (Cambridge: Cambridge University Press, 1977), 4–5.

38. During his brief reign of terror in *2 Henry VI*, Jack Cade describes his interrogation and beheading of Lord Saye as expressions of his "jurisdiction regal" *2H6* 4.7.24–25).

39. Oliver, *Technologies*, 66–67.

40. Hattaway notes that both "father" and "crown" recur in *3 Henry VI* more frequently than in any other play (68 and 60 times, respectively). See Hattaway, *The Third Part of King Henry VI*, 14 and 14n5.

41. Stephen Guy-Bray's remarks about narrative machinery and genetics in *2 Henry VI* are useful for thinking about Henry's attempts to rhetorically construct hereditary legitimacy: "A narrative is, in effect, a machine for producing meaning and for transmitting information. In this context, our contemporary understanding of information is genetic information, the DNA that we fondly hope will explain everything." See Stephen Guy-Bray, "Henry IV, Part 2: The Gayest Play Ever," in *Shakesqueer: A Queer Companion to the Complete Works of Shakespeare*, ed. Madhavi Menon (Durham, NC: Duke University Press, 2011), 139–45, esp. 140.

42. See Oliver, *Technologies*, 39, for a discussion of genetic engineering in the philosophy of Derrida and Jürgen Habermas.

43. Ernst H. Kantorowicz, *The King's Two Bodies: A Study in Medieval Political Theology* (Princeton, NJ: Princeton University Press, 1957).

44. For a discussion of how revenge and the vindication of honor inform succession in *3 Henry VI*, see Peter Lake, *How Shakespeare Put Politics on Stage: Power and Succession in the History Plays* (New Haven, CT: Yale University Press, 2016), 115–19.

45. Lake, *How Shakespeare Put Politics on Stage*, 111. Andrew Griffin observes that similar questions inform *Henry V*'s Salic law speech; see Griffin, "Is *Henry V* Still a History Play?" in *Temporality, Genre and Experience in the Age of Shakespeare: Forms of Time*, ed. Lauren Shohet (London: Bloomsbury, 2018), 83–100, 92. In one of the few extant essays or book chapters devoted entirely to *3 Henry VI*, Edward Berry suggests that York's willingness to forego current kingship so that the crown may pass to his sons is evidence of "compelling paternal love" that the opening scene sets in contrast with Henry's disinheritance of Prince Edward. Berry identifies kinship as "the thematic center of the play." See Edward I. Berry, *Patterns of Decay: Shakespeare's Early Histories* (Charlottesville: University Press of Virginia, 1975), 57–58.

46. Quoted in Oliver, *Technologies*, 73, but without a full citation of Derrida. I have been unable to locate this precise quotation in translations of Derrida. It is likely Oliver's translation of an interview of Derrida by Bernard Stiegler. See Jacques Derrida and Bernard Stiegler, "Spectrographies," in *Echographies of Television: Filmed Interviews*, trans. Jennifer Bajorek (Cambridge: Polity Press, 2002), 113–34, 117.

47. John D. Cox and Eric Rasmussen, eds., *King Henry VI Part 3*, Arden Third Series (London: Arden, 2001), 101.

48. Phelan, "The Same," 66.

49. Derrida, *Death Penalty*, 1:258.

50. For a discussion of what she calls "the shadowiness of paternity" in another of the history plays, see Meredith Evans, "Rumor, the Breath of Kings, and the Body of the Law in *2 Henry IV*," *Shakespeare Quarterly* 60, no. 1 (2009): 1–24, 16. Jean Howard and Phyllis Rackin write, in reference to *1 Henry VI*, that "the invisible, putative connection between fathers and sons that formed the basis for patriarchal authority was always dubious, always vulnerable to subversion by an adulterous wife," though *3 Henry VI* dramatizes other sites of paternity's vulnerability. See Jean E. Howard and Phyllis Rackin, *Engendering a Nation: A Feminist Account of Shakespeare's English Histories*. New York: Routledge, 1997), 64.

51. Berry grounds Shakespeare's connection between the family unit and the state in the Western philosophical tradition, especially Cicero's *De Officiis* (Berry, *Patterns of Decay*, 59).

52. Cox and Rasmussen, *King Henry VI Part 3*, 138.

53. On the utility of forgetting in the construction of historical narratives, see Jonathan Baldo, *Memory in Shakespeare's Histories: Stages of Forgetting in Early Modern England* (New York: Routledge, 2012); and Jonni Koonce Dunn, "The Functions of Forgetfulness in *1 Henry IV*," *Studies in Philology* 113, no. 1 (2016): 82–100.

54. On Warwick's planting metaphors in the context of the history plays' imagery of growing and decaying gardens, see Caroline Spurgeon, *Shakespeare's Imagery and What It Tells Us* (Cambridge: Cambridge University Press, 1935), 216–25.

55. Derrida and Roudinesco, *For What Tomorrow*, 49.

56. The first tetralogy's earliest reference to Richard's deformity occurs in *2 Henry VI*, when Clifford says to Richard, "Hence, heap of wrath, foul indigested lump / As crooked in thy manners as thy shape" (*2H6* 5.1.155–56).

57. Robert Watson remarks that Richard seeks "to establish a royal identity blessed with the stability and integrity of a self that is born and not made"; I argue, rather, that *3 Henry VI* unsettles these categories altogether. See Robert N. Watson, *Shakespeare and the Hazards of Ambition* (Cambridge, MA: Harvard University Press, 1984), 19. Janet Adelman emphasizes Richard's violent disavowal of the maternal body in particular, pointing to Richard's "I am myself alone" moment in *3 Henry VI* as emblematic of how the first tetralogy represents masculinity pitched against "maternal malevolence." See Janet Adelman, *Suffocating Mothers: Fantasies of Maternal Origin in Shakespeare's Plays,* Hamlet *to* The Tempest (New York: Routledge, 1992), 3.

58. Tim Barker, "Aesthetics of the Error: Media Art, the Machine, the Unforeseen, and the Errant," in *Error: Glitch, Noise, and Jam in New Media Cultures,* ed. Mark Nunes (New York: Bloomsbury, 2011), 42–58, 43, 51.

59. Mark Nunes: "Error, Noise, and Potential: The Outside of Purpose," in *Error: Glitch, Noise, and Jam in New Media Cultures,* ed. Mark Nunes (New York: Bloomsbury, 2011), 3–24, 12.

60. On the virtual as potential, see Barker, "Aesthetics of the Error," 54; and Pierre Lévy, *Becoming Virtual: Reality in the Digital Age* (New York: Plenum, 1998), 23.

61. Michael Betancourt, *Glitch Art in Theory and Practice: Critical Failures and Post-Digital Aesthetics* (New York: Routledge, 2017), 37.

62. Nunes, "Error, Noise, and Potential," 13.

63. Barker, "Aesthetics of the Error," 51.

64. Barker, "Aesthetics of the Error," 52, italics original.

65. Nunes, "Error, Noise, and Potential," 3.

66. Evan Choate hints at Richard's function as a glitch when he describes him as "a glimpse behind the 'smiling plenty' of the normative order." See Evan Choate, "Misreading Impotence in *Richard III, Modern Philology* 117, no. 1 (2019): 24–47, 46.

67. Betancourt, *Glitch Art,* 8.

68. Barker, "Aesthetics of the Error," 54, 44.

69. Nunes, "Error, Noise, and Potential," 3–4.

70. Nunes, "Error, Noise, and Potential," 3. See also Barker, "Aesthetics of the Error," 45.

71. Andy Warhol interview, in Gene Swenson, "What Is Pop Art? Answers from 8 Painters (Part I)," *ARTnews,* November 1963.

5. Fuck Off and Die

1. Unless otherwise noted, all quotations of Shakespeare's plays are from William Shakespeare, *The Oxford Shakespeare: The Complete Works,* ed. Stanley Wells and Gary Taylor (Oxford: Clarendon, 1988), cited parenthetically.

2. Disability scholars note that our current notion of disability was introduced in the late seventeenth and eighteenth centuries. Allison P. Hobgood and David Houston Wood defend the "anachronistic" use of this term for early modern studies in *Recovering Disability in Early Modern England* (Columbus: Ohio State University Press, 2013), 1–22. Their introduction, titled "Ethical Staring: Disabling the English Renaissance," also offers a useful account of the development of disabilities studies since its inception in the 1980s. See also Hobgood's discussion of Richard in relation to early

modern medicalization of disability in Allison P. Hobgood, "Teeth before Eyes: Impairment and Invisibility in Shakespeare's *Richard III*," in *Disability, Health, and Happiness in the Shakespearean Body*, ed. Sujata Iyengar (New York: Routledge, 2015), 23–40.

3. For an extended discussion of the implications of Richard's sexual impotence, see Evan Choate, "Misreading Impotence in *Richard III*," *Modern Philology* 117, no. 1 (2019): 24–47. On representations of Richard's impotence in performance, see Constance A. Brown, "Olivier's Richard III: A Re-evaluation," *Film Quarterly* 20 (1967): 23–32; and Antony Sher, *The Year of the King: An Actor's Diary and Sketchbook* (New York: Limelight, 1994).

4. David T. Mitchell and Sharon L. Snyder describe disability as "the material marker of inferiority itself. One might think of disability as the master trope of human disqualification." See Mitchell and Snyder, *Narrative Prosthesis: Disability and the Dependencies of Discourse* (Ann Arbor: University of Michigan Press, 2000), 3. Linda Charnes notes that the figure of the hunchback in particular was stigmatized as ignoble and that a hunched back marked the individual as "downwardly mobile." See Linda Charnes, *Notorious Identity: Materializing the Subject in Shakespeare* (Cambridge, MA: Harvard University Press, 1993), 25.

5. Katherine Schaap Williams, "Performing Disability and Theorizing Deformity," *English Studies* 94, no. 7 (2013): 757–72, 760. Williams extends her exploration of "Disability [as] an idea for theatrical representation" beyond Richard III to other early modern figures, plays, and literature in Katherine Schaap Williams, *Unfixable Forms: Disability, Performance, and the Early Modern English Theater* (Ithaca, NY: Cornell University Press, 2021), 3. For a useful account of how disability studies and performance theory have come to intersect, see Carrie Sandahl and Philip Auslander, "Introduction: Disability Studies in Commotion with Performance Studies," in *Bodies in Commotion: Disability & Performance*, ed. Carrie Sandahl and Philip Auslander (Ann Arbor: University of Michigan Press, 2005), 1–12. Hobgood argues that Richard's disability provides a kind of invisibility—"a lack of perceptibility and presence"—that allows him to plot unperceived (Hobgood, "Teeth before Eyes," 36).

6. Williams usefully describes Richard's fake smiles and tears as "technologies of imitation" (Williams, *Unfixable Forms*, 31).

7. Alison Kafer, *Feminist, Queer, Crip* (Bloomington: Indiana University Press, 2013), 34.

8. Carrie Sandahl, "Queering the Crip or Cripping the Queer? Intersections of Queer and Crip Identities in Solo Autobiographical Performance," *GLQ* 9, no. 1–2 (2003): 25–56, 28. For a more recent study of queercrip performance, broadly conceived, see Robert McRuer, *Crip Times: Disability, Globalization, and Resistance* (New York: New York University Press, 2018).

9. Sandahl, "Queering the Crip," 36. See also Sandahl and Auslander's description of disabled artists' strategies for "turning disability stereotypes and narratives to their own ends" and of how the artist "become[s] an active maker of meaning, rather than a passive specimen on display" ("Introduction," 3).

10. On "coming out as a crip," see Sandahl, "Queering the Crip," 28; and Robert McRuer, *Crip Theory: Cultural Signs of Queerness and Disability* (New York: New York University Press, 2006), chap. 1.

11. Robert McRuer, *"Richard III*: Fuck the Disabled: The Prequel," in *Shakesqueer: A Queer Companion to the Complete Works of Shakespeare*, ed. Madhavi Menon (Durham, NC: Duke University Press, 2011), 294–301, 301.

12. I borrow the term "normate" from Rosemarie Garland-Thomson, *Extraordinary Bodies: Figuring Physical Disability in American Culture and Literature* (New York: Columbia University Press, 1997), 8.

13. Judith Butler, *Bodies That Matter: On the Discursive Limits of Sex* (New York: Routledge, 1993), 122; quoted in Sandahl, "Queering the Crip," 38.

14. Sandahl, "Queering the Crip," 40.

15. McRuer, *Crip Theory*, 35.

16. McRuer, *"Richard III*: Fuck the Disabled," 296.

17. Lee Edelman, *No Future: Queer Theory and the Death Drive* (Durham, NC: Duke University Press, 2004), 3. Edelman summarizes the central claims of *No Future* and elaborates them in a reading of *Hamlet*, "Against Survival: Queerness in a Time That's Out of Joint," *Shakespeare Quarterly* 62, no. 2 (2011): 148–69. For subsequent discussions of queer temporality, see especially Elizabeth Freeman, *Time Binds: Queer Temporalities, Queer Histories* (Durham, NC: Duke University Press, 2010); Jonathan Goldberg and Madhavi Menon, "Queering History," *PMLA* 120, no. 5 (2005): 1608–17; Jack [Judith] Halberstam, *In a Queer Time and Place: Transgender Bodies, Subcultural Lives* (New York: New York University Press, 2005); José Esteban Muñoz, *Cruising Utopia: The Then and There of Queer Futurity* (New York: New York University Press, 2009) and "Cruising the Toilet: Le Roi Jones / Amiri Baraka, Racial Black Traditions, and Queer Futurity," *GLQ* 13, no. 2–3 (2007), 353–67. This 2007 *GLQ* special issue on Queer Temporalities includes an introduction by Elizabeth Freeman and a roundtable discussion, "Theorizing Queer Temporalities," featuring Carolyn Dinshaw, Lee Edelman, Roderick A. Ferguson, Carla Freccero, Jack [Judith] Halberstam, Annamarie Jagose, Christopher Nealon, and Nguyen Tan Hoang (177–95). On debates about queer theory, history, and anachronism, particularly in relation to scholarship on the Renaissance and Shakespeare, see Madhavi Menon, "Queer Shakes," in *Shakespeare: A Queer Companion to the Complete Works of Shakespeare*, ed. Madhavi Menon (Durham, NC: Duke University Press, 2011), 1–27; Melissa E. Sanchez, *Shakespeare and Queer Theory* (New York: Bloomsbury, 2019), 102–110; and Goran Stanivukovic, ed., *Queer Shakespeare: Desire and Sexuality* (London: Bloomsbury, 2017), pt. 1.

18. Edelman, *No Future*, 6–7. Mitchell and Snyder note a similar antisociality in disability: "Disability, like the designation of artistic innovation, derives value from its non-compliance with social expectations about valid physical and cognitive lives" (*Narrative Prosthesis*, 9).

19. Edelman, *No Future*, 3.

20. Edelman, *No Future*, 29.

21. The opening line of this scene, "Once more we sit in England's royal throne," signals that the play ends as it began: around the central prop of the "chair of state" (*3H6* 5.1.1). The phrase "chair of state" appears in the play's opening stage directions.

22. Edelman, *No Future*, 60.

23. Edelman, *No Future*, 25–26.

24. With Edelman's figure of the Child in mind, Joseph Campana notes that in Shakespeare's plays, "Trading in childhood is always trading in futures, but those futures

tend to come at the price of actual children." See Joseph Campana, "Killing Shakespeare's Children: The Cases of *Richard III* and *King John*," *Shakespeare* 3, no. 1 (2007): 18–39, 22. In his role as Lord Protector, Richard will later become a surrogate father to Prince Edward, albeit a kind of anti-father or anti-protector bent on destroying rather than preserving the future of the child. On the threat of surrogate parents in Shakespeare, especially in *Richard III*, see Heather Dubrow, "'I Fear There Will a Worse Come in His Place': Surrogate Parents and Shakespeare's *Richard III*," in *Maternal Measures: Figuring Caregiving in the Early Modern Period*, ed. Naomi J. Miller and Naomi Yavneh (Burlington, VT: Ashgate, 2000): 348–62.

25. Kafer, *Feminist, Queer, Crip*, 34. Marjorie Garber argues that Richard's deformity is itself a deformity produced through the processes of historiography—that it is a "viciously circular manifestation of neo-Platonic determinism." See Garber, *Shakespeare's Ghost Writers: Literature as Uncanny Causality* (New York: Routledge, 1987), 36. Charnes frames the foregone conclusion of Richard's future in terms of "traumatic cultural memory," arguing that the play "reveals how persons are produced to fit the requirements of history's 'traumatic events.' . . . [Richard] must be produced in order to enable and justify the 'cure' that, at least in terms of historiography, has always already preceded him" (Charnes, *Notorious Identity*, 28).

26. Kafer, *Feminist, Queer, Crip*, 2. On the link between race, queerness, and disability, see also 32–33.

27. On eugenics, see Kafer, *Feminist, Queer, Crip*, 29–31.

28. McRuer, *Crip Theory*, 20, quoting from John Nguyet Erni, *Unstable Frontiers: Technomedicine and the Cultural Politics of 'Curing' AIDS* (Minneapolis: University of Minnesota Press, 1994), 41.

29. On the figure of the *muselmann*, see Giorgio Agamben, *Remnants of Auschwitz: The Witness and the Archive*, trans. Daniel Heller-Roazen (New York: Zone Books, 1999), 41–86.

30. Robert McRuer and Abby L. Wilkerson, "Introduction," Special Issue on Desiring Disability: Queer Theory Meets Disability Studies, *GLQ* 9, no. 1 (2003), 1–23, 10. See also Sujata Iyengar, "Shakespeare's 'Discourse of Disability'" in *Disability, Health, and Happiness in the Shakespearean Body*, ed. Sujata Iyengar (New York: Routledge, 2015): 1–19, 2. Carla Freccero uses the phrase "future dead person" in the *GLQ* 2007 special issue on Queer Temporalities (noted above), but she is using it to refer to the human state generally, not to disabled people. See Carolyn Dinshaw et al., "Theorizing Queer Temporalities," 184.

31. Campana, "Killing Shakespeare's Children," 24.

32. Halberstam, *In a Queer Time and Place*, 4; and Kafer, *Feminist, Queer, Crip*, 40–41.

33. McRuer, "*Richard III*: Fuck the Disabled," 299. McRuer's provocative short essay is interested principally in Ian McKellen's performance of the role of Richard in Richard Loncraine's 1995 film but does not pursue a queercrip reading of the play more broadly.

34. On Warhol's dyslexia, see Wayne Koestenbaum, *Andy Warhol: A Biography* (New York: Open Road, 2001), 33–34.

35. Victor Bockris, *Warhol: The Biography* (Cambridge, MA: Da Capo Press, 2003), 15.

36. Simon Watney, "Queer Andy," in *Pop Out: Queer Warhol*, ed. Jennifer Doyle, Jonathan Flatley, and José Esteban Muñoz (Durham, NC: Duke University Press, 1996), 20–30, 25.

37. Andy Warhol and Pat Hackett, *Popism: The Warhol Sixties* (New York: Harcourt, 1980), 13–15.

38. Quoted in Bockris, *Warhol: The Biography*, 107.

39. On temporal drag, see Freeman, *Time Binds*, chap. 2. On Warhol and gender drag, see Alexis Bard Johnson, "The Work of Being Sexed: Andy Warhol on Drag," in *Contact Warhol: Photography without End*, ed. Peggy Phelan and Richard Meyer (Cambridge, MA: MIT Press, 2018), 168–79; and Mandy Merck, "Figuring Out Andy Warhol," in *Pop Out: Queer Warhol*, ed. Jennifer Doyle, Jonathan Flatley, and José Esteban Muñoz (Durham, NC: Duke University Press, 1996), 224–37, 231–35.

40. Quoted in Bockris, *Warhol: The Biography*, 107.

41. "Sydenham Chorea Information Page," National Institute of Neurological Disorders and Stroke, National Institutes of Health, accessed July 8, 2019, https://www.ninds.nih.gov/Disorders/All-Disorders/Sydenham-Chorea-Information-Page.

42. On Warhol's feelings of shame about his appearance and about illness, especially AIDS, see also Jessica Beck, "Love on the Margins: A Case for Andy Warhol and John Gould," in *Contact Warhol: Photography without End,*" ed. Peggy Phelan and Richard Meyer (Cambridge, MA: MIT Press, 2018), 156–67.

43. Bockris, *Warhol: The Biography*, 15, 20.

44. Gerard Malanga, a long-time assistant and associate of Warhol's, recalls that Warhol "said something to the effect that [movie stars] were or could be as powerful as politicians," as quoted in Gunnar B. Kvaran, Hanne Beate Ueland, and Grete Årbu, eds., *Andy Warhol by Andy Warhol* (Oslo: Astrup Fearnley Museum of Modern Art, 2008), 11. One could argue that Warhol foretold the rise of someone like Donald Trump, whose celebrity translated into nonmetaphorical political authority through voters who saw the two forms of power as interchangeable.

45. Carrie Sandahl traces this phrase specifically to Rosemarie Garland-Thomson's work in a National Endowment for the Humanities (NEH) Summer Institute that they both attended. See Sandahl, "Queering the Crip," 55n36.

46. Peggy Phelan and Richard Meyer, "Talking Warhol," in *Contact Warhol: Photography without End,* ed. Peggy Phelan and Richard Meyer (Cambridge, MA: MIT Press, 2018), 14–21, 20.

47. On Warhol's engagement with the *memento mori* tradition, see Peggy Phelan, "Andy Warhol: Contact Sheet, Photography without End," in *Contact Warhol: Photography without End*, ed. Peggy Phelan and Richard Meyer (Cambridge, MA: MIT Press, 2018), 22–43, esp. 34–36.

48. On Warhol's exploitation of the accidents afforded by silk-screen replication, see Jennifer Dyer, "The Metaphysics of the Mundane: Understanding Andy Warhol's Serial Imagery," *Artibus et Historiae* 25, no. 49 (2004): 33–47.

49. Jonathan Flatley, "Warhol Gives Good Face: Publicity and the Politics of Prosopopoeia," in *Pop Out: Queer Warhol*, ed. Jennifer Doyle, Jonathan Flatley, and José Esteban Muñoz (Durham, NC: Duke University Press, 1996), 101–33, 107. Flatley is quoting from David Bourdon, "Andy Warhol and the Society Icon," *Art in America*, January/February 1975, 42–45, 42. Phelan notes that the "rhetoric that overlaps photography and criminality—'shooting,' 'framing,' and 'arresting' perhaps most prominently—suggest the dangerous, if not fatal, photographic effect of portraiture, especially in relation to celebrities." See Peggy Phelan, "Haunted Stages: Performance and the Photographic

Effect," in *Haunted: Contemporary Photography/Video/Performance*, ed. Jennifer Blessing and Nat Trotman (New York: Guggenheim Foundation, 2010), 50–63, 57.

50. Koestenbaum, *Andy Warhol: A Biography*, 71.

51. On Richard's use of "now," see also Katherine Schaap Williams, "Enabling Richard: The Rhetoric of Disability in *Richard III*," *Disability Studies Quarterly* 29, no. 4 (2009): n.p., http://dsq-sds.org/article/view/997/1181; Williams, "Performing Disability," 762; and Philip Schwyzer, *Shakespeare and the Remains of Richard III* (Oxford: Oxford University Press, 2013), chap. 6 (titled "Now").

52. Kafer, *Feminist, Queer, Crip*, 48, 49. Kafer notes that "disabled people, particularly those with intellectual disabilities (or 'developmental' disabilities, as they are often known), are . . . cast as 'unfinished' adults," an adjective that Richard uses here to describe the disjunction between his person and his body (54). Genevieve Love, *Early Modern Theatre and the Figure of Disability* (London: Arden, 2019), connects the temporal disjunctions manifested in Richard's body to the play's bibliographical history (137).

53. Williams, "Enabling Richard," n.p.

54. On Richard's use of "dive" in the context of his other locomotive verbs, see Love, *Early Modern Theatre*, 149. Schwyzer relates the play's pattern of submersion images to a story from Shakespeare's source materials of the princes' bodies being dumped in an area of the ocean called the Black Deeps. See Schwyzer, *Shakespeare and the Remains*, 43, 54–57.

55. Barbara Hodgdon addresses closeted gay identity in her discussion of Ian McKellen's performance of Richard, especially in the stage play directed by Richard Eyre. See Barbara Hodgdon, "Replicating Richard: Body Doubles, Body Politics," *Theatre Journal* 50, no. 2 (1998): 207–25, 218.

56. On Warhol's much-contested public claims of celibacy, see Benjamin Kahan, *Celibacies: American Modernism and Sexual Life* (Durham, NC: Duke University Press, 2013), chap. 5. Warhol claimed to be married to his tape recorder. See Andy Warhol, *The Philosophy of Andy Warhol: From A to B and Back Again* (New York: Harcourt, 1975), 26.

57. Graham Bader, "Political Warhol," in *Andy Warhol by Andy Warhol*, ed. Gunnar B. Kvaran, Hanne Beate Ueland, and Grete Årbu (Oslo: Astrup Fearnley Museum of Modern Art, 2008), 21–27, 23.

58. Flatley, "Warhol Gives Good Face," 105.

59. The theatrical practice of actors pretending to be disabled characters has itself been described as a form of drag—as "disability drag" or "cripping up." See Williams, *Unfixable Forms*, 7–8; Petra Kuppers, "Deconstructing Images: Performing Disability," in *Contemporary Theatre Review* 11.3–4 (2001): 25–40; and Tobin Siebers, *Disability Theory* (Ann Arbor: University of Michigan Press, 2008), 116–17.

60. Rebecca W. Bushnell rightly points out that Richard's image of Edward is one of uxoriousness. See Rebecca W. Bushnell, *Tragedies of Tyrants: Political Thought and Theater in the English Renaissance* (Ithaca, NY: Cornell University Press, 1990), 121.

61. Charnes, *Notorious Identity*, 53.

62. See, for example, Donna J. Oestreich-Hart, "Therefore, Since I Cannot Prove a Lover," *SEL* 40, no. 2 (Spring 2000), 241–60; and Charnes, *Notorious Identity*, 38–41.

63. Ralph Berry, *Tragic Instance: The Sequence of Shakespeare's Tragedies* (Newark: University of Delaware Press, 1999), suggests that Richard's opening soliloquy can be read

as camp, given camp's "mannered projection of self that reflects an intense appreciation of being-as-role-playing" (44).

64. Susan Sontag, "Notes on 'Camp,'" in *Against Interpretation and Other Essays* (New York: Farrar, Straus & Giroux, 1961), 275–92, 283, 275. For a bibliography of criticism on camp, see Heather Love, *Feeling Backward: Loss and the Politics of Queer History* (Cambridge, MA: Harvard University Press, 2007), 168n13.

65. McRuer, "*Richard III*: Fuck the Disabled," 299. I am indebted to Richard Meyer's fascinating essay on Warhol's *Thirteen Most Wanted Men* for my introduction to the figure of the Castro Clone, whom he connects to synthetic masculinity and Warholian repetition. Meyer's essay was formative to my early thinking about cloning, reproduction, queer aesthetics, and drag in *Richard III*. See Richard Meyer, "Warhol's Clones," *The Yale Journal of Criticism* 7, no. 1 (1994): 79–109. Meyer builds on Judith Butler's observation that "heterosexuality only constitutes itself as the original through a convincing act of repetition." See Judith Butler, "Imitation and Gender Insubordination," in *Inside/Out: Lesbian Theories, Gay Theories*, ed. Diana Fuss (New York: Routledge, 1991), 13–31, 23; and Meyer, "Warhol's Clones," 100. Without going so far as to use the term "drag," Charnes and Phyllis Rackin both observe that Richard's performed subjugation to Anne and his offering of his phallic dagger to her comprise a "shifting of bodies and gender roles" (Charnes, *Notorious Identity*, 43) or "his appropriation of the woman's part." See Phyllis Rackin, "History into Tragedy: The Case of *Richard III*," in *Shakespearean Tragedy and Gender*, ed. Shirley Nelson Garner and Madelon Sprengnether (Bloomington: Indiana University Press: 1996), 31–53, 39. Hodgdon notes that in the later scene in which Richard sues to Queen Elizabeth for her daughter's hand, Shakespeare creates "gender inversions of voicing and power" by assigning to Elizabeth criticism that Edward Hall's *Chronicle* lobbies against her. See Barbara Hodgdon, *The End Crowns All: Closure and Contradiction in Shakespeare's History* (Princeton, NJ: Princeton University Press, 1991), 110.

66. Charnes, *Notorious Identity*. My argument disagrees, however, with Charnes's assertion that "[b]y courting Anne, [Richard] includes himself in the social" (40). I quibble somewhat, on similar grounds, with Choate's claim that the wooing scene "reasserts Richard's capacity to occupy and deploy the normative order" (Choate, "Misreading Impotence," 43–44). That order fundamentally relies on sexual procreation, from which Richard is excluded. Rather than becoming socialized or normative, Richard's successful courtship of Anne exposes the fictions on which the social and normative are built and their vulnerability to queercrip fabrication.

67. Sontag, "Notes on 'Camp,'" 288, 283. Joel Slotkin observes the discrepancy between Richard's romantic discourse and his criminal relationship to Henry and Edward as a problem of seriousness, calling his wooing "a grotesque species of understatement, where Richard attempts to fit his truly monstrous crimes into a rhetoric that is not serious enough to hold them." See Joel Slotkin, "Honeyed Toads: Sinister Aesthetics in Shakespeare's *Richard III*," *Journal for Early Modern Cultural Studies* 7, no. 1 (2007): 5–32, 16.

68. Bader, "Political Warhol," 26.

69. Bader, "Policital Warhol," 24.

70. Williams, "Enabling Richard," n.p.

71. Although referring to the opening soliloquy of *Richard III*, Lindsey Row-Heyveld's remark that Richard "is not experiencing the gaze of the audience unknowingly, but actively stage-managing their staring" applies equally to the attention that Richard draws

to his body in this soliloquy. Her study situates *Richard III* in the fascinating context of the "counterfeit-disability" stage tradition and reads Richard's appeal to Anne as principally an appeal to charity. See Lindsey Row-Heyveld, *Dissembling Disability in Early Modern English Drama* (Cham, Switzerland: Palgrave Macmillan, 2018), 135–70, esp. 144.

72. As James Siemon notes, the incident Richard refers to has analogues in Hall and Holinshed. See James R. Siemon, ed., *King Richard III*, Arden Third Series (London: Arden, 2009), 286n76.

73. Vin Nardizzi, "Disability Figures in Shakespeare," in *Oxford Handbook of Shakespeare and Embodiment: Gender, Sexuality, and Race*, ed. Valerie Traub (Oxford: Oxford University Press, 2016), 454–67, 466. Robert Watson similarly refers to Richard's murders as "crimes against lineality" and his rise to kingship a "war on succession" in Robert N. Watson, *Shakespeare and the Hazards of Ambition* (Cambridge, MA: Harvard University Press, 1984), 15, 22. Rackin writes that for characters like Richard III, "the theatrical principle of present performance replaces the historical principle of hereditary status as its defining ground." See Phyllis Rackin, *Stages of History: Shakespeare's English Chronicles* (Ithaca, NY: Cornell University Press, 1990), 75.

74. Following wording in Shakespeare's chronicle sources, the editors of *The Oxford Shakespeare* replace "form" with "face" on the assumption that "form" makes no sense here because Richard is deformed and his father is not. I argue, rather, that "form," which appears in both the First Quarto (1597) and First Folio (1623), are appropriate to Richard's project of cripping history and genealogy.

75. Setting *Richard III* in the context of the rest of the first tetralogy's representations of fathers and sons, Bruce Smith remarks that Richard "can only parody the principles of paternal emulation and sibling rivalry that are played straight by characters like the Talbots, father and son." See Bruce R. Smith, *Shakespeare and Masculinity* (New York: Oxford University Press, 2000), 70.

76. Ramie Targoff traces Shakespeare's close adherence to Thomas More's *History of King Richard III* in the scenes of Richard's election, describing them as "farce." See Ramie Targoff, "'Dirty' Amens: Devotion, Applause, and Consent in *Richard III*," *Renaissance Drama* 31 (2002): 61–84, esp. 71–75, 74.

77. This desire for a simulacrum is echoed by the performance history of the play, in which able-bodied actors playing Richard as disabled have been preferred to disabled actors. See Paul Menzer, *Anecdotal Shakespeare: A New Performance History* (New York: Bloomsbury, 2015), 148–60; and Williams, *Unfixable Forms*, 40–46. Hobgood notes a semi-exception in Peter DuBois's casting of Peter Dinklage as Richard for The Public Theater in 2004 (Hobgood, "Teeth before Eyes," 32–36).

78. Bushnell points out that this scene "paint[s] an image of a passive, womanish Richard" who is "an object of desire" whom others court (*Tragedies of Tyrants*, 123). Robert Heilman observes that Richard's performance in this scene is one that "might be used by a woman coyly yielding to seduction." See Robert B. Heilman, "Satiety and Conscience: Aspects of *Richard III*," in *Essays on Shakespearean Criticism*, ed. James L. Calderwood and Harold E. Toliver (Englewood Cliffs, NJ: Prentice-Hall, 1970), 137–51, 142; quoted in Bushnell, *Tragedies of Tyrants*, 123.

79. Michael Torrey, "'The Plain Devil and Dissembling Looks': Ambivalent Physiognomy and Shakespeare's *Richard III*," *English Literary Renaissance* 30, no. 2 (2000): 123–53, 148.

80. See Garber, *Shakespeare's Ghost Writers*, 39–40. William West does not remark on this scene but notes other moments in which Richard projects his deformity elsewhere, such as his completion of Margaret's curse in act 1, scene 3 with Margaret's name in place of his own and his claim that a "tardy cripple" bore the countermand to Clarence's death sentence. See William N. West, "What's the Matter with Shakespeare?: Physics, Identity, Playing," *South Central Review* 26, no. 1–2 (2009): 103–126, 120.

81. Williams, "Enabling Richard," n.p.; and Nardizzi, "Disability Figures," 466.

82. Row-Heyveld, *Dissembling Disability*, 143.

83. Sontag, "Notes on 'Camp,'" 280.

84. A number of scholars have noted the ambiguity of Richard's disability in *Richard III*, particularly in contrast to his more explicitly described deformities in *3 Henry VI*. See especially Choate, "Misreading Impotence"; Geoffrey A. Johns, "A 'Grievous Burden': *Richard III* and the Legacy of Monstrous Birth," in *Disability, Health, and Happiness in the Shakespearean Body*, ed. Sujata Iyengar (New York: Routledge, 2015), 41–57; Marcela Kostihová, "Richard Recast: Renaissance Disability in a Postcommunist Culture," in *Recovering Disability in Early Modern England*, ed. Allison P. Hobgood and David Houston Wood (Columbus: Ohio State University Press, 2013), 136–49; Genevieve Love, *Early Modern Theatre*, chap. 4; Mitchell and Snyder, *Narrative Prosthesis*, chap. 4; Torrey, "'The Plain Devil'"; West, "What's the Matter with Shakespeare?"; and Williams, "Enabling Richard," "Performing Disability," and *Unfixable Forms*, 32–33.

85. Mitchell and Snyder, *Narrative Prosthesis*, 8. Sandahl and Auslander argue that "disability . . . is performed (like gender, sex, sexuality, race, and ethnicity) and not a static 'fact' of the body" ("Introduction," 2). Showing how the staging of disability in early modern drama demands both performance by and deformation of actors' bodies, Williams' *Unfixable Forms* exploits the notions of fixedness and unfixedness to articulate disability's temporal and representational instability.

86. Dyer makes similar observations about Warhol's paintings of Marilyn Monroe, noting that "there is no original because the original is a promotional shot, a copy of an already famous and disseminated image" (Dyer, "The Metaphysics of the Mundane," 42). Warhol's silkscreens intentionally undermine both the concept of an original work of art and the "aura" that Walter Benjamin attaches to the original in his influential essay, "The Work of Art in the Age of Mechanical Reproduction," in *Illuminations*, trans. Harry Zohn, ed. Hannah Arendt (New York: Schocken, 1969), 217–32.

87. For a discussion of how twenty-first-century democracy is similarly organized by a brutality it disowns, see Achille Mbembe, *Necropolitics*, trans. Steven Corcoran (Durham: Duke University Press, 2019). Mbembe's claim that the violence of colonialism is the "twin," "double," or "nocturnal face" of democratic order suggests a self-other structure that resonates with the figure of the specter I study in chap. 2. He writes, "Two orders coexist within [democracy]" (23, 15, 27, 17).

88. In drawing a parallel between Richard's and Edward's violent ascents to the throne, I contest Ian Frederick Moulton's claim that Richard illustrates how, "detached from patriarchal economies of reproduction, the very phallic power on which patriarchal order depends becomes monstrously destructive." See Ian Frederick Moulton, "'A Monster Great Deformed': The Unruly Masculinity of Richard III," *Shakespeare Quarterly* 47, no. 3 (1996): 251–68, 265.

89. Edelman, *No Future*, 30–31.

90. Jack [Judith] Halberstam, *The Queer Art of Failure* (Durham, NC: Duke University Press, 2011), 96, 110.

91. Kafer, *Feminist, Queer, Crip*, 34. Schwyzer's useful reading of this passage observes overlapping temporal registers that are similar to the phenomenon I describe in chap. 1's reading of Richard II's mirror image. See Schwyzer, *Shakespeare and the Remains*, 217–22.

92. Slotkin notes this collapse of the princes' corpses with Richard's sperm, observing that "he equates their corpses with his own seed, mingling images of death with the already unsavory thought of Richard having sex" (Slotkin, "Honeyed Toads," 24). However, this observation is situated within a misreading of Richard's scene with Queen Elizabeth, one that argues for Richard's successful replication of his conquest of Lady Anne. Elizabeth's decision to marry her daughter to Richmond, her consistent rhetorical control of the scene, and Richard's verbal confusion in the exchanges with Ratcliffe and Catesby that immediately follow disclose his rhetorical and tactical failure.

93. Edelman, *No Future*, 2, 3.

94. Via René Girard, Watson usefully identifies Richard as a sacrificial figure or scapegoat "in whom all evils are gathered so that they may be safely dissipated" (Watson, *Shakespeare and the Hazards*, 16). Girard includes the handicapped among appropriate sacrificial victims. See René Girard, *Violence and the Sacred*, trans. Patrick Gregory (Baltimore: Johns Hopkins University Press, 1977), 12.

95. Muñoz, "Cruising the Toilet," 353. For Muñoz's fuller discussion of queer utopia, see *Cruising Utopia*, especially the chapter on Warhol, "Just Like Heaven: Queer Utopian Art and the Aesthetic Dimension" (131–46).

96. Phelan and Meyer, "Talking Warhol," 15. See also Phelan, "Andy Warhol," 22–43, esp. 25.

97. Peggy Phelan in Phelan and Meyer, "Talking Warhol," 15.

98. On the Richard III Society's bust, see Alice Dailey, "The Art of Recovering Richard III," *Upstart: A Journal of English Renaissance Studies*, August 12, 2013, https://upstart.sites.clemson.edu/Essays/richard-forum/art-of-recovering.xhtml. See also the other essays on the 2012 discovery of Richard's skeleton in the August 2013 issue of *Upstart*. Michael Hardin's remarks about the subjects of Warhol's portraits are equally applicable to these afterlives of Richard: "At the same time that iconization strips the individual of life, it strips the individual of death; being transformed into art or the media gives these icons an immortality that we can *see*." See Michael Hardin, "Postmodernism's Desire for a Simulated Death: Andy Warhol's *Car Crashes*, J. G. Ballard's *Crash*, and Don DeLillo's *White Noise*," *LIT: Literature Interpretation Theory* 13, no. 1 (2002): 21–50, 27.

Postscript

1. Any similarity between this anecdote and Stephen Greenblatt's anecdote about being asked by a fellow airplane passenger to mouth the words "I want to die" is purely coincidental. See Stephen Greenblatt, *Renaissance Self-Fashioning: From More to Shakespeare* (Chicago: University of Chicago Press, 1980), 255.

2. David Bowie, "Lazarus," directed by Johan Renck, January 7, 2016, video, 4:08, https://www.youtube.com/watch?v=y-JqH1M4Ya8. For an account of Bowie's "Lazarus" video in relation to the *ars moriendi* tradition in early modern drama, see Maggie

Vinter, *Last Acts: The Art of Dying on the Early Modern Stage* (New York: Fordham University Press, 2019), 159–68.

3. On this costume and its connection to recurrent symbology across Bowie's career, see the useful—if also largely speculative—essay by Albin Wantier, "Kabbalah, Nuclear Fusion, and Immortality: David Bowie's Signs," in *Bowie*, by Steve Schapiro (Brooklyn: powerHouse Books, 2016), not paginated.

4. David Bowie, "Blackstar," directed by Johan Renck, November 19, 2015, video, 9:59, https://www.youtube.com/watch?v=kszLwBaC4Sw. The decorated skull that appears in the videos for "Blackstar" and "Lazarus" is reminiscent of holy relics like those documented in Paul Koudounaris, *Heavenly Bodies: Cult Treasures and Spectacular Saints from the Catacombs* (New York: Thames and Hudson, 2013).

5. Johan Renck, the video's director, later remarked in the press that Bowie found out during the shooting of "Lazarus" that doctors had declared his liver cancer terminal and were ending his treatment. See, for example, Clarisse Loughrey, "David Bowie: Lazarus Director Says Musician Only Discovered He Was Dying during Last Three Months," *Independent*, January 8, 2017, https://www.independent.co.uk/arts-entertainment/music/news/david-bowie-death-anniversay-last-five-years-lazarus-music-video-a7515581.html.

6. I discuss the cover image, *History's Shadow* (GM1) by David Maisel, and its significant influence on many aspects of this book project in the Acknowledgements.

7. Bowie's musical, *Lazarus*, was directed by Ivo van Hove, the artistic director of Toneelgroep Amsterdam who is well known for his work with Shakespeare's plays, including *Roman Tragedies* (2007) and *Kings of War* (2016), his adaptation of the histories. *Lazarus*'s subsequent 2016 run at the King's Cross Theatre in London was filmed and made available worldwide via livestream on January 8–10, 2021, to mark the fifth anniversary of Bowie's death.

8. Bowie's performances of "Cracked Actor" culminated in his French-kissing the skull, a gesture that is suggestive of Thomas Middleton's *The Revenger's Tragedy* (1606). A track on *Blackstar* titled "'Tis Pity She Was a Whore" makes clear Bowie's familiarity with Jacobean drama.

9. I am indebted to Sondra Rosenberg for the photo of my son as Bowie.

WORKS CITED

Abraham, Nicholas, and Maria Torok. "Notes on the Phantom: A Complement to Freud's Metapsychology." In *The Shell and the Kernel: Renewals of Psychoanalysis*, translated by Nicholas T. Rand, 171–76. Chicago: University of Chicago Press, 1994.

Adelman, Janet. *Suffocating Mothers: Fantasies of Maternal Origin in Shakespeare's Plays*, Hamlet *to* The Tempest. New York: Routledge, 1992.

Agamben, Giorgio. *Potentialities: Collected Essays in Philosophy*. Translated by Daniel Heller-Roazen. Stanford, CA: Stanford University Press, 1999.

——. *Remnants of Auschwitz: The Witness and the Archive*. Translated by Daniel Heller-Roazen. New York: Zone Books, 1999.

Ashby, Richard. "'Pierced to the Soul': The Politics of the Gaze in *Richard II*." *Shakespeare* 11, no. 2 (2015): 201–13.

Augustine, Saint. *Confessions*. Translated by Henry Chadwick. Oxford: Oxford University Press, 1991.

Austin, J. L. *How to Do Things with Words*. New York: Clarendon, 1962.

Bader, Graham. "Political Warhol." In *Andy Warhol by Andy Warhol,* edited by Gunnar B. Kvaran, Hanne Beate Ueland, and Grete Årbu, 21–27. Oslo: Astrup Fearnley Museum of Modern Art, 2008.

Bailly, Jean-Christophe. *The Instant and Its Shadow: A Story of Photography*. Translated by Samuel E. Martin. New York: Fordham University Press, 2020.

Baldo, Jonathan. *Memory in Shakespeare's Histories: Stages of Forgetting in Early Modern England*. New York: Routledge, 2012.

Banks, Carol, and Graham Holderness. "'Mine Eye Hath Play'd the Painter.'" In *Shakespeare and the Visual Arts*, Shakespeare Yearbook Vol. 11, edited by Holger Klein and James L. Harner, 454–73. Lewiston, NY: Edwin Mellen Press, 2000.

Barker, Tim. "Aesthetics of the Error: Media Art, the Machine, the Unforeseen, and the Errant." In *Error: Glitch, Noise, and Jam in New Media Cultures*, edited by Mark Nunes, 42–58. New York: Bloomsbury, 2011.

Barret, J. K. *Untold Futures: Time and Literary Culture in Renaissance England*. Ithaca, NY: Cornell University Press, 2016.

Barthes, Roland. *Camera Lucida: Reflections on Photography*. Translated by Richard Howard. New York: Hill and Wang, 1980.

Bastian, Heiner. "Death and Disaster in the Work of Andy Warhol: A Day Like Any Other." In *Andy Warhol: Death and Disaster*, edited by Ingrid Mössinger, 15–33. Berlin: Kerber Verlag, 2014.

Baudrillard, Jean. *Simulacra and Simulation*. Translated by Sheila Faria Glaser. Ann Arbor: University of Michigan Press, 1994.

Beck, Jessica. "Love on the Margins: A Case for Andy Warhol and John Gould." In *Contact Warhol: Photography without End*, edited by Peggy Phelan and Richard Meyer, 156–66. Cambridge, MA: MIT Press, 2018.

Bellamy, John. *The Tudor Law of Treason: An Introduction*. London: Routledge & Kegan Paul, 1979.

Benedict-Jones, Linda. "Duane Michals: Storyteller." In *Duane Michals: Storyteller*, edited by Linda Benedict-Jones, 18–57. New York: DelMonico Books, 2014.

Benjamin, Walter. "The Work of Art in the Age of Mechanical Reproduction." In *Illuminations*, translated by Harry Zohn, edited by Hannah Arendt, 217–32. New York: Schocken, 1969.

Berger, Harry, Jr. "On the Continuity of the *Henriad*: A Critique of Some Literary and Theatrical Approaches." In *Shakespeare Left and Right*, edited by Ivo Kamps, 225–40. New York: Routledge, 1991.

Berry, Edward. *Patterns of Decay: Shakespeare's Early Histories*. Charlottesville: University Press of Virginia, 1975.

Berry, Ralph. *Tragic Instance: The Sequence of Shakespeare's Tragedies*. Newark, DE: University of Delaware Press, 1999.

Betancourt, Michael. *Glitch Art in Theory and Practice: Critical Failures and Post-Digital Aesthetics*. New York: Routledge, 2017.

Blau, Herbert. *The Audience*. Baltimore: Johns Hopkins University Press, 1990.

——. *The Eye of Prey*. Bloomington: Indiana University Press, 1987.

Blinde, Loren M. "Rumored History in Shakespeare's *2 Henry IV*." *English Literary Renaissance* 38, no. 1 (2008): 34–54.

Bockris, Victor. *Warhol: The Biography*. Cambridge, MA: Da Capo Press, 2003.

Booth, Stephen. "Shakespeare in the San Francisco Bay Area." *Shakespeare Quarterly* 29, no. 2 (1978): 267–78.

Bourdon, David. "Andy Warhol and the Society Icon." *Art in America*, January/February 1975, 42–45.

Bowie, David. "Blackstar." Directed by Johan Renck. Sony Music Entertainment, 2015. Video, 9:59. https://www.youtube.com/watch?v=kszLwBaC4Sw.

——. "Lazarus." Directed by Johan Renck. Sony Music Entertainment, 2016. Video, 4:08. https://www.youtube.com/watch?v=y-JqH1M4Ya8.

Boym, Svetlana. *The Future of Nostalgia*. New York: Basic Books, 2001.

Brown, Constance A. "Olivier's Richard III: A Re-Evaluation." *Film Quarterly* 20 (1967): 23–32.

Brown, Mark. "Richard II Relics Found in National Portrait Gallery Archive." *The Guardian*, November 16, 2010. https://www.theguardian.com/artanddesign/2010/nov/16/richard-second-national-portrait-gallery.

Bulman, James C., ed. *King Henry IV, Part Two*. Arden Third Series. London: Bloomsbury, 2016.

Burns, Edward, ed. *King Henry VI, Part 1*. Arden Third Series. London: Bloomsbury, 2000.

Buse, Peter, and Andrew Scott. "Introduction: A Future for Haunting." In *Ghosts: Deconstruction, Psychoanalysis, History*, edited by Peter Buse and Andrew Scott, 1–20. New York: Palgrave, 1999.

Bushnell, Rebecca. *Tragic Time in Drama, Film, and Videogames: The Future in the Instant*. London: Palgrave Macmillan, 2016.

Bushnell, Rebecca W. *Tragedies of Tyrants: Political Thought and Theater in the English Renaissance*. Ithaca, NY: Cornell University Press, 1990.

Butler, Judith. *Bodies That Matter: On the Discursive Limits of Sex*. New York: Routledge, 1993.

——. "Imitation and Gender Insubordination." In *Inside/Out: Lesbian Theories, Gay Theories*, edited by Diana Fuss, 13–31. New York: Routledge, 1991.

Cahill, Patricia. *Unto the Breach: Martial Formations, Historical Trauma, and the Early Modern Stage*. Oxford: Oxford University Press, 2008.

Camden, William. *Annales*, 1625.

Campana, Joseph. "Killing Shakespeare's Children: The Cases of *Richard III* and *King John*." *Shakespeare* 3, no. 1 (2007): 18–39.

Capers, Bennett. "On Andy Warhol's *Electric Chair*." *California Law Review* 94, no. 1 (2006): 243–60.

Carlson, Marvin. *The Haunted Stage: The Theatre as Memory Machine*. Ann Arbor: University of Michigan Press, 2001.

Cavell, Stanley. "The Avoidance of Love: A Reading of *King Lear*." In *Must We Mean What We Say?*, 267–353. New York: Cambridge University Press, 2002.

Charnes, Linda. *Notorious Identity: Materializing the Subject in Shakespeare*. Cambridge, MA: Harvard University Press, 1993.

——. "Reading for the Wormholes: Micro-Periods from the Future." *Early Modern Culture: An Electronic Seminar* 6 (2007). http://emc.eserver.org/1-6/charnes .html (site discontinued).

Chéroux, Clément. "Ghost Dialectics: Spirit Photography in Entertainment and Belief." In *The Perfect Medium: Photography and the Occult*, edited by Clément Chéroux, Andreas Fischer, Pierre Apraxine, Denis Canguilhem, and Sophie Schmit, 45–71. New Haven, CT: Yale University Press, 2004.

Choate, Evan. "Misreading Impotence in *Richard III*." *Modern Philology* 117, no. 1 (2019): 24–47.

——. "Staged History and Alternative Sir Johns." *Shakespeare Quarterly* 70, no. 3 (2019): 207–29.

Cloutier, Crista. "Mumler's Ghosts." In *The Perfect Medium: Photography and the Occult*, edited by Clément Chéroux, Andreas Fischer, Pierre Apraxine, Denis Canguilhem, and Sophie Schmit, 20–28. New Haven, CT: Yale University Press, 2004.

Connor, Steven. "The Machine in the Ghost: Spiritualism, Technology and the 'Direct Voice.'" In *Ghosts: Deconstruction, Psychoanalysis, History*, edited by Peter Buse and Andrew Scott, 203–25. New York: Palgrave, 1999.

Cortés-Rocca, Paola. "Ghosts in the Machine: Photographs of Specters in the Nineteenth Century." *Mosaic: An Interdisciplinary Critical Journal* 38, no. 1 (2005): 151–68.

Cox, John D., and Eric Rasmussen, eds. *King Henry VI Part 3*. Arden Third Series. London: Arden, 2001.

Crewe, Jonathan. "Reforming Prince Hal: The Sovereign Inheritor in *2 Henry IV*." *Renaissance Drama* 21 (1990): 225–42.

Cunningham, Karen. *Imaginary Betrayals: Subjectivity and the Discourses of Treason in Early Modern England*. Philadelphia: University of Pennsylvania Press, 2002.

Dailey, Alice. "The Art of Recovering Richard III." *Upstart: A Journal of English Renaissance Studies*, August 12, 2013. https://upstart.sites.clemson.edu/Essays/richard-forum/art-of-recovering.xhtml.

———. "The RSC's 'Glorious Moment' and the Making of Shakespearean History." *Shakespeare Survey* 63 (2010): 184–97.

———. "The Talbot Remains: Historical Drama and the Performative Archive." *Shakespeare Bulletin* 35, no. 3 (2017): 373–87.

Daniel, Samuel. *The First Four Books of the Civil Wars between the Two Houses of Lancaster and York*, 1595.

David, Richard. "Shakespeare's History Plays—Epic or Drama?" *Shakespeare Survey* 6 (1953): 129–39.

Davis, Colin. *Haunted Subjects: Deconstruction, Psychoanalysis, and the Return of the Dead*. New York: Palgrave, 2007.

de Grazia, Margreta. "Anachronism." In *Cultural Reformations: Medieval and Renaissance in Literary History*, edited by Brian Cummings and James Simpson, 13–32. Oxford: Oxford University Press, 2010.

Deleuze, Gilles. *The Fold: Leibniz and the Baroque*. Translated by Tom Conley. Minneapolis, MN: University of Minnesota Press, 1993.

Derrida, Jacques. *Archive Fever: A Freudian Impression*. Translated by Eric Prenowitz. Chicago: University of Chicago Press, 1995.

———. *The Beast and the Sovereign*. Vol. 1. Translated by Geoffrey Bennington. Chicago: University of Chicago Press, 2009.

———. *The Death Penalty*. Vol. 1. Translated by Peggy Kamuf. Chicago: University of Chicago Press, 2014.

———. *Specters of Marx: The State of the Debt, the Work of Mourning and the New International*. Translated by Peggy Kamuf. New York: Routledge, 1993.

Derrida, Jacques, and Elisabeth Roudinesco. *For What Tomorrow. . . .* Translated by Jeff Fort. Stanford, CA: Stanford University Press, 2004.

Derrida, Jacques, and Bernard Stiegler. "Spectrographies." In *Echographies of Television: Filmed Interviews*, translated by Jennifer Bajorek, 113–34. Cambridge: Polity Press, 2002.

Di Bella, Maria Pia. "Observing Executions: From Spectator to Witness." In *Representations of Pain in Art and Visual Culture*, edited by Maria Pia Di Bella and James Elkins, 170–85. New York: Routledge, 2013.

DiGangi, Mario. "*Henry VI, Part 1*: 'Wounded Alpha Bad Boy Soldier.'" In *Shakesqueer: A Queer Companion to the Complete Works of Shakespeare*, edited by Madhavi Menon, 130–38. Durham, NC: Duke University Press, 2011.

Dinshaw, Carolyn, Lee Edelman, Roderick A. Ferguson, Carla Freccero, Jack [Judith] Halberstam, Annamarie Jagose, Christopher Nealon, and Hoang Tan Nguyen. "Theorizing Queer Temporalities: A Roundtable Discussion." *GLQ* 13, no. 2–3 (2007): 177–95.

Doane, Mary Ann. *The Emergence of Cinematic Time: Modernity, Contingency, the Archive*. Cambridge, MA: Harvard University Press, 2002.

Doebler, John. *Shakespeare's Speaking Pictures: Studies in Iconic Imagery*. Albuquerque: New Mexico University Press, 1974.

Dubrow, Heather. "'I Fear There Will a Worse Come in His Place': Surrogate Parents and Shakespeare's Richard III." In *Maternal Measures: Figuring Caregiving in the Early Modern Period*, edited by Naomi J. Miller and Naomi Yavneh, 348–62. Burlington, VT: Ashgate, 2000.

Dunn, Jonni Koonce. "The Functions of Forgetfulness in *1 Henry IV*." *Studies in Philology* 113, no. 1 (2016): 82–100.

Dyer, Jennifer. "The Metaphysics of the Mundane: Understanding Andy Warhol's Serial Imagery." *Artibus et Historiae* 25, no. 49 (2004): 33–47.

Edelman, Lee. "Against Survival: Queerness in a Time That's Out of Joint." *Shakespeare Quarterly* 62, no. 2 (2011): 148–69.

———. *No Future: Queer Theory and the Death Drive*. Durham, NC: Duke University Press, 2004.

Ellinghausen, Laurie. "'Shame and Eternal Shame': The Dynamics of Historical Trauma in Shakespeare's Early Histories." *Exemplaria* 20, no. 3 (2008): 264–82.

Erni, John Nguyet. *Unstable Frontiers: Technomedicine and the Cultural Politics of 'Curing' AIDS*. Minneapolis: University of Minnesota Press, 1994.

Evans, Meredith. "Rumor, the Breath of Kings, and the Body of Law in *2 Henry IV*." *Shakespeare Quarterly* 60, no. 1 (2009): 1–24.

Felski, Rita. "Context Stinks!" *New Literary History* 42, no. 4 (2011): 573–91.

Fischer, Andreas. "'A Photographer of Marvels': Frederick Hudson and the Beginnings of Spirit Photography in Europe." In *The Perfect Medium: Photography and the Occult*, edited by Clément Chéroux, Andreas Fischer, Pierre Apraxine, Denis Canguilhem, and Sophie Schmit, 29–43. New Haven, CT: Yale University Press, 2004.

Fischer-Lichte, Erika. *The Transformative Power of Performance: A New Aesthetics*. Translated by Saskya Iris Jain. London: Routledge, 2008.

Flatley, Jonathan. "Warhol Gives Good Face: Publicity and the Politics of Prosopopoeia." In *Pop Out: Queer Warhol*, edited by Jennifer Doyle, Jonathan Flatley, and José Esteban Muñoz, 101–33. Durham, NC: Duke University Press, 1996.

Fleischer, M. H. *The Iconography of the English History Play*. Salzburg: Institut für Englische Sprache und Literatur, 1974.

Forker, Charles R., ed. *The Tragedy of Richard the Second*. Arden Third Series. London: Bloomsbury, 2002.

Foster, Hal. "Death in America." *October* 75 (1996): 36–59.

Foucault, Michel. *Discipline and Punish: The Birth of the Prison*. Translated by Alan Sheridan. New York: Vintage Books, 1995.

Freccero, Carla. *Queer/Early/Modern*. Durham, NC: Duke University Press, 2006.

Freccero, Carla, Madhavi Menon, and Valerie Traub. "Historicism and Unhistoricism in Queer Studies." *PMLA* 128, no. 3 (2013): 781–86.

Freedgood, Elaine. "Ghostly Reference." *Representations* 125, no. 1 (2014): 40–53.

Freeman, Elizabeth. *Time Binds: Queer Temporalities, Queer Histories*. Durham, NC: Duke University Press, 2010.

Freud, Sigmund. "The Uncanny." In *On Creativity and the Unconscious*, edited by Benjamin Nelson, translated by Alix Strachey, 122–61. New York: Harper and Row, 1958.

Fried, Michael. *Absorption and Theatricality: Painting and Beholder in the Age of Diderot.* Chicago: University of Chicago Press, 1988.

——. "Art and Objecthood." In *Art and Objecthood: Essays and Reviews*, 148–72. Chicago: University of Chicago Press, 1988.

——. *Courbet's Realism.* Chicago: University of Chicago Press, 1990.

——. *Manet's Modernism: or, The Face of Painting in the 1860s.* Chicago: University of Chicago Press, 1996.

——. *Why Photography Matters as Art as Never Before.* New Haven, CT: Yale University Press, 2008.

Friedman, Martin. "Foreword." In *Vanishing Presence*, edited by Martin Friedman, Eugenia Parry Janis, Max Kozloff, and Adam D. Weinberg, 6–7. Minneapolis: Walker Art Center/Rizzoli, 1989.

Fulton, Gwynne. "Phantasmatics: Sovereignty and the Image of Death in Derrida's First *Death Penalty* Seminar." *Mosaic: An Interdisciplinary Critical Journal* 48, no. 3 (2015): 75–94.

Garber, Marjorie. *Shakespeare After All.* New York: Pantheon, 2004.

——. *Shakespeare's Ghost Writers: Literature as Uncanny Causality.* New York: Routledge, 1987.

Garland-Thomson, Rosemarie. *Extraordinary Bodies: Figuring Physical Disability in American Culture and Literature.* New York: Columbia University Press, 1997.

Gilman, Ernest B. "*Richard II* and the Perspectives of History." *Renaissance Drama* 17 (1976): 85–115.

Girard, René. *Violence and the Sacred.* Translated by Patrick Gregory. Baltimore: Johns Hopkins University Press, 1977.

Goldberg, Jonathan. *Sodometries: Renaissance Texts, Modern Sexualities.* Stanford, CA: Stanford University Press, 1992.

Goldberg, Jonathan, and Madhavi Menon. "Queering History." *PMLA* 120, no. 5 (2005): 1608–17.

Goodman, Kevis. "Romantic Poetry and the Science of Nostalgia." In *The Cambridge Companion to British Romantic Poetry*, edited by James Chandler and Maureen N. McLane, 195–216. Cambridge: Cambridge University Press, 2008.

Goy-Blanquet, Dominique. *Shakespeare's Early History Plays: From Chronicle to Stage.* Oxford: Oxford University Press, 2003.

Grabes, Herbert. *The Mutable Glass: Mirror-imagery in Titles and Texts of the Middle Ages and the English Renaissance.* Translated by Gordon Collier. New York: Cambridge University Press, 1982.

Greenblatt, Stephen. *Renaissance Self-Fashioning: From More to Shakespeare.* Chicago: University of Chicago Press, 1980.

——. *Shakespearean Negotiations: The Circulation of Social Energy in Renaissance England.* Berkeley: University of California Press, 1988.

Grene, Nicholas. *Shakespeare's Serial History Plays.* Cambridge: Cambridge University Press, 2002.

Griffin, Andrew. "Is *Henry V* Still a History Play?" In *Temporality, Genre and Experience in the Age of Shakespeare: Forms of Time*, edited by Lauren Shohet, 83–100. London: Bloomsbury, 2018.

———. *Untimely Deaths in Renaissance Drama: Biography, History, Catastrophe.* Toronto: University of Toronto Press, 2020.

Grove, Allen W. "Röntgen's Ghosts: Photography, X-Rays, and the Victorian Imagination." *Literature and Medicine* 16, no. 2 (1997): 141–73.

Gunning, Tom. "Invisible Worlds, Visible Media." In *Brought to Light: Photography and the Invisible, 1840–1900,* edited by Corey Keller, 51–63. New Haven, CT: Yale University Press, 2008.

———. "Never Seen This Picture Before: Muybridge in Multiplicity." In *Time Stands Still: Muybridge and the Instantaneous Photography Movement,* edited by Phillip Prodger, 222–72. New York: Oxford University Press, 2003.

———. "Phantom Images and Modern Manifestations: Spirit Photography, Magic Theater, Trick Films, and Photography's Uncanny." In *Fugitive Images: From Photography to Video,* edited by Patrice Petro, 42–71. Bloomington: Indiana University Press, 1995.

Gurr, Andrew, ed. *King Richard II.* Cambridge: Cambridge University Press, 2003.

Guy-Bray, Stephen. "*Henry VI, Part 2*: The Gayest Play Ever." In *Shakesqueer: A Queer Companion to the Complete Works of Shakespeare,* edited by Madhavi Menon, 139–45. Durham, NC: Duke University Press, 2011.

———. *Shakespeare and Queer Representation.* New York: Routledge, 2021.

Halberstam, Jack [Judith]. *In a Queer Time and Place: Transgender Bodies, Subcultural Lives.* New York: New York University Press, 2005.

———. *The Queer Art of Failure.* Durham, NC: Duke University Press, 2011.

Halpern, Richard. "The King's Two Buckets: Kantorowicz, *Richard II*, and Fiscal *Trauerspiel.*" *Representations* 106, no. 1 (2009): 67–76.

Hamilton, A. C. *The Early Shakespeare.* San Marino, CA: Huntington Library, 1967.

Hammill, Graham, and Julia Reinhard Lupton, eds. *Political Theology and Early Modernity.* Chicago: University of Chicago Press, 2012.

Hardin, Michael. "Postmodernism's Desire for a Simulated Death: Andy Warhol's *Car Crashes,* J. G. Ballard's *Crash,* and Don DeLillo's *White Noise.*" *LIT: Literature Interpretation Theory* 13, no. 1 (2002): 21–50.

Harris, Jonathan Gil. *Untimely Matter in the Time of Shakespeare.* Philadelphia: University of Pennsylvania Press, 2009.

Hattaway, Michael, ed. *The First Part of King Henry VI.* Cambridge: Cambridge University Press, 1990.

———. "The Shakespearean History Play." In *The Cambridge Companion to Shakespeare's History Plays,* edited by Michael Hattaway, 3–24. Cambridge: Cambridge University Press, 2002.

———, ed. *The Third Part of King Henry VI.* Cambridge: Cambridge University Press, 1993.

Heilman, Robert B. "Satiety and Conscience: Aspects of *Richard III.*" In *Essays in Shakespeare Criticism,* edited by James L. Calderwood and Harold E. Toliver, 137–51. Englewood Cliffs, NJ: Prentice-Hall, 1970.

Hobgood, Allison P. "Teeth before Eyes: Impairment and Invisibility in Shakespeare's *Richard III.*" In *Disability, Health, and Happiness in the Shakespearean Body,* edited by Sujata Iyengar, 23–40. New York: Routledge, 2015.

Hobgood, Allison P., and David Houston Wood. *Recovering Disability in Early Modern England.* Columbus: Ohio State University Press, 2013.

Hodgdon, Barbara. *The End Crowns All: Closure and Contradiction in Shakespeare's History*. Princeton, NJ: Princeton University Press, 1991.

——. "Replicating Richard: Body Doubles, Body Politics." *Theatre Journal* 50, no. 2 (1998): 207–25.

Holderness, Graham. *Shakespeare Recycled: The Making of Historical Drama*. Hertford-shire: Harvester Wheatsheaf, 1992.

Howard, Jean E., and Phyllis Rackin. *Engendering a Nation: A Feminist Account of Shakespeare's English Histories*. New York: Routledge, 1997.

Humphreys, A. R. *King Henry IV, Part I*. Arden First Series. London: Methuen, 1960.

Hunt, Maurice. "The Politics of Vision in Shakespeare's *1 Henry VI*." *South Central Review* 19, no. 1 (2002): 76–101.

Iyengar, Sujata. "Introduction: Shakespeare's 'Discourse of Disability.'" In *Disability, Health, and Happiness in the Shakespearean Body*, edited by Sujata Iyengar, 1–19. New York: Routledge, 2015.

Janis, Eugenia Parry. "The Bug in Amber and the Dance of Life." In *Vanishing Presence*, edited by Martin Friedman, Eugenia Parry Janis, Max Kozloff, and Adam D. Weinberg, 8–29. Minneapolis: Walker Art Center/Rizzoli, 1989.

Johns, Geoffrey A. "A 'Grievous Burden': *Richard III* and the Legacy of Monstrous Birth." In *Disability, Health, and Happiness in the Shakespearean Body*, edited by Sujata Iyengar, 41–57. New York: Routledge, 2015.

Johnson, Alexis Bard. "The Work of Being Sexed: Andy Warhol on Drag." In *Contact Warhol: Photography without End*, edited by Peggy Phelan and Richard Meyer. Cambridge, MA: MIT Press, 2018.

Kafer, Alison. *Feminist, Queer, Crip*. Bloomington: Indiana University Press, 2013.

Kahan, Benjamin. *Celibacies: American Modernism and Sexual Life*. Durham, NC: Duke University Press, 2013.

Kahn, Victoria. "Political Theology and Fiction in *The King's Two Bodies*." *Representations* 106, no. 1 (2009): 77–101.

Kalas, Rayna. *Frame, Glass, Verse: The Technology of Poetic Invention in the English Renaissance*. Ithaca, NY: Cornell University Press, 2007.

Kantorowicz, Ernst H. *The King's Two Bodies: A Study in Medieval Political Theology*. Princeton, NJ: Princeton University Press, 1957.

Kaplan, Louis. *The Strange Case of William Mumler Spirit Photographer*. Minneapolis: University of Minnesota Press, 2008.

Kastan, David Scott, ed. *King Henry IV, Part 1*. Arden Third Series. London: Blooms-bury, 2002.

——. "Proud Majesty Made a Subject: Shakespeare and the Spectacle of Rule." *Shakespeare Quarterly* 37, no. 4 (1986): 459–75.

——. *Shakespeare after Theory*. New York: Routledge, 1999.

——. *Shakespeare and the Shapes of Time*. Hanover: University Press of New Hamp-shire, 1982.

Keller, Corey. "Sight Unseen: Picturing the Invisible." In *Brought to Light: Photography and the Invisible, 1840–1900*, edited by Corey Keller, 19–35. New Haven, CT: Yale University Press, 2008.

Kerrigan, John. *"Henry IV* and the Death of Old Double (1990)." In *On Shakespeare and Early Modern Literature: Essays*, 66–88. Oxford: Oxford University Press, 2001.

Koestenbaum, Wayne. *Andy Warhol: A Biography*. New York: Open Road, 2001.

Kostihová, Marcela. "Richard Recast: Renaissance Disability in a Postcommunist Culture." In *Recovering Disability in Early Modern England*, edited by Allison P. Hobgood and David Houston Wood, 136–49. Columbus: Ohio State University Press, 2013.

Koudounaris, Paul. *Heavenly Bodies: Cult Treasures and Spectacular Saints from the Catacombs*. New York: Thames and Hudson, 2013.

Kozloff, Max. *Duane Michals: Now Becoming Then*. Altadena, CA: Twin Palms, 1990.

———. "The Etherealized Figure and the Dream of Wisdom." In *Vanishing Presence*, edited by Martin Friedman, Eugenia Parry Janis, Max Kozloff, and Adam D. Weinberg, 30–61. Minneapolis, MN: Walker Art Center/Rizzoli, 1989.

Kracauer, Siegfried. "Photography." Translated by Thomas Y. Levin. *Critical Inquiry* 19, no. 3 (1993): 421–36.

Kuppers, Petra. "Deconstructing Images: Performing Disability," *Contemporary Theatre Review* 11, nos. 3–4 (2001): 25–40.

Kvaran, Gunnar B. *Long Day's Journey into the Past: Gunnar B. Kvaran Speaks with Gerard Malanga*. Oslo: Astrup Fearnley Museum of Modern Art, 2008.

Kvaran, Gunnar B., Hanne Beate Ueland, and Grete Årbu, eds. *Andy Warhol by Andy Warhol*. Oslo: Astrup Fearnley Museum of Modern Art, 2008.

Lacan, Jacques. "Of the Gaze as *Objet Petit a*." In *The Four Fundamental Concepts of Psycho-Analysis*, translated by Alan Sheridan, 67–119. London: Penguin, 1979.

Lake, Peter. *How Shakespeare Put Politics on Stage: Power and Succession in the History Plays*. New Haven, CT: Yale University Press, 2016.

Lamb, Jonathan P. "The Stylistic Self in *Richard II*." *Medieval and Renaissance Drama in England* 28 (2015): 123–51.

Leggatt, Andrew. *Shakespeare's Political Drama: The History Plays and Roman Plays*. New York: Routledge, 1988.

———. "The Death of John Talbot." In *Shakespeare's English Histories: A Quest for Form and Genre*, edited by John W. Velz, 11–30. Binghamton: MRTS, 1996.

Lemon, Rebecca. *Treason by Words: Literature, Law, and Rebellion in Shakespeare's England*. Ithaca, NY: Cornell University Press, 2006.

Lesser, Zachary. *Ghosts, Holes, Rips and Scrapes: Shakespeare in 1619, Bibliography in the Longue Durée*. Philadelphia: University of Pennsylvania Press, 2021.

Lethem, Jonathan. "X, Curator." In *History's Shadow*, by David Maisel. Portland, OR: Nazraeli Press, 2011.

Lévy, Pierre. *Becoming Virtual: Reality in the Digital Age*. New York: Plenum, 1998.

Liebler, Naomi Conn. "'And Is Old Double Dead?': Nation and Nostalgia in *Henry IV Part 2*." *Shakespeare Survey* 63 (2010): 78–88.

Lippit, Akira Mizuta. *Atomic Light (Shadow Optics)*. Minneapolis: University of Minnesota Press, 2005.

Lopez, Jeremy. "Eating Richard II." *Shakespeare Studies* 36 (2008): 207–28.

———. "Introduction." In *Richard II: New Critical Essays*, edited by Jeremy Lopez, 1–48. New York: Routledge, 2012.

Lorenz, Philip. "'In the Course and Process of Time': Rupture, Reflection and Repetition in *Henry VIII*." In *Temporality, Genre and Experience in the Age of Shakespeare: Forms of Time*, edited by Lauren Shohet, 61–80. London: Arden, 2018.

Loughrey, Clarisse. "David Bowie: Lazarus Director Says Musician Only Discovered He Was Dying during Last Three Months." *Independent*, January 8, 2017. https://www.independent.co.uk/arts-entertainment/music/news/david -bowie-death-anniversay-last-five-years-lazarus-music-video-a7515581.html.

Love, Genevieve. *Early Modern Theatre and the Figure of Disability*. London: Arden, 2019.

Love, Heather. *Feeling Backward: Loss and the Politics of Queer History*. Cambridge, MA: Harvard University Press, 2007.

Luis-Martínez, Zenón. "Shakespeare's History Drama as *Trauerspiel*: *Richard II* and After." *ELH* 75, no. 3 (2008): 673–705.

Lupton, Julia Reinhard. *Thinking with Shakespeare: Essays on Politics and Life*. Chicago: University of Chicago Press, 2011.

Mackenzie, Alec. "The Age of the Selfie." *Royal Photographic Society (RPS) Journal* 154, no. 5 (2014): 288–93.

Malkowski, Jennifer. *Dying in Full Detail: Mortality and Digital Documentary*. Durham, NC: Duke University Press, 2017.

Marlowe, Christopher. *Doctor Faustus: A Two-Text Edition*. Edited by David Scott Kastan. New York: Norton, 2005.

Mbembe, Achille. *Necropolitics*, trans. Steven Corcoran. Durham, NC: Duke University Press, 2019.

McGarry, Molly. *Ghosts of Futures Past: Spiritualism and the Cultural Politics of Nineteenth-Century America*. Berkeley: University of California Press, 2008.

McMillin, Scott. "Shakespeare's Richard II: Eyes of Sorrow, Eyes of Desire." *Shakespeare Quarterly* 35, no. 1 (1984): 40–52.

McRuer, Robert. *Crip Theory: Cultural Signs of Queerness and Disability*. New York: New York University Press, 2006.

———. *Crip Times: Disability, Globalization, and Resistance*. New York: New York University Press, 2018.

———. "*Richard III*: Fuck the Disabled: The Prequel." In *Shakesqueer: A Queer Companion to the Complete Works of Shakespeare*, edited by Madhavi Menon, 294–301. Durham, NC: Duke University Press, 2011.

McRuer, Robert, and Abby L. Wilkerson. "Introduction: Special Issue on Desiring Disability: Queer Theory Meets Disability Studies." *GLQ* 9, no. 1 (2003): 1–23.

Melchiori, Giorgio, ed. *The Second Part of King Henry IV*. Cambridge: Cambridge University Press, 2007.

Menon, Madhavi. "Queer Shakes." In *Shakesqueer: A Queer Companion to the Complete Works of Shakespeare*, edited by Madhavi Menon, 1–27. Durham, NC: Duke University Press, 2011.

Menzer, Paul. *Anecdotal Shakespeare: A New Performance History*. New York: Bloomsbury, 2015.

———. "cf., Marlowe." In *Richard II: New Critical Essays*, edited by Jeremy Lopez, 117–34. New York: Routledge, 2012.

Merck, Mandy. "Figuring Out Andy Warhol." In *Pop Out: Queer Warhol*, edited by Jennifer Doyle, Jonathan Flatley, and José Esteban Muñoz, 224–37. Durham, NC: Duke University Press, 1996.

Meyer, Richard. "Warhol's Clones." *The Yale Journal of Criticism* 7, no. 1 (1994): 79–109.

Michals, Duane. "Duane Michals Speaks with Enrica Viganò." In *Storyteller: The Photographs of Duane Michals*, edited by Linda Benedict-Jones, 116–21. New York: DelMonico Books, 2015.

———. "This Is a Real Dream (1984): Duane Michals Interviewed by William Jenkins." In *Storyteller: The Photographs of Duane Michals*, edited by Linda Benedict-Jones, 84–88. New York: DelMonico Books, 2015.

Mitchell, David T., and Sharon L. Snyder. *Narrative Prosthesis: Disability and the Dependencies of Discourse*. Ann Arbor: University of Michigan Press, 2000.

Mitchell, W. J. T. *What Do Pictures Want?* Chicago: University of Chicago Press, 2005.

Möller, Frank. "The Looking/Not Looking Dilemma." *Review of International Studies* 35, no. 4 (2009): 781–94.

Moulton, Ian Frederick. "'A Monster Great Deformed': The Unruly Masculinity of Richard III." *Shakespeare Quarterly* 47, no. 3 (1996): 251–68.

Muñoz, José Esteban. "Cruising the Toilet: Le Roi Jones/Amiri Baraka, Racial Black Traditions, and Queer Futurity." *GLQ* 13, no. 2–3 (2007): 353–67.

———. *Cruising Utopia: The Then and There of Queer Futurity*. New York: New York University Press, 2009.

Musée d'Orsay. "Oscar Gustave Rejlander, *The First Negative*." Curator notes. Accessed February 8, 2021. http://www.musee-orsay.fr/en/collections/works-in-focus /photography/commentaire_id/the-first-negative-23333.html?tx_commentaire _pi1%5BpidLi%5D=847&tx_commentaire_pi1%5Bfrom%5D=844&cHash =0908fda4e9.

Nagel, Alexander, and Christopher S. Wood. *Anachronic Renaissance*. New York: Zone Books, 2010.

Nardizzi, Vin. "Disability Figures in Shakespeare." In *Oxford Handbook of Shakespeare and Embodiment: Gender, Sexuality, and Race*, edited by Valerie Traub, 454–67. Oxford: Oxford University Press, 2016.

Nashe, Thomas. *Piers Penniless His Supplication to the Devil*. In *The Works of Thomas Nashe*, edited by Ronald B. McKerrow, revised by F. P. Wilson, 1:137–246. London: Basil Blackwell, 1958.

National Portrait Gallery. "The Gallery's First Director George Scharf Had a Fascination for the Macabre." Facebook, October 31, 2019. https://www .facebook.com/nationalportraitgallery/videos/423585408341063.

———. "National Portrait Gallery Finds Relics of an English King in its Basement." Press release, November 16, 2010.

Nelson, Victoria. *The Secret Life of Puppets*. Cambridge, MA: Harvard University Press, 2001.

Netzloff, Mark. "Insurgent Time: *Richard II* and the Periodization of Sovereignty." In *Richard II: New Critical Essays*, edited by Jeremy Lopez, 202–22. New York: Routledge, 2012.

Newstok, Scott L. *Quoting Death in Early Modern England: The Poetics of Epitaphs beyond the Tomb*. New York: Palgrave, 2009.

Nicosia, Marissa. "'To Plant Me in Mine Own Inheritance': Prolepsis and Pretenders in John Ford's *Perkin Warbeck*." *Studies in Philology* 115, no. 3 (2018): 580–97.

Norbrook, David. "The Emperor's New Body? *Richard II*, Ernst Kantorowicz, and the Politics of Shakespeare Criticism." *Textual Practice* 10, no. 2 (1996): 329–57.

Nunes, Mark. "Error, Noise, and Potential: The Outside of Purpose." In *Error: Glitch, Noise, and Jam in New Media Cultures*, edited by Mark Nunes, 3–24. New York: Bloomsbury, 2011.

Oestreich-Hart, Donna J. "'Therefore, Since I Cannot Prove a Lover.'" *SEL* 40, no. 2 (2000): 241–60.

Oliver, Kelly. "See Topsy 'Ride the Lightning': The Scopic Machinery of Death." *Southern Journal of Philosophy* 50, no. 1 (2012): 74–94.

———. *Technologies of Life and Death: From Cloning to Capital Punishment*. New York: Fordham University Press, 2013.

Park, Katherine. "The Criminal and the Saintly Body: Autopsy and Dissection in Renaissance Italy." *Renaissance Quarterly* 47, no. 1 (1994): 1–33.

———. "The Life of the Corpse: Division and Dissection in Later Medieval Europe." *Journal of the History of Medicine and Allied Sciences* 50, no. 1 (1994): 111–32.

Parker, Patricia. *Shakespeare from the Margins: Language, Culture, Context*. Chicago: University of Chicago Press, 1996.

Parvini, Neema. *Shakespeare's History Plays: Rethinking Historicism*. Edinburgh: Edinburgh University Press, 2012.

Pasupathi, Vimala C. "Coats and Conduct: The Materials of Military Obligation in Shakespeare's *Henry IV* and *Henry V*." *Modern Philology* 109, no. 3 (2012): 326–51.

Pauli, Lori, ed. *Acting the Part: Photography as Theatre*. New York: Merrell, 2006.

Phelan, Peggy. "Andy Warhol: Contact Sheets, Photography without End." In *Contact Warhol: Photography without End*, edited by Peggy Phelan and Richard Meyer, 22–43. Cambridge, MA: MIT Press, 2018.

———. "Haunted Stages: Performance and the Photographic Effect." In *Haunted: Contemporary Photography/Video/Performance*, edited by Jennifer Blessing and Nan Trotman, 50–63. New York: Guggenheim Foundation, 2010.

———. "The Same: Reflections on Andy Warhol and Ronald Reagan." *Umbr(a): A Journal of the Unconscious* 1 (2002): 65–70.

———. *Unmarked: The Politics of Performance*. New York: Routledge, 1996.

Phelan, Peggy, and Richard Meyer. "Talking Warhol." In *Contact Warhol: Photography without End*, edited by Peggy Phelan and Richard Meyer, 14–21. Cambridge, MA: MIT Press, 2018.

Pitt-Rivers, Julian. *The Fate of Shechem, or the Politics of Sex: Essays in the Anthropology of the Mediterranean*. Cambridge: Cambridge University Press, 1977.

Poole, Kristen. *Radical Religion from Shakespeare to Milton*. Cambridge: Cambridge University Press, 2000.

Poole, Kristen, and Owen Williams, eds. "Introduction." In *Early Modern Histories of Time: The Periodizations of Sixteenth- and Seventeenth-Century England*, 1–17. Philadelphia: University of Pennsylvania Press, 2019.

Prodger, Phillip. *Time Stands Still: Muybridge and the Instantaneous Photography Movement*. New York: Oxford University Press, 2003.

Pye, Christopher. *The Regal Phantasm: Shakespeare and the Politics of Spectacle*. New York: Routledge, 1990.

Rackin, Phyllis. "History into Tragedy: The Case of *Richard III*." In *Shakespearean Tragedy and Gender*, edited by Shirley Nelson Garner and Madelon Sprengnether, 31–53. Bloomington: Indiana University Press, 1996.

——. *Stages of History: Shakespeare's English Chronicles*. Ithaca, NY: Cornell University Press, 1990.

Rank, Otto. *The Double: A Psychoanalytic Study*. Translated and edited by Harry Tucker Jr. Chapel Hill: University of North Carolina Press, 1971.

——. "The Double as Immortal Self." In *Beyond Psychology*, 62–101. New York: Dover, 1941.

Rayner, Alice. *Ghosts: Death's Double and the Phenomena of Theatre*. Minneapolis: University of Minnesota Press, 2006.

Roach, Joseph. *Cities of the Dead: Circum-Atlantic Performance*. New York: Columbia University Press, 1996.

Row-Heyveld, Lindsey. *Dissembling Disability in Early Modern English Drama*. Cham, Switzerland: Palgrave Macmillan, 2018.

Rust, Jennifer R. *The Body in Mystery: The Political Theology of the Corpus Mysticum in the Literature of Reformation England*. Evanston, IL: Northwestern University Press, 2014.

Ryan, Kiernan. "The Future of History: *1* and *2 Henry IV*." In *Shakespeare's History Plays*, edited by R. J. C. Watt, 147–68. New York: Longman, 2002.

Sack, Daniel. *After Live: Possibility, Potentiality, and the Future of Performance*. Ann Arbor: University of Michigan Press, 2015.

Sanchez, Melissa E. *Shakespeare and Queer Theory*. New York: Bloomsbury, 2019.

Sandahl, Carrie. "Queering the Crip or Cripping the Queer? Intersections of Queer and Crip Identities in Solo Autobiographical Performance." *GLQ* 9, no. 1–2 (2003): 25–56.

Sandahl, Carrie, and Philip Auslander, "Introduction: Disability Studies in Commotion with Performance Studies." In *Bodies in Commotion: Disability & Performance*, edited by Carrie Sandahl and Philip Auslander, 1–12. Ann Arbor: University of Michigan Press, 2005.

Sarat, Austin. *When the State Kills: Capital Punishment and the American Condition*. Princeton, NJ: Princeton University Press, 2001.

Schneider, Rebecca. *Performing Remains: Art and War in Times of Theatrical Reenactment*. New York: Routledge, 2011.

Schwyzer, Philip. *Shakespeare and the Remains of Richard III*. Oxford: Oxford University Press, 2013.

Semenza, Gregory M. Colón. "Sport, War, and Contest in Shakespeare's *Henry VI*." *Renaissance Quarterly* 54, no. 4 (2001): 1251–72.

Serres, Michael, with Bruno Latour. *Conversations on Science, Culture, and Time*. Translated by Roxanne Lapidus. Ann Arbor: University of Michigan Press, 1995.

Shakespeare, William. *The Famous Victories of Henry the Fifth*. London, 1598.

——. *The Oxford Shakespeare: The Complete Works*, edited by Stanley Wells and Gary Taylor. Oxford: Clarendon, 1988.

——. *The Tragedie of King Richard the Second As It Hath Been Publickly Acted by the Right Honourable the Lord Chamberlaine His Seuantes*. London, 1608.

Sher, Anthony. *The Year of the King: An Actor's Diary and Sketchbook*. New York: Limelight, 1994.

Sherman, Donovan. "'What More Remains?': Messianic Performance in *Richard II*." *Shakespeare Quarterly* 65, no. 1 (2014): 22–48.

Shortslef, Emily. "Acting as an Epitaph: Performing Commemoration in the Shakespearean History Play." *Critical Survey* 22, no. 2 (2010): 11–24.

Shuger, Debora. "The 'I' of the Beholder: Renaissance Mirrors and the Reflexive Mind." In *Renaissance Culture and the Everyday*, edited by Patricia Fumerton and Simon Hunt, 21–41. Philadelphia: University of Pennsylvania Press, 1999.

Siebers, Tobin. *Disability Theory*. Ann Arbor: University of Michigan Press, 2008.

Siemon, James. *Shakespearean Iconoclasm*. Berkeley: University of California Press, 1985.

Siemon, James R., ed. *King Richard III*. Arden Third Series. London: Arden, 2009.

Slotkin, Joel. "Honeyed Toads: Sinister Aesthetics in Shakespeare's *Richard III*." *Journal for Early Modern Cultural Studies* 7, no. 1 (2007): 5–32.

Smidt, Kristian. "Shakespeare's Absent Characters." *English Studies* 61, no. 5 (1980): 397–407.

Smith, Bruce R. *Shakespeare and Masculinity*. New York: Oxford University Press, 2000.

Sontag, Susan. "Notes on 'Camp.'" In *Against Interpretation and Other Essays*, 275–92. New York: Farrar, Straus & Giroux, 1961.

——. *On Photography*. New York: Picador, 1973.

——. *Regarding the Pain of Others*. New York: Picador, 2003.

Spencer, Charles. "Delicate Debauchery." *The Telegraph*, April 21, 2000.

Spurgeon, Caroline. *Shakespeare's Imagery and What It Tells Us*. Cambridge: Cambridge University Press, 1935.

Stanivukovic, Goran, ed. *Queer Shakespeare: Desire and Sexuality*. London: Bloomsbury, 2017.

Stanley, Arthur Penrhyn. "On an Examination of the Tombs of Richard II. and Henry III. in Westminster Abbey." *Archaeologia* 12 (June 26, 1873): 309–27.

States, Bert O. "Death as a Fictitious Event." *The Hudson Review* 53, no. 3 (2000): 423–32.

Stewart, Susan. *On Longing: Narratives of the Miniature, the Gigantic, the Souvenir, the Collection*. Durham, NC: Duke University Press, 1993.

Swenson, Gene. "What Is Pop Art? Answers from 8 Painters (Part I)." *ARTnews*, November 1963.

"Sydenham Chorea Information Page." National Institute of Neurological Disorders and Stroke, National Institutes of Health. Accessed July 8, 2019. https://www.ninds.nih.gov/Disorders/All-Disorders/Sydenham-Chorea-Information-Page.

Targoff, Ramie. "'Dirty' Amens: Devotion, Applause, and Consent in *Richard III*." *Renaissance Drama* 31 (2002): 61–84.

Taylor, Diana. *The Archive and the Repertoire: Performing Cultural Memory in the Americas*. Durham, NC: Duke University Press, 2003.

Thomas, Keith. *Religion and the Decline of Magic: Studies in Popular Beliefs in Sixteenth and Seventeenth Century England*. New York: Oxford University Press, 1971.

Torrey, Michael. "'The Plain Devil and Dissembling Looks': Ambivalent Physiognomy and Shakespeare's *Richard III*." *English Literary Renaissance* 30, no. 2 (2000): 123–53.

Traub, Valerie. "Prince Hal's Falstaff: Positioning Psychoanalysis and the Female Reproductive Body." *Shakespeare Quarterly* 40, no. 4 (1989): 456–74.

Tucker, Harry, Jr. "Introduction." In *The Double: A Psychoanalytic Study*, xiii–xxii. Chapel Hill: University of North Carolina Press, 1971.

Vinter, Maggie. *Last Acts: The Art of Dying on the Early Modern Stage*. New York: Fordham University Press, 2019.

Wagner, Matthew D. *Shakespeare, Theatre, and Time*. New York: Routledge, 2012.

Wall, Jeff. "Jeff Wall in Conversation with Martin Schwander." In *Selected Essays and Interviews*, 229–38. New York: Museum of Modern Art, 2007.

Walsh, Brian. *Shakespeare, the Queen's Men, and the Elizabethan Performance of History*. Cambridge: Cambridge University Press, 2009.

——. "'Unkind Division': The Double Absence of Performing History in *1 Henry VI*." *Shakespeare Quarterly* 55, no. 2 (2004): 119–47.

Wantier, Albin. "Kabbalah, Nuclear Fusion, and Immortality: David Bowie's Signs." Preface to *Bowie*, by Steve Schapiro. Brooklyn: powerHouse Books, 2016.

Warfield, Katie. "Digital Subjectivities and Selfies: The Model, the Self-Conscious Thespian, and the #realme." *International Journal of the Image* 6, no. 2 (2015): 1–16.

Warhol, Andy. *The Philosophy of Andy Warhol: From A to B and Back Again*. New York: Harcourt, 1975.

Warhol, Andy, and Pat Hackett. *Popism: The Warhol Sixties*. New York: Harcourt, 1980.

Warren-Heys, Rebecca. "Death and Memory in Shakespeare's *2 Henry IV*." *HARTS & Minds: The Journal of Humanities and Arts* 1, no. 3 (2013–14): 1–15.

Watney, Simon. "Queer Andy." In *Pop Out: Queer Warhol*, edited by Jennifer Doyle, Jonathan Flatley, and José Esteban Muñoz, 20–30. Durham, NC: Duke University Press, 1996.

Watson, Robert N. *Shakespeare and the Hazards of Ambition*. Cambridge, MA: Harvard University Press, 1984.

Weil, Herbert, and Judith Weil, eds. *The First Part of King Henry IV*. Cambridge: Cambridge University Press, 1997.

West, William N. "What's the Matter with Shakespeare?: Physics, Identity, Playing." *South Central Review* 26, no. 1–2 (2009): 103–26.

Whitver, H. Austin. "Materiality of Memory in Shakespeare's Second Tetralogy." *SEL* 56, no. 2 (2016): 285–306.

Williams, Katherine Schaap. "Enabling Richard: The Rhetoric of Disability in *Richard III*." *Disability Studies Quarterly* 29, no. 4 (2009): n.p. http://dsq-sds.org /article/view/997/1181.

——. "Performing Disability and Theorizing Deformity." *English Studies* 94, no. 7 (2013): 757–72.

——. *Unfixable Forms: Disability, Performance, and the Early Modern English Theater.* Ithaca, NY: Cornell University Press, 2021.

Wills, David. *Killing Times: The Temporal Technology of the Death Penalty.* New York: Fordham University Press, 2019.

Wolf, Matt. "Sly yet Sweet Falstaff in 'Henry IV, 1 and 2.'" *New York Times*, May 11, 2005. https://www.nytimes.com/2005/05/11/arts/sly-yet-sweet-falstaff-in-henry-iv-1-and-2.html.

Worthen, W. B. *Shakespeare, Technicity, Theatre.* Cambridge: Cambridge University Press, 2020.

Zimmerman, Susan. *The Early Modern Corpse and Shakespeare's Theatre.* Edinburgh: Edinburgh University Press, 2005.

INDEX

Page numbers in *italics* indicate illustrations.